Devil's Contract

THE HISTORY OF THE FAUSTIAN BARGAIN

ED SIMON

MELVILLE HOUSE
BROOKLYN • LONDON

Devil's Contract: The History of the Faustian Bargain

First published in 2024 by Melville House
Copyright © 2023 by Ed Simon
All rights reserved
First Melville House Printing: May 2024

Melville House Publishing
46 John Street
Brooklyn, NY 11201

and

Melville House UK
Suite 2000
16/18 Woodford Road
London E7 0HA

mhpbooks.com
@melvillehouse

ISBN: 978-1-68589-207-4
ISBN: 978-1-68589-103-9 (eBook)

Library of Congress Control Number: 2024934237

Designed by Beste M. Doğan

Printed in the United States of America

1 3 5 7 9 10 8 6 4 2

A catalog record for this book is available
from the Library of Congress

Devil's Contract

To Meg

Dr. Johann Georg Faust (c. 1480 – c. 1540), itinerant German alchemist, astrologer and magician of the Renaissance, main character in Christopher Marlowe's *The Tragical History of Doctor Faustus* (1604) and Goethe's *Faust* (1808). © Quagga / Alamy.

CONTENTS

When all the world dissolves,

And every creature shall be purified,

All places shall be hell that are not heaven.

—MEPHISTOPHELES

IN CHRISTOPHER MARLOWE'S

DOCTOR FAUSTUS (1593)

APPOINTMENT AT DEPTFORD

Listen to me: You'll never go wrong
If you pile it on, pile it on, and still pile it on.
Bewilder, confound them with all your variety,
The public's the public, they're a hard lot to satisfy.
—Johann Wolfgang von Goethe, *Faust I* (1808)

The book which you are currently reading, *Devil's Contract: The History of the Faustian Bargain*, is your autobiography—mine too. That's because in our willingness to occasionally betray our principles for personal gain the story of the man who sold his soul to the Devil for power and knowledge is our own story. No matter how saintly we may be, all of us lapse, all of us are imperfect creatures who are content to sometimes sign on the dotted line of a diabolical compact. There are resonances with that ancient story whenever we are bedeviled by particularly alluring delusions, whenever our endless appetite for justifying our delusions is indulged.

That legend of the Devil's contract is the most alluring, the most provocative, the most insightful, the most *important* story ever told. It concerns a humanity strung between Heaven and Hell, the saintly and the satanic; how a man could trade his soul for powers omnipotent, signing a covenant with the Devil so that he could briefly live as a god before being pulled down to Hell. Frequently associated with Christopher Marlowe's *Doctor Faustus,* that Elizabethan play wasn't the origin of that myth, but his is certainly a sterling example of that eternal script. Yet long before that Renaissance play and long afterwards, we can find the inky traces of Faust's damned signature in a multitude of works both high and low, canonical and popular. More disturbing than that is the way that the Devil's hoof-prints can be found across the wide swatch of history, in our willingness to embrace power and engage in exploitation, to summon self-interestedness and to conjure cruelty.

———

Examine some of those Mephistophelean hoof-prints as discovered at a Southwark, London construction site in 1989. The Rose Theatre, where Marlowe's play premiered in the late sixteenth century, was torn down in 1606 where it would be subsumed beneath layers Jacobean,

Interregnum, and Restoration, then Hanoverian, Regency, and Victorian, until Thatcher-era contractors building a soulless corporate office tower uncovered the bottom level of this strata of London history. Workers sifting through dirt found the tell-tale signs of a theater, from the preserved remains of charred hazelnut shells once sold as snacks to the broken clay pots used to collect tickets. The ruins of the theater once again had sunlight upon them. Now the remains of the Rose are within the basement of said soulless office tower looming above the Thames, the rare active archeological site which also invites audiences to enjoy a show atop the detritus of the theater where plays were first performed four centuries ago.

The earliest performances of *Doctor Faustus* were dogged by supernatural associations; audience members claimed that during the scenes of magical conjuration the playwright's words compelled demons to appear. "How am I glutted with conceit of this!" marvels Faustus in the first act of Marlowe's play, "Shall I make spirits fetch me what I please, / Resolve me of all ambiguities, / Perform what desperate enterprise I will?" Ostensibly a description of the dark arts' powers, but applicable to any art's strange abilities, certainly those of the theater. How did Marlowe differ from Faustus? For he could compel spirits of the imagination to fetch what he wanted, to perform what he wanted, to generate a seeming universe from nothing but words and gestures. And, like Faustus, Marlowe too would have his punishments, stabbed to death through the eye in a Deptford tavern, purportedly after arguing over the bar tab a year after the premier of his most celebrated play.

Should subsequent legends be trusted, *magic* apparently happened in what today looks like scarcely more than a pile of sifted rubble. During performances of *Faustus,* Latin incantations and magical circles inscribed upon the stage floor were said to be capable of conjuring forth demons just as if the actors were necromancers. From those circles traced with a staff into the dirt of the floor, it was believed that a wizard could summon the citizens of Hell to appear—Azazel with his curved goat horns, the snorting, red-eyed bull Moloch, or insect-winged Beelzebub, his mandibles sticky with blood. Maybe even Mephistopheles, that demon novel to the Faust legend, who first appears as if a decomposing corpse with flesh decayed away from his skull and maggots sifting through his eye-sockets and nose, only to later conduct himself in the more respectable shape of a Franciscan mendicant. Now, for any visitor to the theater built upon the corpse of its predecessor, the thin line of lurid blood-red neon light which demarcates the rough circle of the Rose theater's original foundation appears unnervingly like those magic circles affixed with strange alchemical symbols and numbers in which Renaissance necromancers would attempt to call upon all of the cursed demons of Pandemonium and where Satan came hidden on opening night to critique how well he'd been rendered by the playwright.

When I attended a performance at the Rose of another

Renaissance play known for its occult themes—think Scotland, witches, murdered kings—it was that neon light along the periphery of the darkened, damp, and musty smelling subterranean hole that most kept my attention, that luminescent circle offset in the darkness of the basement's most distant corners, bordered by the rubble of centuries still being sifted. The production was good, albeit in the now de rigueur tic for modernization, but sitting on the rafters in that basement that smelled of water and earth, the Weird Sisters and Macbeth were far less fascinating to me than what I couldn't see, just somewhere on the dark edge of vision, beyond a ribbon of neon intended to let me know where the walls of the Rose had once been.

Imagining that premier of *Doctor Faustus* more than four hundred years ago—and all of that is inaccessible to us in that strange and distant country of the past—I couldn't help but entertain those diabolical legends about Marlowe's audience that evening. *There, in that black space above the periphery, was that where Satan sat on the rafters, disguised as a ruffled Elizabethan gentleman in black and red velvet?* But no, Satan is not real, those stories are antitheatrical Puritan agitprop, folktales intended to frighten the credulous. No demons were conjured in any production of *Faustus*, for they are but characters, and characters are mere fiction. And yet, when the wizard's clown reads "Sanctabulorum . . . Mephistopheles" (nonsense Latin, incidentally) and a demon does appear, even the skeptic in me wonders what an infernal story deftly told may conjure.

The morning following that 2013 production of Marlowe's play, I traveled to Deptford to meet the playwright himself. When Marlowe was martyred in an upstairs room of Eleanor Bull's tavern, Deptford was part of Kent and was regarded as a sordid, distant environ of the capital, a seedy dockyard town south of London governed by dissolute merchants. Walking down its High Street, I found that four centuries have only moderately softened that reputation. Making my way past claustrophobic pubs with their bubbled-windows and the dark abyss of their propped-open doors, the greasy fried odor of fish and chip shops and the tinny Brit Pop playing within, I spent the better part of an hour vainly looking for St. Nicholas's churchyard while nervously eyeing grey skies and the cool wind blowing in off the Thames, for in those days I didn't avail myself of a smartphone's convenience.

Though it was July, in my memory it was only ever October, Deptford a morass of confusing, crooked, coble-stoned streets punctuated by centuries-old dissenting churches and small brick rowhouses whose curtains were tightly pulled shut. Surely there were green leaves on the trees, but in my memory, all of those branches are skeletal, bones stripped of flesh withered beneath a sky the color of brackish water. My Gothic disposition only intensified after I finally found Marlowe's graveyard, the opposing red-brick columns marking the entrance to the grounds topped by a pair of grinning skulls hewn from stone, their toothless grins and eyeless sockets a *memento mori* installed a century after the most famous resident was tossed into an anonymous pauper's tomb. A redbrick, ivy-covered wall demarcates the graveyard from the realms of the living, upon which is affixed a small white marble plaque mourning the poet's "untimely death," while proclaiming that somewhere within this earth are the remains of Marlowe, his bones intermingled with other subjects in the kingdom of death. "Cut is the branch that might have grown full straight" reads Marlowe's epitaph. It's from *Doctor Faustus*.

Examining the dual voids in the carved skulls welcoming me to St. Nicholas's reaffirmed what I found so fascinating about this story of a contract with the Devil, for walking upon that hallowed ground, atoms of Marlowe now slick with the dirt on the soles of my shoes, and the part of me that is skeptical of skepticism couldn't help but feel antique occult enthusiasms, that sense that there may be something beyond this veil of our reality, something that we can access but that we can't control.

———

My desire to write a cultural history of the Faust legend goes back a few years earlier than my pilgrimage to the Deptford churchyard, around the time that I attended an adaptation of the play entitled *faustUS* staged by the theater collective 404 Strand in my hometown of Pittsburgh. Basing the script on the shorter, so-called "Text A" of

Marlowe's play, a tauter and more cryptic work that cuts the slapstick that mars more traditional productions of *Doctor Faustus*, the performance was hallucinatory, ritualistic, psychedelic, incantatory. A work of conjuration. With the audience invited to sit in an ad hoc theater-in-the-round constructed on the stage of the Kelly Strayhorn Theater, we all faced a rusted iron-cage in which the action of the play would be set. I was in the front row.

My most distinctive memory of that performance was the actor who played Faust, shirtless and sinewy, glistening with sweat beneath the oppressive stage lights, hoisting a shaggy, bestial mask of a horn-twisted ox over his head, and wildly gesticulating to thrash metal so loud that my fillings were humming, the necromancer then taking a full loaf of white bread out of its antiseptic bag and shredding it into the gapping maw of the bovine mask, bits of spongy whiteness spraying onto all of us sitting in the front row. It was bizarre and impossible not to watch, part avant-garde performance art and part pagan ceremony. The physicality of the performance made it seem otherworldly, alien, and dangerous. Walking out into the autumn air of Pittsburgh's East Liberty, a neighborhood of Gilded Age high-rises and Gothic skyscraper cathedrals that are intercut with alleyways and corner bars, I vowed that one day I would sign a contract to pen my own Faustian tale. That was the only production of Marlowe's play that I've seen. The sort of thing Satan might just come to see if he was wondering how he might be depicted.

Marlowe's scant seven plays are seldom produced today; the 2007 staging of *Tamburlaine the Great* mounted by the Shakespeare Theater Company in Washington DC or the riveting film adaptation of *Edward II* directed by Derek Jarman in 1991 notwithstanding. When compared to his contemporary, competitor, and possible colleague William Shakespeare, who four centuries after his death has productions mounted every day, of every year, in every major city on Earth, who is not just a writer but *The Bard*, the standard by which capital-L Literature is evaluated, Marlowe can seem an afterthought, a footnote, even if he is distantly the second most popular Elizabethan playwright whose work is still performed.

Yet I'd argue that Marlowe, whose mighty blank verse prefigured and in many instances surpassed that of The Bard, is every bit the equal of Shakespeare. Between the two, Marlowe is in some ways the more antiquated, a man who despite his reputation for atheism had an inclination toward the Medieval. That, however, is what ironically gave the arch-heretic such a profound sense of the numinous, for whatever his own relation to the Lord, Marlowe can't be accused of not taking an interest in the holy and transcendent, the sacred and the ecstatic. Of course Shakespeare had his own sense of the numinous—it was impossible not to in the Renaissance. But as a kind of divine blasphemer, Marlowe endures as a parallel universe Bard, a kind of shadowy counter-Shakespeare, the great, queer, sacrilegious poet and playwright of damnation.

Tamburlaine the Great's iconoclasm and *The Jew of Malta*'s irreverence aside, no work of sacred heresy in Marlowe's oeuvre is as profound as *Doctor Faustus*. His quisling scholar selling his birthright for the pottage of trickery and illusion may be modernity's operative metaphor, but Marlowe was hardly the originator of the myth. As you'll read in the chapters ahead, Marlowe adapted the historical Johann Faust from German folkloric tradition, though the myth of a contract with Satan existed centuries before that unfortunate alchemist first crossed potassium nitrate with sulfur. Nor of course was Marlowe's rendition the final word, as thousands of permutations of the basic story have been produced over the half-millennium, from Goethe to the musical *Damn Yankees*, Thomas Mann to the Dixie-fried pablum of the execrable Charlie Daniels Band number "The Devil Went Down to Georgia." High culture like Franz Liszt's *Faust Symphony* and Gustav Mahler's *Symphony No. 8*; pop culture from the comic book *Ghost Rider* to the Jack Black flick *Tenacious D in the Pick of Destiny*.

"The figure of Faust is—after Christ, Mary, and the Devil—the single most popular character in the history of Western Christian culture," writes Jeffrey Burton Russell in his classic *Mephistopheles: The Devil in the Modern World*. And of those characters, Faust is the most fully human to us, in his arrogance and his failure, his negotiations and his capitulations, in the whole litany of abuse which the cankered soul is capable of inflicting upon itself.

Russell's contention is far from hyperbole, and amending the word "character" to "narrative," I'd say that there are few archetypal scripts in our culture as essential as the legend of a man selling his soul to the Devil. Thousands of works of literature and film, music and art, grapple with the bargain whereby somebody trades what's most human for power or wealth, influence or knowledge. Only the myth of Adam and Eve being cast out of Eden competes with Faust in terms of influence, and that story is arguably an early variation on the Devil's contract.

Which is what makes the relative dearth of critical treatments of the variable legend so surprising. There are to be sure a multitude of books, tracts, monographs, and papers on the best-known versions of the legend; academic appointments have been made based on studies of Marlowe, and tenure has been secured with an expertise on Goethe, but the whole megillah as it pertains to Faust, whether that's his name or we call him something else, has yet to be told. My own modest attempt is this book, for though Marlowe, Goethe, and Mann might all be inside, it's not a book about Marlowe, Goethe, and Mann, it's not even really a book about a singular character named "Faustus."

And though it is ostensibly a history, and this narrative moves onward rather chronologically, I prefer to think of the story it tells as being about a character who is outside of time, who lives parallel to past, present, and future. An eternal story. Because what this book is concerned with are

the implications— culturally, politically, theologically—of
these highly symbolically charged narratives concerning
the abjuration of a soul, of the ceding of what's intrinsic
to us, of the capitulations and negotiations which make up
any failed life, which is to say every life. More than a history, then, *Devil's Contract* is an account of what it means
to be human in all of our failings.

Increasingly an account of humanity *right now*. For
all the legend's archaicism, the muttered Latin and the alchemical conjuration, Faust's story has always been estimably modern, perhaps the first modern story. Unlike Adam
and Eve, with their inscrutable Bronze Age story composed
in an idiom so ancient and foreign that centuries of theologians have disagreed on what the implications of each
facet of the tale might mean, the details in the Faust legend
are inescapably of our time. This is, after all, the story of
a *contract*. The dénouement of most versions of the Faust
story involves the signing of a legally binding document, an
experience foreign to the authors of Genesis but replete in
our own lives, whether interacting with human resources
or clicking on an agreement with our phone company.
Faust's tale may deal in the numinous and the transcendent, but it's also about bureaucracy and paperwork, our
contemporary hell and its sacrament, respectively. We recognize Faust in a manner that no character in the Bible can
ever be our contemporary.[1]

An issue of signing on the dotted line is superficiality
when it comes to Faust's significance to modern readers,

however, because more than any other myth the tale of the
Devil's contract is a succinct encapsulation of the human
predicament over the past five centuries, right as modernity
was gestated, born, thrived, and is now in the throes of its
own death.

———

Marlowe staged his play at the very beginning of what is
increasingly being called the Anthropocene, the geologi-
cal epoch in which humanity was finally able to impose its
will (in an almost occult manner) upon the earth. There
are costs to any such contract, as the wisdom of the legend
has it, so that it's worth considering after five centuries of
human domination of the planet that we might now be facing our own collective appointment at Deptford. We seem
to finally be facing the final act, the apocalyptic tenor of
our times, from climate change to nuclear brinkmanship
making the continued survival of humanity an open question, our sad predicament the result of hubris, and greed,
and vainglory. It may be appropriate to rechristen this age
the Faustocene. Because whether or not the Devil is real,
his effects in the world are. When it comes to "truth" and
"facts," the two words are not synonymous, and I wouldn't
at all be surprised if I could make out the smoke of some
devilish chimera beyond the neon-line of the Rose Theater,
deep within a darkness so all-encompassing that not a
squib of light is capable of escaping.

Devil's Contract

CHAPTER ONE

SIMON MAGUS: ARCH-HERETIC, SUPREME NECROMANCER

And the star that leads the way is your star.
—The Gospel of Judas (c. 300 CE)

Five months after the first nuclear explosion at the Trinity Test Site in Alamogordo, New Mexico—the demonic birth of our modern world—in another desert some seven thousand miles away, two Egyptian farmers made another explosive discovery. Muhammad and Khalifah Ali al' Samman were either digging for fertilizer or grave robbing—accounts differ—outside the small town of Nag Hammadi when they unearthed a large, rough-hewn, red jar, the opening of which was sealed shut with an upturned bowl affixed by a slather of bitumen. Simultaneously fearing jinn and hoping for gold, the two men of the al' Samman clan broke open the jar, a shower of flaked papyrus dust briefly shimmering in the intense heat of the midday sun. Neither gold nor genies were inside, but rather dozens of codices, leather-bound sheafs of frayed, brittle, and fragmentary papyri.

In a sense, the papyri of Nag Hammadi confirmed the al' Sammans' desires and fears, for the canon within that jar was as if both gold and jinn, the largest compendium of ancient Christian heretical thought to ever be found, a veritable dark shadow-bible of writings with exotic titles like the Gospel of Judas, the Hypostasis of the Archons, and the Gnostic Apocalypse of Peter. Familiar names appear throughout these scriptures—Abraham, Moses, Mary, Christ—but the overall sentiment of this hidden bible is far different from that which has been received by posterity.[1] As diverse as these writings are, they share some postulates: that the true nature of reality is hidden, that ours is a corrupted and fallen world, and that certain exemplary individuals are capable of intimating the true nature of our existence. A powerful and revolutionary form of faith; the creed of the romantic and the mystic, the poet and the contemplative, the sorcerer and the mage. The faith of Faust.

The papyri discovered at Nag Hammadi are collectively known as Gnostic writings, after the Greek word for "Knowledge" (which is to be contrasted with "Faith"). Gnosticism has always been a contested term, but has

generally connoted a dark, mysterious subcurrent in early
Christian history which supplied a counternarrative to the
New Testament gospels. Drawing from a variety of ancient
Greek and Persian philosophical movements, the Gnostics
promulgated a confusing variety of theologies across an
even more confusing variety of denominations. The la-
bel "Gnostic" grouped together variety of baroque early
Christian cosmologies under a single designation, though in
actuality this wide-tent heresy includes dozens of radically
different groups with bizarre names such as the Sethians,
the Basildeans, the Valentinianists, the Thomasines, and
so on. Most likely the Nag Hammadi texts, which give detail on several of these denominations, were transcribed no
later than the fourth century, works that were possibly bur-
ied by monks of the nearby Chenoboskian monastery after
the steadfastly orthodox bishop St. Athanasius banned all
apocryphal scripture in the fourth century. What all these
groups shared was a sense that this visible world isn't our
real world, and that it's a devilish one, too, so that the God
who is worshiped by most people is very distant from the
actual holy deity.

For seventeen centuries of stony sleep the fifty-two
tractates of Nag Hammadi lay entombed in this ancient
Egyptian graveyard. Despite their sometimes wild diversity,
the Gnostics were nonetheless united in the belief that the
world of our everyday experience was the creation of a demonic Demiurge, and that a greater, truer God lay beyond.[2]
Despite their often stunning diversity, what was clear at

Nag Hammadi was that this had been a cracked, eccentric faith that bore little similarity to Christianity as it developed; a mystical and at times magical religion that emphasized the fallenness of this world and the corruptibility of the devilish god whom the Gnostics believed others had confused with the true Lord.

An alternative Christ in the Gospel of Thomas instructs that the "Kingdom is inside of you, and it is outside of you;" while in the Gospel of Philip the Messiah loved Mary Magdalene "more than all the disciples and used to kiss her on the mouth." Whether the denominations, sects, and cults represented by the various gospels, epistles, apocalypses, and wisdom tracts discovered at Nag Hammadi belong to a cohesive tradition is debatable, but to orthodox Christians such beliefs were at best alien and at worst blasphemous. Yet the Gnostics were not above condemning others as heretics, for in an enigmatic and highly fragmentary work from Nag Hammadi entitled Testimony of Truth there is a denunciation of a sacrilegious thinker responsible for "schisms," who "belongs to the darkness of the world."

Simon Magus—the wicked sorcerer, the nefarious wizard, the conjurer, magician, necromancer. The Arch-Heretic. Faust's story begins with Simon Magus, for his is the forerunner of all Faustian bargains, the first to sell his soul to the Devil (or, more paradoxically as the story has it, to sell his soul to God). Whoever wrote the Testimony of Truth was referencing a group known as the Simonians after their founder, a sect accused of any number of impieties and obscenities, of practicing semen- and blood-besmirched orgies as religious rituals, and who called upon supernatural entities to acquire profane powers. Over the centuries, Simon's reputation has accrued a litany of occult details—it's been said that he was capable of levitation and raising the dead, the manipulation of illusions and the conjuration of demons. What makes the brief reference to Simon in the Testimony of Truth so surprising is that it's an example of a Gnostic denunciation of a man who was often described by orthodox Christians as Gnosticism's founder, though that was obviously a means to slur them both. Endlessly enigmatic as Simon has been, presumably charismatic, too, since he was able to draw a multitude of followers during his lifetime, neither the Christians nor the Gnostics claimed him.

I've long had a bit of an unusual interest in the Magus, for at the very least us Simons must stick together. There's something singular in seeing your own name associated with such a figure, maligned by the early Christians as the cankered father of lies. That he was often used as a convenient cipher for Medieval anti-Judaism (despite being a Samaritan) has only deepened my sympathy. I've always envisioned Simon in the manner that he was depicted by an anonymous twelfth-century carver of the Romanesque tympanum of Porte Miègeville at the Basilica of Saint-Sernin in Toulouse, France. Here a distinctly Orientalized wizard, with turban and curly beard the hue of the pale limestone from which the cathedral is constructed looks toward the heavens which he will be denied, a pointy-eared devil behind his right shoulder, the Latin inscription reading that "Confounded by his magical art, Simon is defeated by his own weapons." Hard for me not to have sympathy.

Before attempting the Faustian corpus, before studying ancient magic or even ancient religion, the following fact must be kept in mind—these people of millennia past were not like us but with more dirt. Their beliefs were different, their prayers were different, their faith was different, their very thoughts were different, and yet we still live within their long shadows. The flattening of history, the reduction of experience, all tends to re-create the past through the misapprehensions of the present, but that's as if to stare through a mirror darkly. To fully inhabit this epoch in which everyone believed in the supernatural, where it was a matter of course that there were invisible consciousnesses higher than yours, that messages and meaning were encoded into everything no matter how seemingly inert, is to grasp toward a kingdom that none of us now living can ever really acquire the keys for.

No doubt both the contemporary faithful and their critics will argue that there are plenty of people who believe they have some connection to this enchanted realm, yet the possibility of doubt always exists for us moderns—even apparent believers—that we can't inhabit the consciousness of those who existed within a truly charged reality. Our image of Simon, or Christ, or Peter, are intimations from a past we can never fully comprehend, mere traces of a forever inexplicable way of being. They are exiles of a nonexistent country, beings who existed before theology tried to convince the newly doubtful of the veracity of faith. For Simon, there was no need of syllogism, argument, or discourse, his was not a realm of logical debate about the particulars of God, but rather the shining, mystical, ecstatic experience of that same thing.

As with Christ, somebody like the Magus can only be peripherally seen. Whoever Simon happened to be, now he's become a cipher, a symbol, a fable, a parable, and he's been that way for nearly two thousand years. Maybe once there was a man whom this legend was based on, squatting in a wool chiton dusty with the red clay of Samara and quickly scooping stewed chickpeas with unleavened and charred barley cakes from a rough, earthenware bowl. Maybe this man talked to his disciples about this new faith of Christ or maybe he talked about his own spiritual visions. Maybe he was regarded as a great healer or possibly his reputation as a wicked magician was earned. Perhaps there were two or three Simons merged over time by that kiln of misinterpretation and faulty memory, invention and duplicity, fantasy and vision. None of it matters, whoever the "real" Simon was is irrelevant—as with Christ. For a figure who dwells at those crossroads between faith and knowledge, religion and magic, piety and blasphemy, the greatest work of conjuration Simon ever accomplished was to become something so much greater than a mere man. He became a story. Whoever Simon Magus was—whoever

Christ really was for that matter—just understand that
when he felt the buzzing sense behind the eyes of being
grasped by some power that would descend upon him, that
force was something with a name, something that could
speak back.

What Simon coveted was the ability to command that
voice. His was a bargain, a wager, a bet, a contract. A covenant, not with Satan, but with that equally malevolent deity known as God. For the Magus, then, such power could
lay within. The power to manifest himself; the ability to
create himself. As is recorded in an extant passage from
the Simonian work *The Great Declaration*, the Magus understood the purpose of divinity as being "producing himself by himself," to be "manifested to himself [by] his own
Thought." More than a mere man, Simon Magus was an
archetype. Not necessarily the first of the magicians—the
ancient Chaldeans who ruled Babylon a half-millennia before Christ long had a reputation in that discipline—but
Simon was the first real *personality* to whom a talent for
the dark arts can be ascribed.[3]

These accounts can differ in the details and accusations,
not unusual for this time, but the broad contours of Simon's
biography are that he was a Samaritan (a Levantine religion historically related to Judaism) who was converted to
Christianity by Philip the Evangelist, but who hoped to use
the promise of his baptism not for the purpose of salvation,
but rather to selfishly gain the miracle-working abilities of
the saints. What makes this story unsettling is that Simon's

strategy *works*; through his conversion he perfects the ability to perform magic. Ancient works, both canonical and apocryphal, can be comfortable with this discomfort, can be conversant with the copacetic relations between magic and faith. The complex nature of this twined relation between the sacred and the demonic can feel very alien to some contemporary readers, especially if they're reared in American Christianity with its almost hysterical fear of the occult (but blindness to its own magical thinking). It's precisely this tension between the divine and the diabolical which animates Simon's bargain, and which makes it such an enduring story.

This unsettling parallel between the celestial and the satanic is in evidence across the non-canonical second-century *Infancy Gospel of Thomas*, which is notably not a Gnostic work. This scripture covers the lacuna of Christ's prepubescent biography, filling in gaps obscured in the New Testament, but the portrait which emerges is disturbing. Wholly human and wholly God, the young Christ is ill-suited to his supernatural abilities, with the child's personality evoking Damien from *The Omen* more than the Messiah. For example, the young Christ fastens a number of clay statues of birds which he then endows with life, using them to terrorize the denizens of Nazareth. He afflicts the neighbors of Mary and Joseph with blindness when he is angry. Most cryptically, Christ murders two children who have displeased him, only to resurrect his playmates later. All of this is more in keeping with the Antichrist than Christ. Or, as is perhaps more generous and more the point, it's in keeping with a human child who happens to be cursed with being the Lord, which is what Christ was. "When Joseph saw the understanding of the child, and his age . . . he thought himself again that he should not be ignorant," writes the author, "and he took him and delivered him to another teacher." What's imparted in this enigmatic text is the fundamental strangeness of the sacred, the ways in which human good and evil can be very distant from that divine kingdom.

Necromancer or not, Simon Magus was closer to Christ than any of us are. The uncomfortable relationship of Simon's faith and magic is clear in a disquieting extended passage about his life in the New Testament Book of Acts. Written by the same gentile author who penned the Book of Luke, Acts enumerates the activities of the Church in the immediate aftermath of Christ's resurrection and ascension. Acts 8:9-24 speaks of a "certain man, called Simon" who had "bewitched the people of Samaria." In keeping with the extra-scriptural tradition which accumulated about Simon Magus, the author writes of how the followers of the sorcerer understood him to be an emissary of the power of God (some apocryphal texts claim that he was worshiped). Conversion to Christianity does nothing to quell Simon Magus's trickery. If anything, this bad Samaritan's witnessing of the miracles performed by the apostles convinced him that he should acquire their same powers, and so he implores the Holy Ghost to descend unto him and grant him those abilities.

So covetous is he of the apostolic gifts of hand laying and tongue speaking that he offers both Peter and John payment if they'll grant these skills to him (from which the sin of "simony"—the buying of Church offices—derives its name). Peter, traditionally the first pope and a frequent enemy of Simon Magus, tells the magician that "Thy money perish with thee, because thou hast thought that the gift of God may be purchased with money." The gospel lesson seems clear: Simon has confused magic with faith, and the saving power of God with devilish tricks and delusions, so he is cast out and exiled. Simon's miracles are seen as tricks and his theologies as delusions, a man not of religion, but of illusion. If faith is an issue of acceptance, than magic is one of will, and Simon was a wizard, not an evangelist. An anxiety is apparent, especially as concerns the concept of a bargain. The wizard has entered into a contract, but there is an uncomfortable parallel with the prayers of the faithful. What makes his bargain even more disturbing is that Simon has entered into covenant with the very same God as the faithful, albeit for wicked reasons.

Luke is silent about the ultimate destiny of Simon, but other works only slightly younger than the gospel are less circumspect. Justin Martyr, among the second-century theologians who defined orthodoxy and are known as the Church Fathers, claimed that Simon came to Rome where he established a cult with his lover, a former prostitute named Helen—that particular name endures in later manifestations of the Faust myth—and that his sorcery led the credulous pagans to worship him as a god.[4] Helen appears to be not merely a scurrilous invention of Justin Martyr, but a figure who appears in the writings ascribed to the Gnostic Simonians, the supposed followers of the Magus. Pairs of conjoined male and female evangelists weren't unheard of in the ancient Mediterranean, another departure from our common myth of the isolated and sexless mystic.[5]

Many of these figures were paragons of chastity, but Simon's Helen was a woman who was a courtesan, a harlot, a whore—though that was precisely the point. In the Simonian corpus, the Magus had apparently argued that the initial emanating Thought of God was feminine (there are antecedents to this belief in both Judaism and Platonism), but that after the fall such an essence was imprisoned in the physical form of a multitude of women, reincarnated one after the other and culminating in Helen. It was only by a flouting of morality that this divine soul could find liberation, hence the justification for Helen's employment in the oldest profession. Hippolytus of Rome, yet another Church Father, writes as way of proffered explanation in his second-century *Refutation of All Heresies* that Simon was simply "enamored of this wench . . . and it was out of respect for his disciples that he invented this fairy-tale."

An even more scurrilous tradition about Simon Magus developed in later extra-biblical scriptures that if not heretical were certainly not canonical.[6] These works present a detailed narrative of Simon's life in Rome after his conversion to Christianity and make clear that even while much of his magic was derived from classical paganism, his baptism effected a transformation that allowed him to produce "miracles" which cheapened God's grace. In both works, Simon is pointedly contrasted with his great adversary, the apostle Peter. Notable that Peter's original name was Simon, for a rather pithy psychoanalytic argument should be made of how much we're to understand the infernal magician as an aspect of the disciple's psyche. In this way, Simon is a shadow self to Peter, a sort of Id whom the apostle must battle. And Peter does battle Simon, whether the latter is merely symbolic or not. The Acts of Peter depicts a veritable "prayer battle" between Simon and Peter, after the magician uses his abilities to levitate above the Roman Forum, and the apostle furiously implores God to dash the Samaritan down, who then plummets to the ground while the Emperor Nero looks on. The Magus is later stoned by an enraged crowd.

—

"O Simon Magus," wails the Italian poet Dante in the nineteenth canto of "Inferno," the first third of the fourteenth-century epic *The Divine Comedy*, "O forlorn disciples, / Ye who the things of God, which ought to be / The brides of holiness, rapaciously / For silver and gold do prostitute."

Dante's Simon was he who established simony, that sin of purchasing Church offices, of no small account to the oft-corrupt clergy of Medieval Catholicism whom the poet denounced. "Now it behoves for you the trumpet sound" writes Dante, for here in the penultimate eighth circle of Hell do the simonists eternally abide. It is with simony that the Magus introduced one of the most characteristic aspects of the Faust legend, that of the contractual exchange. To conjure demons was one thing, but with the sin of simony our machinations with the Devil would be translated into contract and bargain, the financial logic of debt and payment.

Not that such dry particulars need to be dwelled upon, because his story—that battle floating over the Forum, for example—is also irresistibly visual. On illuminated vellum or small-gemmed mosaic, stretched canvas or fresh-washed fresco, it's that Luciferian fall that's most memorable. Simon's fate, or at least a version of it, can be seen in the colored engravings of the fifteenth-century German encyclopedia the *Nuremberg Chronicle,* where a group of suspiciously Teutonic-looking Romans in Medieval garb stare agog at the unfortunate red-robed Samaritan who is pulled aloft and molested by a trio of caprine and chiropteran demons, a fair-haired angel with sword levitating even higher, as if heaven and hell should fight over who gets to immolate the magician's cursed soul. Or, look at the minor Dutch master Jan Rombouts's *The Fall of Simon Magus* (c.1522), and now displayed at the Museum Leuven, in Belgium,

whereby the magician is shown in green velvet tunic and
red cape, pushed from the heavens by a cackling hag of
a demon with withered paps, the necromancer shrieking
in horror before he splatters on the Roman ground. Born
so far before Milton or Byron, there is no Romantic hero-
ism; like Faust he gets what he deserves. Here was a figure,
mysterious and censored though he may have been, at the
very origins of Christianity, who points toward something
hidden and hermetic in the religion.[7]

By the sixteenth century, Faust had replaced Simon
as the standard-bearer of the diabolical contract, but the
Magus endures as a symbol of occult perdition. Dante's first
American interpreter, Henry Wadsworth Longfellow, was
drawn to the tragic story of Simon and filtered it through
a distinctly Romantic sensibility. Both Longfellow's
now largely unread *Christus: A Mystery* of 1851 and his
1880 lyric "Helen of Tyre" reference the doomed heretic,
"Simon, the Seer" who shall deliver his beloved "From this
evil fame, / From this life of sorrow and shame, / I will lift
thee and make thee mine . . . And Helen of Troy . . . shalt
be / The Intelligence Divine!" The shamed necromancer is
also alluded to by twentieth-century writers such as Jorge
Luis Borges, predictably drawn to the esoteric and drawing on Simon in his iconic short story "Three Versions of
Judas," as well as in the private writings of the science fiction writer Philip K. Dick, who occasionally believed all
of us to be victims of a Gnostic demiurge that occluded
our reality, namely that that we're all really living in the

first century. "The distinction between sanity and insanity is narrower than the razor's edge," Dick self-perceptively wrote, "sharper than a hound's tooth, more agile than a mule deer." If Simon Magus has provided inspiration for our most metaphysically baroque of writers, then he's also had his own unexpected film entrances, an occasional subject of Hollywood features such as in the schlocky 1954 Victor Saville–directed sword-and-sandals flick *The Silver Chalice*, where he is played by a muscular, scenery-chewing Jack Palance, the only notable aspect of that movie being that it was Paul Newman's first. Martin Scorsese succinctly described *The Silver Chalice* in a 1978 interview with *Film Comment* as "a bad picture." A better film is the 1999 Ben Hopkins movie *Simon Magus,* in which the wizard's name is appropriated for the titular character, a Jewish holy fool living in a nineteenth-century Polish shtetl who has his own disturbing interactions with the devil, the entire picture a potent allegory of the nihilism at the core of modernity, and what the ultimate conclusions of that technological modernity shall be.

Such rancor as imparted to Simon is attributable to his understanding that there is an inner power that can connect with outer forces, that the supernatural need not only be the object of our worship but can also be a field of our command. "I am the first power, who am always, and without beginning," Simon supposedly said as recorded in the fourth-century *Recognitions of Clement*, and despite the hubris, it is a sense that has motivated not just magic, but later iterations of that way of thinking ranging from science and technology to art and literature. Ultimately it's important to remember that whatever his occult powers, the sorcerer's fate was still the hard ground of the Roman Forum. Simon's narrative isn't just one of moralizing censure; for there is a thread that should be far more disquieting to the religious believer (and all the best spiritual stories are disquieting). Irenaeus dismisses the faith of Simon by saying that the Magus had supposed that the "apostles themselves performed their curse by the art of magic, and not by the power of God," but the line separating magic from religion is porous. Though it's clear that Simon was capable of necromancy before his conversion, Philip's baptism didn't cause the cessation of such magic, and even increased its power.

Arguably Simon has a bit of a point when it comes to the Apostles. They could cure the ill, speak in tongues, and finally engage in prayer-battle against the magician himself: if anything, the magic of faith was simply more powerful. Magic itself is hardly a repudiation of God, rather such practices are confirmation of the supernatural, no matter how distasteful or torrid more rational theologians might find incantations and conjurations to be.[8] Observing the similarities and continuities between magic and religion is not to denigrate either; far from it, it's to note that a transcendent realm amenable to intervening in the affairs of humanity is an axiom of both systems. There's much that Simon Magus shares with later iterations of the Faust myth—the overweening hubris, the prideful desire, the violent conclusion, and even women named Helen. What's different is that despite his reputation for necromancy, nowhere does Simon Magus interact with Satan. Read together, there's a suggestion that there's not much difference between abusing the grace of the Lord or the Devil's magic. Whether or not you sell your soul to Satan or to God, *you've still sold your soul*. The numinous realm, the astral plane, the transcendent dimension—*the sacred*—is a terrifying kingdom, defined by its difference from everything that is safe and familiar and human. What distinguishes Peter and Simon, the Apostles and the magicians, is less what supernatural reality they're interacting with then their reasons for doing so.

Between knowledge and faith, both Simon and Faust desired the former, and in that way both were Gnostics. Most importantly, both the Gnostics and magicians like Simon understood this world as irrevocably fallen, ironically taking evil even more seriously than orthodox Christianity. At its mystic core, Gnosticism was an attempt to reconcile the conundrum of theodicy—the question of why evil exists in the world—which forever bedevils monotheism. That classic theological puzzle maintains that the obvious existence of evil in the world is inexplicable. Evil makes it difficult to reconcile God's omnipotence and His omnibenevolence.

To wit, during the century that Simon and Peter sparred, petty criminals would be nailed to crosses outside of Rome's beautiful marble Esquiline Gate, heavy iron nails splintering wrist bones, the weight of bodies pulled down by gravity slowly asphyxiating the guilty until air could no longer escape lungs, not even a scream. During the Jewish Rebellion of 70 CE when the persecuted of Judea rose against Roman occupation, the Jewish historian Josephus records that the empire was so unforgiving that "Most of the victims were peaceful citizens, weak and unarmed, butchered wherever they were caught." When it came to God's Temple itself, the "heaps of corpses grew higher and higher, while down the Sanctuary steps poured a river of blood and the bodies of those killed at the top slithered to the bottom." Meanwhile, in the capital of Empire, the condemned were famously shouldered into the pit of the Colosseum, where a multitude of wild beasts including lions, bears, and wolves would sink fang and claw into the soft flesh of woman, child, and man, for the ritual blood lust of the cheering crowd forever famished for bread and circuses.

Not that this has much changed in two millennia, as the Holocaust and Hiroshima demonstrate. Evil has a way of making belief in a good and powerful God difficult. This can be phrased by the theologians in syllogism and hermeneutics, but it's simply understood by everybody else through experience. A multitude of ingenious solutions to theodicy have been proposed over the past two millennia, but the Gnostics had perhaps the greatest exoneration of God—He didn't create this world. As Philip K. Dick noted in his cracked 1981 exegesis *VALIS*, "It is sometimes an appropriate response to reality to go insane." The *insane* response of the Gnostic as alluded to before was that this corrupted, filthy, fallen, and wicked world was not the spawn of a God worth worshiping, but rather of a lesser deity whom both the Jews and Christians mistook for the real divinity who exists in some heaven as far away from us as to be unreal. For the Gnostics the name of the demiurge was variable, such as Samael or Yaldabaoth, but really they were all talking about Yahweh. The God of the Hebrew Scriptures, the Gnostics maintained, was really the Devil. As the bloodletting of Jerusalem and Rome was a manifestation of the evil of Empire, so was disease, famine, and natural disaster the result of the Emperor of this dimension, the Devil whom believers erroneously call God. Rather than being conventional necromancers, the Gnostics were austere and stoic rejectors of this world and its prince, understanding everyday life to be a Faustian bargain. To eat, to sleep, to work, to procreate, to live, to exist, to be—all of it was to give over a measure of your life to the Demon who had tricked us into worshiping him as the Lord. Our being itself is Faustian.

There is something to this, something almost poignant, even tender, about this impossible dilemma of how to live in a fallen world, where the sacred itself is always

mysterious, foreign, dangerous. But, if there was a Simon
Magus, the identification of him as being somehow the
"founder" of Gnosticism is almost certainly at best a gross
simplification and at worst theological slander. In an important regard the necromancer's rebellion against God by
using the very gifts of that same deity indicates a similar
spiritual sensibility.[9] The perspective of a Simon, however,
was much darker than even the Gnostics, who thought that
the god who created our corrupted world was the Devil.
They believed, at least, in another God who existed in a
higher sphere that was perfectly good even if powerfully
distant, but for Simon there wasn't any higher heaven—
this was all there was. It's not that the Lord of this world
was Satan, it's that there was never any difference between
God and the Devil anyhow. And so when Simon Magus
prostrated himself before the apostles, he understood that
his baptism was a variety of selling his soul to the Devil,
and he hoped to foment his own revolution against that
heavenly status quo. For Simon, any kind of bargain with
God was a Faustian one.

In his 1983 novel *The Encyclopedia of the Dead* the
brilliant Yugoslav novelist Danilo Kiš, who wrote with the
precision of parable and the parsimony of prayer, has his
fictionalized Simon Magus intone that "The Kingdom of
Heaven rests on a foundation of lies . . . Their scriptures
are composed of false words and mysterious laws" and
that God is nothing but "a tyrant, a vindictive tyrant." The
Magus's was a radical theodicy, the deployment of divinity

against divinity itself, a rebellion against the unfeeling tyranny of God. Such a revolution was bound to fail, for the inviolate law understands that no rebellion can be accomplished on the authoritarian's terms. Impossible not to admire Simon at least partially, for his failure is our own. After all this time, after the myths and inventions, stories, dreams, fantasies, and nightmares, the parable of Simon Magus reminds us that the difference is between magic and religion, between God and the Devil is imperceptible. Nothing remains of Simon Magus some twenty centuries later, except two curious depressions in the grooved basalt along a walkway in the basilica Santa Francesca Romana in the Campitelli district of Rome, a building that is a suturing of the Romanesque, Renaissance, and Baroque, as jumbled together as the myths with which we order our lives. At Francesca Romana, tradition has held, the prayers of Peter were so intense when he was engaged in his night-battle with Simon that the saint's knees and shins wore away the stone of the path in a single evening. I rather prefer an alternative possibility: it was here that Simon would be dashed down to the ground, the supplicating sinner forced to finally genuflect on bended knee before the demiurge of this fallen realm.

CHAPTER TWO

CHRIST IN THE DESERT: TWO MILLENNIA OF LENT

The doors of heaven and hell are adjacent and identical.
—Nikos Kazantzakis, *The Last Temptation of Christ* (1952)

Sotheby's, the venerable British auction house, has its American headquarters on York Avenue along the edge of the Upper East Side, situated halfway between the comparative calm of Carl Schurz Park and the cacophony of Memorial Sloan Kettering hospital. On January 27th, 2023 a wealthy art patron, as is such a person's wont, would have traded York Avenue's ambulance wails and honking taxis for the relative silence of Sotheby's glass, modernist monolith, and successfully bid forty thousand dollars—a steal—for a marginal painting by a marginal artist that nonetheless conveys the strangeness of its biblical subject with quiet sublimity.

Lodewijk Toeput was born in Flanders, but spent his life in Italy, where he worked under the name "il Pozzoserrato," so that the sixteenth-century painter's work is a delightful fusion of two different Renaissance styles, a combination of the epic scope of Florence with the human intimacy of Amsterdam. Il Pozzoserrato's *Landscape with Scenes from the Life of Christ*, the painting auctioned in lot 478 on that day, was most likely painted in Italy sometime in the last decade of the sixteenth century. Borrowing the hazy blue *sfumato* of his Italian antecedents and his fellow Netherlandish painters (especially Brueghel), and Toeput imagines a vast rustic tableau of massive primeval trees and violently gashed valleys, a first-century Judea that appears more as if a particularly lush Tuscany. A triumphal Roman arch, in ruins and covered in encroaching ivy, is admired by several small figures toward the right of the composition. In the grey-tinged lunar-blue background there are the towers of a fantastic city. And there, toward the bottom center of the painting and again atop a high peak of jagged rocks depicted on the far left are two instances of Toeput's titular subject.

In the valley below, a haloed Son of Man commands Thomas to probe the side-wound of his resurrected body, while on the peak above Christ stands with the Devil, the third of the temptations presented to the Messiah during his forty-day-long vigil in the wilderness.[1] All the figures, despite their supernatural import, are dwarfed by the vista. They're easy to overlook at first. Christ appears as the man that he was, but then so does the Devil—a prosaic, forgettable, normal figure.

———

From the Flemish miniaturist Simon Bening's sixteenth-century representation of the Devil as a bird-footed, becloaked bestial monstrosity to the French lithographer Gustave Doré's iconic hard-bodied, bat-winged fallen angel of the nineteenth century, Satan is oft-depicted as something bizarre. Toeput was hardly the first artist to imagine the Devil coming in the guise of a man; there is nothing revolutionary in *Landscape with Scenes from the Life of Christ,* but that sartorial decision does result in a composition that underscores the human nature of Christ's temptations. Not that Toeput or any other artist who has taken the temptations of Christ as a subject has much from the biblical narrative to draw upon.[2]

As recounted in Matthew, which is my preferred version because it evidences a logic of ever more consequential challenges, Satan appears to the weary and worn Christ and commands him to transform the stones of the desert into bread, which the Messiah refuses to do, answering that "Man does not live by bread alone." Then the Prince of Lies takes Christ to the very parapet of the Temple in

Jerusalem, imploring him to jump, the presumption being that a chorus of angels bearing Him to the ground would prove that Jesus is indeed who He claims to be. To such a challenge, Christ tells the Devil "Thou shalt not tempt the Lord thy God." Finally, Lucifer brings Christ to the top of a tall peak in the desert, and shows Him all of the kingdoms of the world; if Christ will only supplicate Satan, then the Devil will offer all to Jesus. "Get away Satan!" is Christ's response, and with that the Son of Man has proven Himself true and faithful when confronted by every temptation presented by the Prince of Perdition. This, then, is the rough scaffold of the tale; the gospels aren't consistent in the ordering of the temptations (the second and third are switched in Luke, for example).

That he rejected such offers makes all the difference; both the crucifixion and the resurrection would have been impossible without the passing of this test in the desert. Though the ministers and theologians may blanch at the identification of this story as a variation on the Faust trope, they'll be positively apoplectic when I claim that the encounter in the Judean wilderness is the most important moment in the entirety of the New Testament, not because it depicts Christ as winning this contest, but because it implies an alternative where Jesus might have succumbed. What logically follows is an entire gospel of power derived from asking what it would mean for God to sign a contract with the Devil.

Part of the innate mystery of scripture is the lack of detail, so different from what our contemporary novelistic imaginations demand. Satan isn't described at all in any of the synoptic gospels—Mark doesn't even identify him as such, only cryptically referring to the figure as the tempter.[3] No horns or wings, no cloven hooves or forked tail. Naturally that absence of specificity has allowed for a multitude of artistic interpretations, from the animalistic creature in Bening to the Byronic hero of Doré, but despite Toeput's liberties (the Judean Desert doesn't look like Flanders, for example), there is something all the more unsettling in the Devil appearing in the guise of a man. Christ sits among the jagged rocks of the Judean Desert, a place of disorienting jutting precipices and deep caverns gashed into the rough and broken flesh of the earth, of scalding noonday sun and freezing midnight. His only companions are the locusts and scorpions, the spiders and the centipedes; Christ's dark weathered skin is sun-blistered, his nut-brown face burnt by the wind and the heat—sand cuts like a prayer into the dried surfaces of his russet eyes, dirt clings like a parable to his swollen grey hands, small cuts cover his bruised arms and legs like the scratched words of a psalm. And what of Satan, what does he look like? Not monster, but a man—maybe a monk or mystic, possibly identical in appearance to the Messiah. Same short-shorn black curly hair, same red-streaked beard, equal in short stature, missing matching teeth, clothed in identical rough, woolen tunics.

For forty days before the adversary would appear, Christ lives a scripture of pebbles, stones, and rocks, a Bible of silt, gravel, and dirt. A true Bible of this fallen world.

This is the scene into which *Ha Satan*—Hebrew for "The Adversary"—does announce himself to the Son of God. Crucially, this test of wills between God and the Devil is itself a form of disputation; the two are involved entirely in source-quoting material from the Hebrew Scriptures, a battle not of supernatural powers as with Simon and Peter, but of exegetical acumen. Through the entire story, there is the question of if the Devil knows exactly who it is that he's tempting. For that matter, there is the conundrum of whether Jesus really knows who He is.[4]

Connecting Christ's biblical temptation in the desert to the Faust legend is a controversial assertion—no doubt the ministers and theologians will be annoyed that I've done so. Yet what do Matthew, Mark, and Luke recount other than a failed attempt on the part of the Devil to enact a Faustian negotiation, a contract which Christ completely rejects? After all, Satan has offered certain gifts in exchange for Christ's fealty.

This is the story of a failed Faustian bargain, yet a Faustian bargain all the same. What a bizarre story then, the tale of the Devil commanding God to bow down. What exactly does it mean for the mere creature to entice the Creator to transgress? There is, to be sure, a certain melancholy to the idea, where even He who embodies ultimate Goodness can be tempted by evil. There are shades of this anxiety in the Hebrew Scriptures, where in that immaculate book of Job the Great Adversary who is Satan tricks the Lord into punishing a pious man. Yet in the tale of

Jesus's temptation in the desert, there is something else, a sense of God's humanity, for Christ incarnate is equally man as He is God, so in all our failings, all of our possibilities of temptation, we have a deity who can share in our own fallibility and fallenness.[5] *So what exactly does it even mean for Satan to tempt God?*

Whether or not Jesus thought himself to be God is an issue of faith. That the authors of Matthew, Mark, and Luke didn't think that Jesus was God—for the first two were clearly religious Jews for whom such a concept would be absurdity—is obvious from reading the texts themselves.[6] Why would Satan offer the world to the very being who created it? Notable that of the four gospels of the New Testament only the otherwise metaphysically inclined John doesn't include the story of the temptation, for in that work it's clear that the author views Christ as not only the Messiah, but as an incarnation of God.

Perhaps by that point the Devil knew better. Yet the synoptic gospels are canonical, and in the bulk of the Christian traditions which receive them as inspired there is a creedal belief in Christ being God, so the story of the temptation can't but be read as a Faustian bargain presented to the Lord. This clearly presents certain *philosophical issues.* That Satan believed he was capable of successfully tempting God is *important*, but that he could have succeeded is *crucial.* Christianity's scandalous paradox of absurdity always has been, and always will be, Christ's being wholly human and entirely God at the same time, and since a man could be ensnared by the temptations offered by Satan, it would follow that Jesus must have been prey to this possibility.

"The temptation of Christ was harder, unspeakably harder, than the temptation of Adam," argued the Lutheran theologian Dietrich Bonhoeffer during a lecture at the University of Berlin in 1932, delivered as the Weimar Republic was collapsing and the Third Reich, which would eventually execute the radical minister, was coming into power. "Adam carried nothing in himself which could have given the tempter a claim and power over him. But Christ bore in himself the whole burden of flesh, under the curse, under condemnation; and yet his temptation was henceforth to bring help and salvation to all flesh." When the Devil tempted Christ to sell him His soul—was that a prayer of a sort?—far more was in balance than merely a *human's soul*, but rather *humanity's soul*.

Christians believe that God and man are unified within the person of Christ, so that the temptation of Jesus in the desert becomes the crescendo of the cosmic drama, where literally everything is at stake. And yet there is a strange dramatic irony in the story, for what use is telling God that He can acquire the very world which He crafted? If we're to suspend our disbelief and pretend that Christ is really God, then it must be admitted that Jesus clearly could turn stones to bread, safely propel Himself from the pinnacle of the Temple, and easily leash king and emperor. What use is offering anything to an omnipotent being?

The nature of temptation wasn't literal so much as it was intellectual; within this Faustian bargain, Christ and Satan were arguing over the nature of *power*. This was a philosophical debate, a hermeneutic battle, an exegetical temptation. The entire point is that Satan knows that Christ can perform those miracles, but that to compel Him to fulfill those requests he'd force God to admit His naked, cynical, authoritarian understanding of power's exercise. Christ wins this debate—he abrogates any Faustian contract—by refusing to exercise His power.

What the temptation in the wilderness presents are two different models of authority as explored through the narrative of the bargain. The Devil's understanding of power is the world's understanding—it's most of our understandings as we effectively live our lives, whether our stated values are Christian or socialist, democratic or liberal. Note, however, that our hypocrisy does not invalidate our stated values—exactly the opposite. Satan's conception of power is that of the figure who decides whose bellies are full, who drafts the lists of who is protected by the law and who is punished by it. "Sovereign is he who decides the exception," writes the notorious Nazi legal philosopher Carl Schmitt in his tract *Political Theology: Four Chapters on the Concept of Sovereignty,* and it's the relativist and totalitarian ethic of the Devil, the first rugged individualist and the ultimate dictator. A system enraptured by the world, the flesh, and the Devil.

Christ, by contrast, tells Pontius Pilate that "My kingdom is not of this world." If the Devil finds the desert to be
a Hobbesian state of nature, than Christ rather uncovers
in the ascetic quietude and stoic silence of the wilderness
a sliver of the utopian empire, an intimation of Christ's
prophesied millennium. To be omnipotent and yet to reject
all the familiar trappings of power—to reject tremendous
wealth and military strength—is to paradoxically court a
variety of power almost inconceivable to the limited human
mind. Jesus could have given in because he is a man; Christ
never could because He is not.

That is the conundrum of Christianity's cracked metaphysics. The promise of the story is that such a kingdom
of heaven is available to all of us; the tragedy of human
history is that almost all of us are incapable of quite reaching it. Because who, if hungry, wouldn't turn those stones
to bread (or something better) at least some of the time, if
offered the possibility? The temptation in the wilderness is
the Faustian bargain that Christ declined, but which the
rest of us continually sign. Everyone—even the saints—
will compromise for a bit of piggishness, a bit of pleasure,
a bit of power, depending on how those things are defined.
Even Saint Francis must have been churlish, occasionally,
Gandhi sometimes gluttonous. The crux of Christ's wilderness temptation is that he was the only human who so
completely and totally resisted any such temptations, but
only because he was also God. Such a psychological Jesus
is innately attractive, for the dueling temptations within the

soul speak to our post-Freudian understanding, the sense
of the bifurcated personality in which some regions of the
brain can countenance avarice, pride, and cruelty, while at
the same time another part of the mind enables the most
tender kindnesses.

The temptation as an internal drama is apparent in the
Russian painter Ivan Kramskoi's scandalous 1872 *Christ
in the Desert,* now exhibited in the Tretyakov Gallery of
Moscow (a metropolis known for its own Faustian bargains). Displaying Kramskoi's adept understanding of
how to paint light, each rock, pebble, and stone glows
with a focused and disturbingly precise illumination, the
sky slightly transitioning from a cold blue to the barest of
pinks. An undeniably human Christ sits downcast with
clasped hands upon the rubble in the chill of the Judean
desert, a blue shawl over his red tunic, an expression of
utmost exhaustion on his face. Nothing is triumphant, victorious, martial, or glorious in this Christ. He is a man,
and a tired and pathetic man at that. Many of the spectators who first saw Kramskoi's Christ at Pavel Tretyakov's
gallery were horrified by his base humanity, but this has
always been the case for those committed to the respect-
ability of a fundamentally unrespectable faith. They lack
the faith to justify the existence of a dismal, ugly, twisted,
and crucified God. Leo Tolstoy, a man who over the course
of his life tried to make his peace with the scandal of this
absurd religion said of Kramskoi's composition that "This
is the best Christ I know."

Important to find the best Devil as well. Of the two figures in the scene, Satan is at least as fascinating as Christ,
and he's been made to appear as both clawed demon and
suave interlocutor, animalistic creature and Romantic an-
tihero. The Renaissance Flemish painter Juan de Flandes
gave one of the truest portraits of the Devil in his 1500
Temptation of Christ in the Wilderness, held at the
National Gallery of Art in Washington DC. Christ in blue
robe is the predictable bearded and long-haired figure that
we've come to expect, but the horned Satan walks through
the cool of this garden's evening in the rough brown,
hooded cowl of a Franciscan monk, a pair of rosaries being
fingered by his right hand. Easy to forget that the one being
who can't help but be a believer is the Devil. An atheistic
Satan is a contradiction.

Believing in God and worshipping God are two entirely
different things, of course. Satan can't help but believe in
the Lord because he knows that God is real. He's seen Him,
waged war against Him.

———

Such faith was the seventeenth-century British poet John
Milton's great subject. Milton's 1667 epic *Paradise Lost*
is a massive poem of eleven thousand lines in blank verse
that is preposterously canonical and wonderfully heretical,
an explication of Lucifer's faith. *Paradise Lost* is Milton's
most celebrated work, and for good reason—it has all the

good lines. *Paradise Regained,* by contrast, is of interest largely only to specialists; a work of less than a third the length of its more famous sibling, and first printed in 1671.[7] *Paradise Regained,* though, is intrinsic to Milton's thought, a work which completes the epic of damnation, and whose narrative dross fills out the skeleton plot of Christ's temptation in the desert (we are told what Mary and the apostles are doing while Christ is in the wilderness, what other demons are doing at the same time, and so on). Nominally a Puritan, an ever-variable term, Milton was a poet who tended toward baroque allusion, description, and turn of phrase.

Paradise Regained is an epic which reads as if it were written by a Puritan, a triumph not of the purple but of the plain. Milton's second great epic sings "not of arms / But to vanquish by wisdom hellish wiles." Any attempt at temptation which Satan makes to Christ—neither appeals to pride, power, or knowledge are capable of swaying Jesus from his mission—fails. Ever the Puritan, Milton's Christ is the greatest of all iconoclasts, following the "first of all Commandments, Thou shalt worship / The Lord thy God, and only him shalt serve." There is no selling your soul if you never owned it in the first place.

Satan draws on the examples of past rulers to entice Christ into abjuration: first, Alexander the Great, the brilliant Macedonian military commander.[8] Alexander is a perfect countermelody to Christ, a man who with the same three decades of time conquered the entire world while

Jesus merely suffered an excruciating and ignominious criminal's death. This is the lesson of Christianity; Christ's death was a greater conquering victory than all the martial, armor-plated elephants which Alexander could muster to traipse through the verdant Hindu Kush.

The next alternative model of power whom Satan proposes to entice Christ is Judas Maccabeus, hammer of the pagans and warrior for God. Judas Maccabeus is more complicated a case than Alexander, a righteous man whose often brutal violence was in glorification of the one true Lord. And yet what the story of Christ in the wilderness and *Paradise Regained* posit is that temporal power—even if used for good—is always contaminated, is always apt to blunder into pride, avarice, wrath. Only the pure spiritual rebellion of a Christ is capable of true subversion against the princes of this world, and only He was truly capable of accomplishing it.

"They err who count it glorious to subdue / By Conquest far and wide, to over-run / Large Countries, and in field great Battels win," which is to say that honor is not defined in the manner that we expect—victories—but in a more mysterious, less measurable manner. Milton's own politics were republican; his metaphysics arguably, if surprisingly, materialist. If we can explicate the relationship between base and superstructure in Christ's anarchism, the answer is ambiguous, a suggestion that the problem isn't necessarily who own the factories and farms, or who leads the armies and the navies, but the idea of control itself. The politics of power in the New Testament are so ethereal, so subtle and difficult to conceive (even more to enact), that for the skeptic it can sound like navel-gazing justification for the status quo and for many Christians as inscrutable dictate fit for God, only worth platitudinous parroting, but otherwise which we're free to ignore. The temptation in the desert is unnerving because it seems so slant to us humans who sign Faustian contracts every day, with every pettiness, every cruelty, every ungraciousness, every wickedness, both large and small.

"It's one thing to want to change the way people live," says David Bowie's Pontius Pilate in Martin Scorsese's *The Last Temptation of Christ*, "but you want to change how they think, how they feel . . . It's against the way the world is. And killing or loving, it's all the same. It simply doesn't matter how you want to change things. We don't want them changed." For the Roman governor of Judea, power always flows from the barrel of a gun (or the tip of a sword). All temporal power is hierarchical, all temporal power is about dominance in some manner, all temporal power demands degradation. Whether Judeans or Romans in charge, Jews or pagans, democrats, communists, or fascists, the exercise of power presumes winners and losers.

The answer to Pilate is in Nikos Kazantzakis' novel from which Scorsese adapted his film, when Christ says that if the "soul within us does not change . . . the world outside us will never change. The enemy is within, the Romans are within, salvation starts within!" Scorsese's controversial adaptation of this novel is so powerful in part because it admits that Pilate's isn't the absurd position (truth is a different issue). It is telling that in the dramatization of the desert temptation, Satan appears to Christ (as played by Willem Defoe) in three guises—that of a snake, a lion, and finally a pillar of flame, the last of which has Pilate's cold British accent. The ways of Satan are the ways of this world, for he is its prince (by God's design) after all. To exist in society is to sign the Faustian contract; the best we can do is to try and ameliorate some of the suffering that is the by-product of our appetites and consumptions and privileges.

Yet to fully embrace and choose God's kingdom is so difficult as to seem impossible, much less desirable. Both the film and its source were judged blasphemous because they acknowledge this reality, but ironically its full implications are made manifest because Kazantzakis and Scorsese take Christ's humanity, and not just his divinity, seriously. Notably the "temptation" of which the title refers is not the famous incident in the desert, but rather a chimera invented by Kazantzakis, a vision imparted to Christ at Golgotha when Satan momentarily tricks him into thinking that He was not the Son of God, that his death does not offer redemption, and that he shall be privy to the simple pleasures of an average man. Much of both the novel and the film is concerned with the subsequent biography that Christ imagines; his marriage to Mary Magdalene, his children, his work as a carpenter, his contented old age. All of this is a sort of devilish fever-dream, a whole life compressed into the few short moments between Christ's anguished cry demanding to know why his Father has forsaken him and his glorious declaration that the great work has been accomplished. "What's good for man isn't good for God!" says Judas—the hero of *The Last Temptation of Christ*. It's a poignant, beautiful, and heartbreaking moment, that Christ could resist pride and power, but not the simple life of a regular man, and yet this too must be resisted if the work is to be accomplished.

—

Kazantzakis' novel is the greatest literary treatment of Christ in the twentieth century and Scorsese's adaptation the most perfect cinematic, but it's the interlude in Fyodor Dostoevsky's 1880 *The Brothers Karamazov,* often published separately as "The Grand Inquisitor," that is the most potent disputation on the temptations since the synoptic gospels themselves. As an allegory about two different forms of power—the Satanic which reigns in our world and the millennial which is promised to us—it is unparalleled.

During this conversation between two brothers, Ivan and Alexei Karamazov, the former, a staunch political radical and metaphysical materialist, delivers an unusual parable to the latter, a novice Russian Orthodox monk. Ivan invents a story imagining the return of Christ in the fifteenth century, arriving in Seville at the height of the

Spanish Inquisition of the zealous Dominican friar Tomás
de Torquemada, when the fragrance of saffron and lemons
in that learned city of winding stone paths and Arabesque
minarets had been replaced with the gamey stench of burnt
flesh, accused heretics immolated in the autos de fé of the
Prado de San Sebastián while the church bells rang.

"He comes silently and unannounced," says Ivan, and
yet all recognize Christ, for the "population rushes toward
Him as if propelled by some irresistible force . . . it surrounds, throngs, and presses around, it follows Him . . .
Silently, and with a smile of boundless compassion upon
His lips." The resurrected Christ works miracles among
the poor and hungry, the desperate and suffering of Seville,
teaching not with the empty words of faith but the living
gospel of works. Soon the Messiah's return comes to the attention of the Grand Inquisitor, and for the second time in
his ministry Jesus is arrested and brought before religious
authorities.[9] The Grand Inquisitor visits the Son of Man
in His dank cell, and so this prince of the Church who
has prayed to Christ, adored icons of Christ, imagined the
suffering of Christ is now in front of Christ. "Thou hast
no business to return and hinder our work," the Inquisitor
tells Christ.[10]

What Dostoevsky so brilliantly conveys are not just
the ways in which ecclesiastical authority hypocritically
shrouds itself in the robes of Christ while dismissing His
gospel of social justice, but indeed in which all authority and power does so, because by contrast Jesus offered

a terrifying and incommensurably difficult ethic of pure existential freedom. As posited by the Grand Inquisitor, Christ came not as a representative of organized religion, but as something transcendent and anarchic, and for most people the condition of existing as a naked soul is too much to bear. "The most agonizing secrets of their consciences— all, all will they bring to us, and we shall resolve it all, and they will attend our decision with joy, because it will deliver them from the great anxiety and fearsome torments of free and individual decision," says the Great Inquisitor. Christ presents the uncomfortable freedom of the question, but the Church rather offers the soothing slavery of the answer, and that makes all the difference. The Grand Inquisitor provides a gloss on the infamous temptations of the desert, and the entirety of the interlude is presented as a modernized version of that event. According to the cleric, Christ was wrong to reject each one of the temptations given by the Devil, that "wise spirit, the dread spirit of death and destruction."

—

Man may not be able to live on bread alone, but when you're hungry you can't eat roses; to demand the angels hoist you upward after you jump from the pinnacle may seem like a cheap trick, but the crowd loves circuses even more than bread, and according to the priest, to reject the potential of absolute sovereignty is a hideous irresponsibility. For

Torquemada "seriously regards it as a great service done
by himself, his brother monks and Jesuits, to humanity,
to have conquered and subjected unto their authority that
freedom, and boasts that it was done but for the good of
the world."[11]

What makes the Grand Inquisitor's homily so disquieting is that he's convincing. Not in the violence of the pyre
per se, but in advocating for the benefits of authority over
rebellion, empty solace over terrifying freedom, the answer
over the question. And so the Grand Inquisitor condemns
Christ to the flames, Jesus having long served any benefit to the Church, now to be entirely dispensed with, the
promised return not salvation but a mere nuisance. During
the entirety of the story, Christ never speaks to the Grand
Inquisitor, but "the captive has been attentively listening
to him all the time, with His eyes fixed penetratingly and
softly on the face of his jailer." The priest is disturbed by
the silence, he desires denunciation, bile and invective.
Instead, after a period of quiet, Christ rises "slowly and
silently approaching the Inquisitor, He bends towards him
and softly kisses the bloodless, four-score and-ten-year-
old lips. That is all the answer." The seemingly repulsed
Inquisitor nonetheless lets Christ leave the Spanish jail cell,
merely telling Jesus to never return, and though we don't
see anything approaching redemption for the cruel cleric,
Dostoevsky writes that the "kiss burns in his heart."

Like all genuine literature, the power of "The Grand
Inquisitor" is in its divine ambiguities. The French

philosopher Louis Althusser uncomplicatedly refers to
the "anti-socialist theme of the 'Grand Inquisitor'" in his
book *On the Reproduction of Capitalism: Ideology and
Ideological State Apparatuses,* particularly the dismissal
of turning stones to bread (for would not the truly hungry rightly wish for such a power?) and he's not wrong to
identify the profoundly conservative strain in Dostoevsky's
wider thinking, yet *The Brothers Karamazov* revels in
beautiful paradoxes far more than it affirms. Russian philosopher Mikhail Bakhtin rather acknowledges in his classic *Problems of Dostoevsky's Poetics* how the interlude is
"nevertheless full of interruptions" marked by the "very
unexpectedness and duality of its finale, [which] indicate
an internally dialogic disintegration at its very ideological
core." In other words, parsing the politics of the parable is
irrelevant; rather, Dostoevsky evidences a kind of trans-
politics, for the work has less to say about responding to
partisan squabbles than it does to a broader conception of
what it means to live in a fallen world, where every negotiation and interaction is a Faustian bargain.

Dostoevsky was intellectually many things, but he
took the metaphysical implications of atheism seriously, far
more seriously than the bourgeois dictates of the so-called
"New Atheists," those High Church Sunday School rebels,
ever did. "If there is no God, anything is permitted" says
Ivan Karamazov, and he's right. No amount of putting our
thumb on the cosmic scale changes that; we can't kill God
and nicely arrive at pedestrian liberal values. At the same

time, Dostoevsky's work acknowledges how the problem of evil makes untenable any rational belief in God's existence. As Ivan tells Alyosha, faith in God is "not worth the tears of . . . one tortured child who beat itself on the breast with its little fist and prayed in its stinking outhouse, with its unexpiated tears to 'dear, kind God!' It's not worth it, because those tears are unatoned for." *And he's clearly, obviously, and absolutely right.* Honesty compels us to admit this, and Ivan is if anything a profoundly honest man. Which is the enigma at the heart of *The Brothers Karamazov*, and of Christianity (but not always the Church)—the answer which Christ gives isn't rational, logical, or utilitarian, it's a kiss. Love may not answer or justify anything, but it's the only genuine and complete resistance that we have.

—

How the Prince of this World conducts his affairs is entirely through the language of strength, power, and domination, and in our own million little temptations and tribulations we too can err on behalf of those values. Satan's system can be described in a multitude of ways, but for the past three centuries his hand has largely been an invisible one, operating through industry and technology, markets and capitalism. Whether *The Brothers Karamazov* critiques nascent nineteenth-century socialism is an issue for Dostoevsky's biographers, but that a rejection of the Grand Inquisitor's offers necessitates a rejection of the Moloch

whom economists call "the free market" is incontrovertible. Capitalism does and always will require the reduction of the human to commodity, product, services. No
good works but goods; no humans but consumers. If the
mechanical god of the Industrial Revolution was one of
greased gears and fearsome levers, the parsimonious and
intricate steam lord of extraction and manufacture, then
increasingly he is a deity of silicon and diode, transistor
and algorithm, though the dark supplications remain ever
the same.[12]

This is the philosophical position of Satan in the desert
and the ethics of the Grand Inquisitor in Seville; in such
a world, anything is permitted, and not only does this
Moloch not care about the death of a single innocent child,
the beast will continually sacrifice millions of them in the
name of all unholy capital. Questions of ethical consumption under capitalism are legion, of course, but it does us
no harm to admit that most of us must make varying levels
of peace with this system that oppresses, for whether we
tithe the full price of our soul, Satan requires something of
us until millennium. Yet there are those who reject those
temptations that Christ was offered, even if it's not possible
to do so as completely as he did. The Zapatistas of Chiapas
and the partisans of occupied Zuccotti Park; blessed Oscar
Romero celebrating the Eucharist for peasants in the sweltering Nicaraguan noonday sun and Dorothy Day at the
Catholic Worker House in the Bowery ministering to those
holy fools of the homeless, and the junkies, and the drunks.

Meanwhile, further uptown, and in that warm winter of 2023, some anonymous and successful bidder watched as Lodewijk Toeput's *Life of Christ* was wrapped in heavy canvas and secured with twine, to be loaded into an Aston Martin DBX or a Porsche Cayenne, later to be privately displayed above a mantlepiece at a summer home in Lake Tahoe or a condo near Miami Beach. Christ's temptations themselves purchased, the owner of the Toeput must have walked out of Sotheby's onto York Avenue's chorus of blaring honks, into the low winter sun and ever-warming days of our last era, after having finished his paperwork and signed the contract that transferred ownership of God's image.

CHAPTER THREE

OF SAINTS AND SUCCUBI: MEDIEVAL DIABOLICAL CONTRACTS

A monk should surely love his books with humility, wishing their good and not the glory of his own curiosity; but what the temptation of adultery is for laymen and the yearning for riches is for secular ecclesiastics, the seduction of knowledge is for monks.
—Umberto Eco, *The Name of the Rose* (1980)

A mong the lilting hills of Lower Saxony, a province decorated with spruce and pine conifers from the plains to the sea, there is a stalwart Romanesque Abbey in the countryside not far from the town of Bad Gandersheim. Like the Faust legend itself, Gandersheim Abbey is composed of many different parts from disparate time periods, a jumble of the Romanesque, the Gothic, and the Renaissance, an architectural commonplace book of northern European Christian history rendered in lime and

sandstone, oak and spruce wood. Established in the ninth
century, some of the original austere Romanesque façade
remains, ingested by the abbey in the same way that a folktale consumes and grows over the centuries with the addition of new characters, turns of phrase, tropes, or settings.

When its most famous occupant, Canoness Hrotsvitha,
arrived in the tenth century, Gandersheim Abbey had
already served God, Lower Saxony, and the Ottonian
Dynasty (not necessarily in that order) for almost a hundred years, a fortification for Christianity here in the most
frigid part of northern Europe where only a few generations
before the locals had traded Thor's Hammer for Christ's
cross. Hrotsvitha would be among the most celebrated ab-
besses in Christendom, surpassed in Germany only be the
great visionary, composer, and philosopher Hildegard von
Bingen, both women intrinsic to the renaissance of wom-
en's mysticism during the Middle Ages.[1]

Within those thick and secure Saxon walls, Hrotsvitha
commanded a coterie of scholarly nuns, making the tenth-
century abbey a famed center for devotion and leaning.
Walking through the grey and brown winter grounds of
Gandersheim, her weathered and deeply lined red face
framed by her immaculate white habit, a vellum missal
clasped in withered hand, Hrotsvitha would assemble a remarkable curriculum vitae, authoring books such as *Gesta
Oddonis,* a secular history of the Teutonic dynasty that
supported the abbey; *The Book of Drama* composed of six
closet plays revising the misogynist works of the ancient

Roman writer Terrence; and finally *The Book of Legends,*
eight hagiographies including one entitled "Theophilus,"
which is the first familiar version of the Faust legend as it
came to be received.

Christ may have been unsuccessfully tempted by the
Devil, and Simon Magus may have drawn upon God for
his abilities, but it was in the German nun's imagining of
the historical Byzantine bishop Theophilus that the major
tropes of the Faust myth began to coalesce. A cursed scholar's desire for power and knowledge, the signed contract,
the damnation (and last-minute pardon)—all placed into
Leonine hexameters. At lauds prayers—Hrotsvitha feared
the Devil; at prime— Hrotsvitha fought the Devil; at ves-
pers—Hrotsvitha vanquished the Devil; at compline—
Hrotsvitha thought on the Devil. The abbess did all this
not with incantation but in writing, by calcifying the assortment of legends about St. Theophilus, the Cilician
bishop who in the sixth century apparently acquired his
ecclesiastical position through diabolical intercession.

———

True to his name, meaning "Love of God," Theophilus was
at first a dutiful, humble, charitable servant of the Lord.
As vicar, Theophilus's flock maintained a "united devotion
in the tender affection of their hearts" toward the cleric
whom "they cherished . . . as a dear father," according to
Hrotsvitha in *The Book of Legends.* Upon the death of

the beloved archdeacon of Adana, Theophilus was elected
bishop, though ever humble, the simple vicar of God refused
the offer, seeing himself as unworthy of such a position.
Narratively, Theophilus' humility ironically manifests itself
as an inverted form of tragic hubris, for the man appointed
in his stead acquired the office through simony, and in due
course stripped the vicar of his modest clerical appointments. Ever the do-gooder, Theophilus sees this as more
opportunity for him to devote his attentions heavenward,
and yet the human soul is never so completely forgiving.

Hrotsvitha writes that the "savage enemy of all human-
kind soon came to loathe this patient soul, and with that
same cunning with which he had erstwhile deceived our
first parents, he assailed the inmost heart of this just man,
bringing before his frail mind very often the quiet delights
of his former position." True to the meaning of Christ's
temptation in the desert, Hrotsvitha understood that not
even the most seemingly righteous, just, kind, holy, or pious
of people can resist the Devil always and forever, which was
the case with Theophilus, who in due course searches out a
sorcerer, with the abbess specifying that this nameless figure
is a Jew, the author abundantly privy to the prejudices of
Christianity. This necromancer leads the once-holy man in:

> hellish persuasions, at dark of night secretly
> through the city and brought him to a place
> filled with many specters, in which were the
> inhabitants of hell, clad in white garments and

many of them holding candles in their hands.
In their midst sat enthroned the iniquitous
prince, who is the king of death and the son of
perdition, persuading his damnable agents with
cunning deceit to cast over all unremittingly
their nets of wonted cleverness, nets ready to
capture all.

This spooky, nocturnal scene is the first in Western literature in which an actual contract with the Devil is signed,
where the soul of man is traded to Satan in exchange for
some profane benefit, all of it made in exacting legal language (none of which Hrotsvitha quotes, but that its terms
are enumerated upon parchment is unequivocal). Though
necromancers had been conjuring demons to do their bid-
ding for millennia, the innovation of a signed contract signals a paradigm shift and establishes a tale that's obviously
Faustian in structure.

Despite Faust appearing as if a refugee from a more
superstitious epoch, and regardless of the Middle Ages
reputation for credulity, the appearance of a *contract* demonstrates the enshrinement of rationality. Scholastic philosophy, which would dominate the universities of Europe
a few centuries after Hrotsvitha, would make logic the
center of its theology. Western Christendom understood
God's universe as not just divine, but ordered, logical, and
rational. A contract is an argument, and it reflects this
trust in reason. Furthermore, a contract is supposed to be

fair—and despite the Devil's machinations, he is rather explicit about the ultimate destination of the condemned spirit.[2] A literalism concerning the promises and power of contracts is threaded throughout Theophilus' ultimately happy story.

Because it shouldn't be forgotten that he is *Saint* Theophilus of Adana, undoubtedly the only person canonized by the Church who also happens to have sold his soul to Satan. That he is counted among those who instantly arrived in heaven upon death is entirely due to his repentance, which itself was made possible by the logic which motivates contracts. After a period when his heart withers from Satanic malignancy, Theophilus realizes the horror of what he's done, and calls out in genuine sorrow to the "Mother of Christ and powerful Queen of heaven and radiant, spotless temple of the Holy Spirit," an early instance of the Marian devotion that marked Medieval Catholicism (and indeed modern Catholicism), which regards Virgin Mary as the benevolent intercessor who may mediate the affairs of God and man.

For days the bishop holds vigil, bitterly imploring the Virgin Mary to help save him from Hell, when finally the Mother of God arrives. Despite "all the faults, which perchance thou hast perpetrated against me, I in kindliness of heart now forgive thee freely." Still, Mary's forgiveness means nothing without procuring the paper on which Theophilus' signature has been affixed; she does, and it's duly burnt, freeing the soul of the now-saved vicar.[3] An early example of the Virgin acting as a supernatural

intercessor, a softer, human link between us and her divine
Son.[4] Both Mary and Hrotsvitha have been often anach-
ronistically repurposed as feminist icons, though the nun
does conceive of a variety of feminine spirituality based in
"motherly affection," as she describes it, a muscular but
nonetheless loving understanding of divinity which is a
counterbalance to the dominating, Luciferian ethic of our
profane existence. Arguably, Hrotsvitha was the progenitor
of not just Faust, but of Mary.

Still, despite the motherly nature of Hrotsvitha's
Marian devotions, it's a faith willing to hit first. This is
the Mary as delightfully depicted in a Book of Hours (a
devotional guide for the individual penitent) illuminated by
the English scribe William de Brailes in which a beatified
and berobed Virgin with a satisfied smile punches a short,
paunchy, positively goofy looking Satan square in the face
with her right hand while she snatches back Theophilus'
contract with the left. De Brailes' small insert, which is in
the upper left-hand corner of a page in the Book of Hours in
which the legend is recounted, renders the scene in browns,
reds, and whites, an earthy color for an earthy story. The
grimace on the hairy Devil's face as Mary smacks his or-
bital is, for lack of a better critical term, *funny*. Common
Medieval iconography of the Devil, in which he was more
often a squawking, farting, drooling idiot than a figure of
Marlovian terror or of Miltonic pathos, has been repurposed for our age of pussy grabbers and #MeToo revelations as a means of satirical resistance. The Book of Hours

illumination appeared in Twitter memes and Facebook posts, Mary's sly smile as she beaned Satan reminiscent of the type of revenge that a woman might want to take on a pig at work or at the bar after the day is done.

Fully human and yet also the Mother of God, Mary has often occupied a space in the theological imagination that encourages egalitarian radicalism. Whether or not it's accurate to call Hrotsvitha's tale "feminist," there is a revolutionary quality in the idea that this human being—a woman!—could successfully mount an attack on Satan.[5] This is the Mary of the Magnificat, the portion of Luke adapted as a canticle by several Christian denominations and incorporated into the liturgy. Among the most ancient of Christian hymns, Mary declares in the Magnificat that not only has God shown the power of the powerless by elevating her into Christ's Mother, but that the Lord "hath pulled down the mighty from their seat: And hath exalted the humble and meek. / He hath filled the hungry with good things: and the rich he hath sent empty away."[6] The Virgin Mary—feminist, communist revolutionary, or at least that might be what we desire.

The Book of Legends tempers this a bit, since Mary can't unilaterally save Theophilus, and she attacks the Devil because she must procure the contract in question, the destruction of which is required for the priest's redemption. At its conclusion, Hrotsvitha writes of that "despairing and sinful man, who yet learned to bewail his own transgressions and had striven to chastise himself amid worthy lamentations."

Thus Theophilus, who sold his soul to Satan, became a saint—note the appallingly low standards by which men were congratulated, then as now. The intercession of the Virgin Mary and Theophilus's salvation differentiate this tale from Marlowe's far more despairing version and its terrifying Elizabethan Devil, who also portends modernity's growing nihilism. Hrotsvitha's cheerier plot is, however, echoed in Goethe's eighteenth-century *Faustus*.

Such are the charged enchantments of the Faust legend, flitting in and about literary history. In drawing the strange tale of Theophilus to a close, Hrotsvitha's words were recorded on vellum of sheep or goat's skin scraped clean and tanned, stained with ink of charcoal gum and tannic acid, like all Medieval literature written onto the corpses of God's creatures, the resultant manuscript an intricate mechanism of ligament and tendon, the Word become flesh. The gutting and skinning of the goat and its treatment with a variety of potions, its kid now a miracle of transubstantiation, the universe of literature evoked from such base materiality, all of it a sacrifice. An incantation.

That manuscript of *The Book of Legends* made its way from Gandersheim to the library of Regensburg's cloister of St. Emmeram where, like a grave-robber excavating a tomb, the humanist scholar Conrad Celtes would find her book in 1493, during the height of the historical Johann Faust's necromantic career. Hrotsvitha's words were finally published throughout Europe by the benefit of the still-novel printing press, with engravings by Albrecht Dürer. Even while

Hrotsvitha's book moldered on a German shelf awaiting its resurrection like a body on the Day of Judgment, the legend of Theophilus remained a mainstay of Medieval mythmaking, by far the most popular Faustian narrative in the centuries before the eponymous fifteenth-century sorcerer.

—

The French troubadour Rutebeuf's 1261 *The Miracle of Theophilus,* the earliest extant play in that language, was presumably written without knowledge of Hrotsvitha's poem, evidence of the enduring fascination that people had with the diabolical contract motif. Notably, Rutebeuf added another element of the legend in the form of an incantation uttered in an incomprehensible language:

> Bagahi laca bachahe
> Lamac cahi achabahe,
> Karrelvos,
> Lamac lamec bachalvos,
> Cabahagi sabalvos,
> Baryolas.
> Lagozatha cabyolas,
> Samahac et famyolas,
> Harrahya.

You should be careful if reading this book aloud, because according to Rutebeuf that's the exact combination of syllables required to conjure Satan.

Within *The Miracle of Theophilus,* the titular saint calls upon the services of a sorcerer named Salatin—an obvious slur against Saladin, the Islamic commander during the Second Crusade—who uses this strange invocation to compel Satan to appear. What exactly any of these nonsense syllables might mean has been a topic of considerable scholarly disagreement (possibly it's an imitation of Hebrew, Arabic, Greek, or Latin), though Medieval literature frequently deployed this sort of nonsense sound-poem to give a work a sense of infernal verisimilitude. Such language hits the ear with an uncanniness, as if it was derived from some alternate dimension, as if it finds its origin in Hell.[7] Incidentally, the so-called "Bagabi Chant" became a mainstay of Wiccan devotions in the twentieth century, and no less a wizard than Aleister Crowley hypothesized that the absurdity of the words themselves was intrinsic to their supernatural import. All the more disquieting in that Rutebeuf's miracle play—itself a sort of liturgical ritual—must have generated an anxiety among those who saw Theophilus' drama on stage, fearful that Salatin's words might conjure an actual devil or two.

—

During the decades that Hrotsvitha was placing Theophilus's tale into hexameters, an esteemed French scholar named Gerbert of Aurillac began a remarkable career that included the importation of the abacus and Arabic numerals into European mathematics, and the design of intricate armillary spheres that made possible complicated astronomical calculations. For such heterodox intellectual borrowings from Moorish Al-Andalus, he was also predictably accused of infernal predilections. What makes this more interesting is that Gerbert is primarily known by a different name which he chose in the last year of the first millennium, when in 999 he ascended to the throne of St. Peter and became Pope Sylvester II, the pontiff who sold his soul to the Devil.

While in some legends a Devil's contract secures his ascension to the papacy, it's most often understood that Gerbert's desire isn't for power so much as for knowledge, and so another aspect of the Faustian legend is made manifest, along with the inclusion of not just incantations, but diabolical magic books known as grimoires. Educated by the remarkably tolerant, diverse, and learned scholars from Islamic cities of Seville and Cordova upon the southern coast of Spain, Sylvester supposedly acquired grimoires during those studies.[8] No doubt much of the diabolical legend that accrued about the future Pope Sylvester II was based in bigotry and suspicion, the scholar viewed warily by members of the Catholic curia who distrusted such syncretism. Arguably there was also a profound distrust of Gerbert's empirical and mathematical enthusiasms, such projects bearing more than a bit of similarity to what would be recognized as magic.

Yet it's also an ahistorical category mistake to assume that magic was ever easily separable from what we'd come

to call science during the Middle Ages, and no doubt
Sylvester was familiar with any number of grimoires that
he studied during his Spanish sojourns, even if the future
pope himself wasn't a demonologist. Perhaps he encountered the astrological manual *Ghâyat al-Hakîm*, translated into the Latin *Picatrix* by the thirteenth century, or a
Greek copy of the demonology manual *The Testament of
Solomon*. Whether this learned man who introduced base
ten numbers and the abacus to the West had discourse with
the Devil, he no doubt *believed* in that Devil, and his contemporaries believed he knew more of such a being than he
was willing to admit.

The most popular source for the legend about the
Pope's Faustian contract are from a twelfth-century
work by William of Malmesbury entitled *History of the
Kings of England*. True to the English national vocation
of Francophobia, William portrays the first French pope
as a willing tool of Satan, a necromancer and sorcerer
who benefited from "Saracen" magic. William writes that
Sylvester had "surpassed Ptolemy with the astrolabe, and
Alexandreaus in astronomy, and Julius Firmicus in astrol-
ogy," but that he had also "acquired the art of calling up
ghostly forms from Hell." Additionally, the reader is told,
Gerbert used such Islamic magic to, among other things,
construct a massive mechanical brazen head capable of
prophecy and conjuring a beautiful succubus with whom
he enjoyed perverse conjugal relations.

The brazen head features in other Faustian legends

into the Renaissance, a detail sometimes attributed to the thirteenth-century English Franciscan, theologian, and proto-scientist Roger Bacon. A type of gear-punk computer which William describes as the "head of a statue, by a certain inspection of the stars when all of the planets were about to begin their courses, which did not speak unless spoken to, but then pronounced the truth either in the affirmative or the negative," the device indeed predicted Gerbert's demise, though its oracular pronouncement contained the customary fatal ambiguity misinterpreted by its subject. Being told that the Devil would only claim his soul while he was in Jerusalem, the pope avoided the place of Solomon's Temple and Christ's crucifixion, while neglecting to note that the church Santa Croce in Gerusalemme references that holy city in its name. The Devil's contracts might be fair, but he's not above a technicality, and so when Sylvester was saying Mass at Santa Croce, a coterie of demons arrived to rip his limbs apart and play marbles with his eyeballs in front of the horrified congregants. An inglorious end.

Writing a century after the pope had lived, William's consideration of his scholarly career is surprisingly not unfair; the historian admits that Gerbert's talents may be God-given and the legends of diabolical contracts merely superstitious folklore. A certain Cardinal Beno of Santi Martino e Silvestro was less charitable a century after Sylvester's death, sadistically recounting that when Gerbert's blood was spilled upon Santa Croce's altar, the pontiff "begged his hands and tongue (with which, by offering to demons, he had dishonored God) be cut to pieces." Brazen heads or not, the most fascinating detail about Sylvester's intercourse with the Devil is his literal intercourse with a succubus. Predictably, the historians and pamphleteers who wrote about the pope were similarly drawn to this prurient aspect of the legend. Texture is supplied, even the comely demoness's name of Meridiana, though such accountings are disappointingly far from pornographic. From Simon Magus's Helen to Faustus's Helen of Troy, the dangerous demonic seductress has often been a character in diabolical contract stories, a bit of erotic charge under the guise of sexual moralizing, enlivening the tale with at least implied exploitative possibilities. Whatever Hrotsvitha's feminist sensibilities may have been, Faust legends more generally prick the desires of their male readers, who while publicly eschewing the Faustian example privately thrill to the powers the sorcerer acquires, especially those of sexual prowess.

Meridiana intercedes between the necromancer and the Devil, with the additional facet that theirs was a fruitful intellectual partnership enlivened by sexual possibilities. Walter Map, a thirteenth-century Welsh courtier among the Plantagenets, added to the legend of Pope Sylvester in his gossipy compendium *Trifles of the Courtiers*, describing Meridiana as a "woman of wondrous beauty, sitting upon a great cloth of silk and with a huge heap of money before her" from whom the future pope "profited to the full from his double instruction, both of the bed and of the benches." Pillow talk with this succubus enabled not only Gerbert's increase in temporal power, but his supernatural knowledge as well. In Rheims where he had first ascended to the position of bishop, and perhaps Meridiana instructed Gerbert in the occult philosophies of Hermes Trismegistus, or the forbidden knowledge of the *Sefer Raziel HaMalakh*. Theirs was a relationship of ink and semen, this cardinal prince of Rome and scarlet lady of Babylon, and lest that phrasing seem suspect, consider the generative nature of both fluids, the union of brain and genitals in such tales.

Not that Sylvester wasn't warned. "It is forbidden for a man to sleep alone in a house," notes the Talmud in the tractate entitled Shabbat151a, "lest Lilith get hold of him." There was a long-standing theurgical anxiety about succubi and cum, as in the Talmud warning about nocturnal emissions and in the more graphic writings in the Kabbalistic *Zohar*. Succubi, female demons such as Meridiana, were believed to extract semen for use in the creation of new devilish creatures, something that had been their vocation back to the first of their kind, Satan's partner Lilith. The succubi who often populate Faustian legends— from Meridiana to the demoness who appears as Helen of Troy in the Elizabethan play—can be directly linked to Lilith, who appears by name in Goethe's version, and was originally an ancient Canaanite goddess who was long a figure of terror in Jewish apocrypha.[9] Popular a generation ago as the official avatar of the feminist Lilith Fair rock concert, the goddess (slurred by both Jews and Christians as a demoness) has long been a symbol of resistance to patriarchal authority, an ambiguous figure to the end.

———

Lilith enters Jewish and Christian mythology as a bit of a rounding error, a rabbinic attempt to reconcile contradictions in the Book of Genesis. Because the Bible offers two clashing tales of creation—Adam and his partner are first having been described as simultaneously generated from the earth, and only later is the more famous story about Eve drawn from Adam's rib recounted—Lilith was introduced as a means of correcting such an obvious disjuncture. In reality, the shaggy inconsistencies of Genesis are almost certainly the result of redaction, of several different authors' words being melded into one (non-cohesive) whole, but for the authors of Midrashim and the Talmud, a potential solution to the narrative problems was to assume that this wasn't a contradictory story, but really two separate stories of creation. It was argued that only the second account of creation concerned Eve, and that the first was of an entirely separate woman—Lilith.[10]

Such are the misogynistic vagaries of the Lilith legend. Even before Eve was created, the story supposes, this first woman demanded that when fucking Adam, she be on top, and for such perfidy Lilith, made from the same soil as her equal husband, would be damned. The cosmos for a sexual position. According to the rabbis, Adam's refusal to cede his dominance compelled Lilith to leave Eden—in some versions then partnering with the devil Samael—but in almost every telling from the eleventh-century *Alphabet of Ben-Sirach* to the *Zohar* (of disputed age) Lilith became the first succubus, a beautiful demonic temptress. The supple lamia, the dread siren, even the fanged vampiress all have their mother in Lilith.

What of Pope Sylvester II, wailing for his demoness lover? Who did he see? A 1460 illustration of the story in a manuscript of the thirteenth-century Dominican historian Martin of Poland's *Latin Chronicle* shows a distinctly Orientalized Sylvester—black hair, black beard—dimly smiling in papal tiara, while a devil gesticulates before him, the creature's hairy grey flesh exhibiting multiple demonic faces, including on the anus and genitals. Nightmares of *vagina dentata* aside, perhaps when Sylvester closed his eyes before damnation he saw Meridiana as the ancient Babylonian relief now held by the Louvre, the statue of Lilith surrounded by her screech-owl familiars carved some two millennia before Christ, depicting a beautiful woman of wide hips and large breasts who nonetheless has feet that are the clawed talons of some mighty raptor. Or, maybe, Sylvester had a premonition of the Norwegian Edvard Munch's 1895 painting *Love and Pain*, with its dignified gentleman face down as an almost featureless woman appears to either be embracing him or attempting to devour him, her long beautiful red hair flowing over him as if coagulating blood. Maybe those were the visions which Gerbert of Aurillac saw when he closed his eyes, before they were ripped from their sockets by the demons of Santa Croce and traded about the interior of the sanctuary like dice under the cross.

Before anyone with the name "Faust," and his myth was popular in the Middle Ages, the legend's overweening concern with *words* made manifest by a people fully enraptured by the idea of scripture, by this faith that language itself made reality (and could unmake it as well). A soul is sold to the Devil, after all, not in a gentleman's promise, but with a signature affixed to a contract, and the benefit is also words in the form of knowledge, at least for a bit. The central importance of the contract in Medieval Faust legends—its stipulations laid out as elegantly as a syllogism—attests to this.[11] It would be a mistake, however, to understand Medieval reason as the anemic version we think of today, the parsing of logical fallacies and the valorization of "critical thought." For Medieval mystics and philosophers alike, language was the thorough-structure of reality which composed the universe, so just as it was a medium in which God dwelled, so would it be where Satan resided. Hence the importance of spells, conjurations, incantations, and grimoires to the sorcerer's vocation.

Consider Herman the Recluse, a thirteenth-century Dominican of Bohemia who violated his vows of chastity, obedience, and poverty, and so was walled alive in a dank cell of the Podlazice monastery. Convincing his superiors to free him if he was able to produce a massive, sumptuous, illuminated Bible in a single night, the monk contracted with Lucifer to do the work for him. The result was the *Codex Gigas*—literally the "Giant Book"—the largest manuscript of the Middle Ages, weighing around 165 pounds and requiring the sacrifice of at least 160 donkeys to make up its vellum pages. Beautifully illustrated, it's been said that Satan left his signature in the form of a two-foot-tall self-portrait on recto 290. Not unlike De Brailes' Devil, there is something a little funny about the picture in the *Codex Gigas*, except this demon is ominously in on the joke. Clawed arms akimbo and taloned legs spread-eagle, this crouching red and green devil has a wicked smile punctuated by a forked tongue, penetrating reptilian eyes that don't quite seem to have been colored by human hand, though perhaps the legend just starts to get to you.

Today, nothing of Theophilus remains and Sylvester's contract has been lost. But the *Codex Gigas* has made its way to the archives of the Tre Kronor castle in Stockholm, Sweden. Some are able to still trace their finger along the red and black lines of Satan's serpentine curves, a living connection to the bargain which made such an illustration possible. The Word become flesh, at least of a type. If you see Faustus, it's always been most true that you can find him in a library.

CHAPTER FOUR

GREAT RECKONINGS, SMALL ROOMS: SEARCHING FOR THE HISTORICAL FAUST

How he did oblige himself for a certain time unto the Devil,
and what happened to him, and how he at last got his just reward.
Rare revelations are also included.
—Anonymous, *History and Tale of Doctor Johannes Faustus* (1587)

On May 21, 1991 the celebrated, forty-one-year-old University of Chicago Divinity School professor Ioan Petru Culianu attended a used-book sale in the lobby of Swift Hall along the southern edge of an ivy-covered, gothic quad, the academic building appearing like nothing so much as a secular monastery. An expert on occultism, Culianu was the author of works like *Eros and Magic in the Renaissance* and *The Tree of Gnosis: Gnostic Mythology from Early Christianity to Modern Nihilism*, and a protegee of his countryman, the great scholar of religious studies Mircea Eliade. A refugee from Romania, Culianu had long run afoul of the communist left and the fascist right, especially since in the months following the revolution which saw dictator Nicolae Ceausescu executed alongside his wife in 1989 the scholar was more than willing to excoriate the Faustian bargains which united the illiberal right and left in his home country.

Culianu was a thinker whose fascination with the occult combined the personal and the scholarly, explored in hundreds of papers on everything from divination to erotic magic. A writer who in addition to his scholarly output wrote dozens of Borgesian short stories that had the uncanny feeling of predicting future events in his native country; a professor who was known to perform Tarot card readings for his graduate students at Hyde Park parties. Such explorations, as a cursory reading of magical history demonstrates, come at a profound cost. "Since sorcery was a *crimen exceptum*," writes Culianu in *Eros and Magic in the Renaissance*, "and dealings with the evil demons of Satan's hordes were ascribed to sorcerers, it followed naturally that any form of magic invoking demons was held to be suspect and was to be persecuted."

On that morning toward the end of the semester the professor would have spent a few minutes examining what was on offer at the book tables; maybe the grad student mainstays of Michel Foucault's *Discipline and Punish* or Jean Baudrillard's *Simulacra and Simulation,* perhaps a find like Colin Wilson's *The Occult: A History* or Dame Frances Yates's *The Rosicrucian Enlightenment*. Culianu would have then walked up marble steps, past bulletin boards and the faculty offices, doors affixed with *New Yorker* cartoons and postcards depicting a Caravaggio or Bosch seen at the Uffizi or the Prado while doing sabbatical research.

Finally, shortly after noon, he would have entered the last bathroom stall on the third floor. A few minutes later an assassin's .25 caliber bullet pierced the back of his head and exited through a nostril. The assailant had most likely lain in wait by standing atop the toilet of the adjacent stall. A clean kill—Culianu's murderer was never apprehended.

There are few places more inglorious to be martyred than in a public bathroom stall, but then Golgotha was an inglorious place as well. Holiness in the mundane, the sacred in the profane, the incarnational poetics of divinity trapped in the messy realities of humanity. All aspects of comparative religion that Culianu understood well.[1] And his killer—an agent of the Romanian national intelligence service or an initiate in an occult group sacrificing the professor as part of a Black Mass (both possibilities considered by the FBI)—would have walked past all of the same tweedy, rumpled things on his way to the bathroom where he (or she) would await the professor's arrival. Journalist Ted Anton, in a piece published eighteen months after Culianu's murder in the now-defunct *Lingua Franca*, describes a wizardly figure, a man fluent in "eight

languages, the author of seventeen books, and the holder
of three Ph.D.'s" whose entire philosophical project was
based in the contention that "multiple universes exist, that
the mind creates reality, and that magic can outperform
modern science."

Culianu is a thinker that, whatever the merits of his
tremendously learned research, it's hard not to be a bit
obsessed with, at least if you're of a certain disposition.
That his unsolved murder is potentially the only foreign
assassination of an American academic on American soil is
something out of a true crime novel or an espionage story;
that law enforcement seriously proffered the hypothesis
that his killing may have been a Black Mass ritual sacrifice is a detail more fit for a horror film.[2] Working as a
scholar of Renaissance literature and philosophy, Culianu
figured prominently in my own academic writing, so naturally when I was spending a summer in Hyde Park as part
of a National Endowment for the Humanities seminar, I
made a pilgrimage to Swift Hall's third-floor bathroom.
Because the bathroom is arrestingly mundane—the same
water-stained, linoleum-tiled, broken-toileted space that's
common in many workplaces—it can seem incongruous
to think of it as a sacred space, and yet everywhere that a
sacrifice happens is a sacred place.[3]

Fair arguments can be made that there is something
prurient and exploitative in all of this, that whatever the
circumstances of the scholar's murder (and Anton makes
a compelling circumstantial case that he was killed by an

operative of the Securitate tied to Bucharest), this is primarily a personal and political tragedy rather than a gothic tale. Yet despite making this point in a critical review of Anton's book *Eros, Magic, and the Murder of Professor Culianu*, scholar Claire Fanger admits that the "myth of Faust would have to enter in some manner into any accurate telling of Culianu's life."

A brilliant scholar meddles with dark forces, acquires secret knowledge, and faces a terrifying fate. The body of the Faust myth is skeletal enough to have accommodated many historical Fausts and ready-made to embrace a tale like Culianu's. The Devil's contract, as has been shown, long predates the association of such a bargain with anyone who has the name "Faust"—*and yet there was such a historical personage*, who indelibly marked the legend with his identity, so that his patronym became synonymous with selling your soul to Satan. Macabre to imagine it, but if Culianu had a moment to think of it before that bullet pierced his brain, would he have made the connection?

As with Culianu or Marlowe, the actual Johannes Faustus endures behind the accumulated detritus of his legend, a real man who was the distant inspiration for all the plays and novels, operas and songs. This man apparently also suffered a violent end. Some traditions have it that while working within a white-washed and brown-roofed house in Baden-Württemberg the necromancer Johann George Faust was eviscerated by a legion of demons, but it's not clear just when this auspicious event happened.

Faust's tortured last hours, to an imaginative mind, conjure
flesh being peeled from muscles, ligaments twisted apart,
bones snapped and eyes gouged, but for all of the blood
stains displayed to tourists on warped wooden floors in
half-timbered taverns and inns from the Alps to the Baltic,
certainty on where the magician's doom was met is also
a matter of disagreement. A massive compendium of the
legend's variations by the German philosopher Alexander
Tille in the nineteenth century lists fifty separate potential locations for Faust's demonic murder, including the
aforementioned Baden-Württemberg and Regensburg,
Wittenberg, Cologne, and Königsberg, while Leo Ruickbie
notes in *Faustus: The Life and Times of a Renaissance
Magician* that Satan may have come to collect his due on
several different possible dates between 1538 and 1541.

Regardless of the *when* or the *where,* most compilers
of the lurid pamphlets known throughout the German-
speaking lands of the Holy Roman Empire as *teufelsbücher,*
or "Devil's books," were clearer on the *how.* Johannes Gast,
in a 1548 tract, writes that Faust was "allotted a miserable,
lamentable end, for he was suffocated by Satan," while in a
1555 sermon the theologian Philip Melanchthon described
how after a night of unnatural shrieks and rumblings a
group entered the magician's chamber to find that demons
had "twisted the dead man's face against his back." The
anonymous English translator of a German account, known
only as "P. F. Gentleman," is far more detailed—Faust's eyes
are found in opposite corners of the room, his teeth in a pile

of horse dung, and his brains which once comprehended divine secrets are smeared across the wall. The Renaissance's greatest wizard was "most monstrously torn, and fearful to behold." Despite variations on the *where, when,* or even *how,* there is consensus on the *why*—nobody can be expected to get away with dealing with the Devil forever.

Numerous inconsistencies plague a reliable biography of Faust, but what's more remarkable is that there is a historical man behind that myth to begin with. This ghostly figure precedes Thomas Mann's experimental composer in his 1947 novel *Doctor Faustus,* he lived long before the titular Romantic hero of Johann Wolfgang von Goethe's nineteenth-century *Faust,* and he almost abuts, but not quite, Marlowe's doomed figure in *The Tragical History of Doctor Faustus* first performed in 1594. More than any other document, the narrative which Marlowe relied on is *Das Faustbuch,* or *The Faustbook,* printed by Johann Spiess in Frankfurt in 1587 and possibly written by him as well; a volume designed to entertain, edify, and help readers "protect themselves from similar maculations of the most shameful sort."

In bright red gothic print, the front piece announces Spiess's rendition to be an authoritative account some four decades after Faust had either been killed in an alchemical experiment or been dismembered by demons—again the sequence depends on whose authority you trust. The real man, it seems, has always been more of a shadow than the fiction. Ruickbie estimates that since the sixteenth century around 20,000 books have fictionalized the notorious bargain which lends itself to the adjective "Faustian."[4] Faust has become an archetype, and an archetype can't be a man—yet Faust *was* a man, albeit a specter, a shadow, a stranger.

There was an alchemist known as Faust who Latinized his name to Faustus. He may have been christened George Sabellicus. Most everything else is conjecture, invention, or mere possibility. Maybe Faust was from Heidelberg, or Knittlingen, or Roda; born of woman (in some accounts a virgin) in 1466, or, based on good evidence, in 1481. The character could have developed over time as writers confused two separate itinerant magicians. Dozens of grimoires, diabolical books of incantations and conjurations claim him as their author, but all of them are elaborate and often much later forgeries.

Of course, the Devil's contract is the most characteristic part of Faust's biography, the one thing that everybody knows, even though that detail is a latter interpolation. Selling his soul to the Devil is what's most striking in the tale, readers and audiences thrilling to that bargain for all the reasons anybody immerses themselves in stories of imps and devils, with an understanding of the human reasons Faust justifies what he does. Faust worships the idol of the self and is willing to pursue knowledge, power, wealth, and pleasure while also being aware of what it will cost him.

That there was *somebody* who inspired this legend is incontrovertible. He first enters the record in 1507, in that tumultuous gloaming between the discovery of America and the start of the Reformation, noted in a letter written by the Benedictine abbot and occultist Johannes Trithemius, a resident of that hermetic canton of Basel. Trithemius refers to the magician as the "prince of necromancers." Despite Trithemius own less than savory reputation, he concludes that Faust was a "vagabond, an utterer of vain repetitions, and a wandering monk who, lest he have the temerity to profess further in public places things so abominable and contrary to the Holy Church, is deserving of chastisement by whips."

The necromancer appears across letters, pamphlets, and books during his ostensible lifetime; first in the form of the popular *teufelsbücher* printed in the decades immediately following his death, and then of course the novels, plays, operas, movies, and comics that mark his apotheosis in the realm of the mythical, the actual man no longer even a shadow. During the sixteenth century, there are glimmerings of Faust—a sighting in Prague, an account in Krakow, an incident in Wittenberg. Martin Luther discusses him in the charmingly titled collection *Table Talk,* the first time Faust is connected to an infernal contract. Within the same 1507 letter by Trithemius, the abbot records that the magician was expelled from a teaching position at a school in Kreuznach, as he was guilty of committing a "kind of nefarious fornication." In 1513, Trithemius's friend the humanist scholar Conrad Mutianus Rufus encountered the astrologer while they were both staying at a Thuringian inn; he mockingly dismissed Faust as the "demigod of Heidelberg."

By 1535 accounts confirm that Faust was near Münster

during the infamous Anabaptist rebellion when religious radicals abolished private property and mandated Old Testament law while establishing a communist theocracy. Defeated by a combined force of Lutherans and Catholics (the first ecumenical partnership), Anabaptist leaders like John of Leiden were burnt at the stake, while his corpse was exhibited for five decades in an iron cage hanging from the steeple of St. Lambert's Church. As for Faust's role, the *Waldeck Chronicle* of Daniel Prasser, written in 1650, records that the magician entered the Catholic encampment and prophesized that "without doubt, the city of Münster would be captured by the Bishop that same night," so that perhaps such fortunes lay in their own sulphureous bargains. Münster's collapse reverberated throughout Christendom, the radical example of the Anabaptists seemed to confirm warnings about the relativistic potential in the doctrine of the "priesthood of all believers," as Luther had first imagined the Reformation.[5] Faust's association with Münster makes some sense in this way, even if Prasser indicates that the devilish contracts happened to be on behalf of the status quo (same as it ever was). Such a link between Faust and heresy could have been part of the justification of his notoriety.

Faustian stories were widely read because of the shocking supernatural tales which they told. Melanchthon claimed that Faust had flown over Venice, a city that even during the Renaissance was associated with a certain mystery, before crashing near St. Mark's Square, perhaps narrowly drowning in a canal. The preacher knew that his audience would connect Faust to that far more ancient magician, the arch-heretic Samaritan Gnostic wizard Simon Magus who in the first century engaged in a flying battle with the apostle Peter over Rome before similarly falling to the earth. Other aspects of the early legend include Faust's guardianship of a canine familiar. Johannes Gast, who admits to never having met Faust, notes in his *Sermones Convivales* of 1548 that the necromancer "led a dog and a horse, I believe them to have been demons . . . The dog sometimes assumed the likeness of a servant," with the author making clear that this was simply what "I was told." In another passage, Gast recounts how Faust was able to torture a group of monks by projecting a poltergeist into their monastery. Even more remarkably, through the manipulation of magic circles, ideograms, and incantations, during the chill of a Wittenberg winter Faust produced the illusion of a sumptuous pleasure garden of delectable fruits and fragrant flowers, providing a dinner for gathered nobles.

Impressive though all of this may be, casting demons and conjuring specters wasn't unusual in the Renaissance (or at least belief in such things wasn't out of the ordinary), an era that for all of its connotations of rebirth was more a golden age for academic magic than it was for enlightened science. While it's the Middle Ages that are slandered as "dark," the Renaissance was the greatest period for alchemical and astrological thinking, an appreciation for ethereal and mystical Platonism threaded through the new learning of humanism.[6] Intellectuals studied the Jewish mysticism of Kabbalah as well as the neo-paganism of the mythical Hermes Trismegistus, mastering the manipulations of spells, the drafting of magic circles to imprison spirits, and divinatory calculation with strange glyphs.

Nothing is out of the ordinary in Faust's conjurations—readers would have *believed* them to be real. All those chapbooks about Faust could be placed on the shelf next to contemporaries like the German alchemist Cornelius Agrippa with his *Three Books of Occult Philosophy* or the Swiss physician Paracelsus. The honor roll of the Renaissance is filled with wizards, but Faust remains the most famous, more Prospero than mere alchemist. Agrippa, Paracelsus, the Italian heretic Giordano Bruno, Elizabeth's court astrologer John Dee—none of the writings attributed to Faust are as significant as books by these men, and yet Faust's name is an adjective while those others are largely forgotten.

———

"The life of a Renaissance magus was not a safe one," quipped Frances Yates in a 1966 essay in *The New York Review of Books*, while tallying those either censured or, if you're as unlucky as Bruno, burnt at the stake. Always at risk of punishment, so that the idea of Faust becomes useful to those more staid magicians. *"We're not Satanic, it's Faust who is Satanic."* While Agrippa and Paracelsus anxiously explained how their practical magic was not of the black variety, the *teufelsbücher* lustily detail Faust's machinations with the chthonic. A convenient mirror, since all the rest of his contemporaries can displace their fears about their own legitimacy onto him. Because shapeshifting dogs and chimerical gardens aside, the word "Faustian" connotes a certain thing above all others, and that's the notorious contract with the Devil. Such contracts were replete during Faust's day, strongly associated with witches, the signing of a woman's name into the Devil's book signaling her as being indentured to the prince of darkness. Only Johann Faust, however, became synonymous with that theme.

Yet it would be reductionist to assume that only the man with that cursed name was its inspiration. The Faust legend emerges from the Renaissance milieu of high magic, the hermetic corpus and occult sciences that animated the gloaming-realm between science and theology, and it's long endured so that later figures, such as Culianu, are easily recognizable as being Faustian. Even in the High Middle Ages some thinkers developed a reputation for necromancy, though during that period a magically fertile Platonism was in eclipse, its axiomatic claims about all observable reality merely a pale reflection of a transcendent realm awaiting Renaissance humanism.

Roger Bacon, the brilliant thirteenth-century English Franciscan who was integral to the development of empirical science and the inductive method was rumored to be a sorcerer, and such feats as the alchemical transmutation of base metals into gold, the invention of robotic automatons, and the construction of a brazen head were attributed to him, as they had been to Pope Sylvester II in the previous century.[7] Responsible for the popularization of everything from eyeglasses to gunpowder, Bacon's technological innovations must have appeared miraculous; he wrote that so "many secrets of nature and of art are thought magical by the unlearned, and the magicians trust foolishly in symbols and incantations to bring them power; pursuing them, they leave behind the work of nature and of art for the sake of the error of incantations and symbols."[8]

Copernicus, Tycho Brahe, Kepler, Galileo, Wilhelm Gottfried Leibnitz, and Isaac Newton were all scientific thinkers with occult fascinations, and though only the first two could have been an influence chronologically on the initial Faust myth and Marlowe's version of it (not that there is evidence of that per se), it's not unreasonable to see all of them as in symbiotic interdependence with the more general figure of the magus as he developed through early modernity and naturally intersected with the legend of the Devil's contract. Magic had become a respectable discipline for study with the rise of Renaissance humanism and a variety of what's known as Nco-Platonism associated with Florentine scholars like Giovani Picco della Mirandolla and Marsilo Ficino. They signaled the advent of figures much more properly understood as "real" sorcerers (or people who desired to be sorcerers) than Medieval proto-scientists like Bacon and Llull.

Many of these same figures, such as Agrippa and Trithemius, are explicitly part of the Faust legend, or are featured in the historical records of Johannes Faust. Agrippa, for example, took great pains to differentiate his own magical practice from the sort associated with Faust, steadfastly claiming it to be Christian, orthodox, and moral. Admitting in the introduction to *Three Books of Occult Philosophy or Magic* that those who study magic are often believed to "sow the seed of heresies, offend the pious, and scandalize excellent wits," he denied that he was a "sorcerer, and superstitious and devilish," rather claiming that "Magicians, as wise men, by the wonderful secrets of the world, knew Christ, the author of the world, to be born, and came first of all to worship him; and that the name of Magic was received by philosophers, commended by divines, and is not unacceptable to the Gospel."

Regardless of such protestations, perhaps written with Faust in mind, Agrippa's detractors nonetheless accused him of being a sorcerer and of entering an infernal covenant. One popular story had it that as Agrippa lay on his deathbed in Grenoble, France he conjured demons to ferry him to his new home. The brilliant Swiss alchemist, philosopher, and physician Paracelsus was, despite his own empirical commitments, also associated with demonological endeavors.[9] Both Agrippa and Paracelsus' teacher Trithemius also had the occasional stench of bitumen and sulfur, methane and nitrous about them. Such were the paradoxical vagaries of the sixteenth and seventeenth centuries, when the line between philosophy and magic, science and necromancy was wafer-thin.[10] Regardless of contemporary skeptics and rationalists' squeamishness on this score, science evolved out of magical thinking, and at this crossroads was the figure of Faust, simultaneously the cursed magician and curious scholar.

But why then among all those instances of the Devil's contract before Faust, and besides all the other wizardly characters who have a bit of the diabolical about them, is it this relatively minor German sorcerer who has become so associated with the legend? I'd suggest that such a connection persists because of our innate attraction to Mephistopheles, the other central character in the Faust corpus. While many early narratives about the magician attribute the contract to Satan himself, in Spiess's *Faustbuch* the Devil employs that unique emissary with his multi-syllabic name, who when called upon first appears as a dragon, then a fiery sphere, a moldering corpse, and ultimately as a brown-robbed monk.

Scholar Jeffrey Burton Russell explains that Mephistopheles is "not a traditional Judeo-Christian or folkloric name but a brand-new coinage," sounding a bit Greek or Latin, and perhaps trying to evoke Hebrew as well. Several different etymologies are offered, with elements of the name recalling the Latin *mephitis* meaning "sulfurous" or the Hebrew *tophel* for liar, but Russell concludes that the "originator and his intentions are unknown, so the derivation of the name is uncertain," unless of course that just happens to be the actual demon's name. In the abecedarium from Azazel to Ziminair, Mephistopheles is a singular and untraceable entry. A disquieting sense of verisimilitude in that we're privy to some secret arrangement of letters formed in a location below, especially when considering how incantation has always relied on hidden words.

Mephistopheles presents a cool, detached, almost ironic affect; in Marlowe's play, when the demon first appears it's in the form of a decomposing corpse—maggots crawling out of nostrils, flesh clinging to a raw pate. Faust compels Mephistopheles to return in a more pleasing form, so the demon comes back wearing the cowl of a Franciscan mendicant. "Why this is hell, nor am I out of it," Mephistopheles says, for regardless of appearance we're all just bones encased in meat, the only difference between the living and the dead being the rate of decomposition. "Hell hath no limits," explains the demon, "nor is circumscrib'd / In one self place; but where we are is hell, /And where hell is, there must we ever be," whether in Krakow or Heidelberg, Prague or Wittenberg.

A man who has been transformed into a legend must speak in a powerful enough register for us to still hear him more than five centuries later. Should Faust's story have any enduring resonance, it's this—his legend is about the difference between appearances and reality, and in a disenchanted age both he and his demonic interlocutor become an "elegant symbol of the modern," as Russell writes. When Marlowe's play premiered, it was said that the Devil himself was in the audience to make sure that he was presented fairly, and that the stage incantations led to the conjuring of an actual demon among the actors. A play where Faust hears Homer, sees Helen of Troy, all of them phantoms, "Rather illusions, fruits of lunacy; / That make men foolish that do use them most." Renaissance necromancers claimed to communicate with the dead, but clerics said that those were just devils in disguise; a wizard prepared a sumptuous course of delicacies grown in his garden, but they were all filth and ash; for five hundred years we've retold the story of Faust, but the real man is only as tangible as the bare knowledge that he existed.

A transmutation of flesh into words, of matter into ideas, of man into metaphor, but nonetheless an ever-shifting symbol, an allegory difficult to parse because its meaning won't stay put. As none other than Culianu put it in a paper for the French journal *Review of the History of Religions*, such a "hollow plot can be put to any imaginable use, and Faust can be anything, from a pimp to a benefactor of humanity . . . One is amazed how much can be achieved by means of a hollow plot." Faust's story is ultimately about the burdens of artifice, but the curse is that this living man accrued so many stories about himself that he transitioned into legend and in the process erased the particulars of his soul. Language is the true medium of such magicians, for as another sorcerer intoned—*words, words, words.* "At the very moment I am concluding these pages," wrote Culianu, "new Fausts are being born, perhaps too many." Now the imagined Faust is the real Faust. If you search for him, then he is already here. Take heed.

CHAPTER FIVE

A DEVIL TOO MANY:
KIT MARLOWE
AND THE CONJURING
OF DR. FAUST

Despair in God and trust in Beelzebub.
Christopher Marlowe, *The Tragical History of the
Life and Death of Dr. Faustus* (1593)

Established in 1550 by Calvinist refugees fleeing
Spanish oppression in the Low Countries, London's
Nederlandse Kerk was one of the most prominent
of the so-called "Stranger Churches" founded by sixteenth-
century continental Protestants who were welcomed by the
English crown.[1] The Dutch Church was, and remains, a
handsome and stolid structure of grey granite and plain interiors, a sanctuary for the stern, doctrinaire, and industrious
Reformed Christians who would gather daily in their dour

black and their modest ruffled collars for prayer and scripture reading. As a place of communion, the Dutch Church
was to be contrasted with another institution less than a mile
away in Cheapside, at the corner of Friday and Bread Streets
not far from St. Paul's Cathedral, where one day Christopher
Wren's glorious dome would arise over the squalor of East
London. There, in the shadow of St. Paul's tall Medieval
steeple was a pub of some ill repute, but still sallied with
literary associations, known as the Mermaid Tavern.

"A pure cup of rich Canary wine," imagined the poet
Ben Jonson, "Which is the Mermaid's now, but shall be
mine." Jonson was only one of the literary figures of the
late Elizabethan era who could be found affixed to a stool
at the tavern, a glass of sack or a pewter of port in his
pink hands. Over a bowl of roasted chestnuts or some meat
pies, the greatest writers of the English language's greatest
century drank, conversed, fought. A very different congregation from the Dutch Church. Behind the half-timbered
walls of the pub, espied beyond the bubbled glass of its
windows, might be the young raconteur Jack Donne before he became the respectable Dr. John Donne, the brilliant playwrights John Fletcher and Francis Beaumont, the
explorer William Strachey who survived a Bermuda ship-
wreck on his way to the Virginia plantations in 1609, and
a certain Stratford-born actor and writer who would draw
inspiration from the previous man's account of being ma-
rooned in paradise following a tempest.

On the evening of May 10, 1593, some anonymous

hand mimicked Luther and nailed to the door of the Dutch Church fifty-three lines of blasphemous verse threatening the congregation, signing it "Tamburlaine" after the most famous character of the most famous playwright of the day. Maybe the evening when that happened, Christopher Marlowe would have been enjoying some ale, perhaps a capon, in the safe environs of the Mermaid Tavern a few blocks away. "Ye strangers yt doe inhabite in this lande," begins the note before moving on into more inflammatory language, for "Weele cutte your throtes, in your temples praying / Not paris massacre so much blood did spill."[2] Not quite Marlowe's "mighty line," the immaculate blank verse which he perfected and which his competitor William Shakespeare appropriated, but still a passable approximation of iambic pentameter.

Whoever wrote the missive that has come to be known as the "Dutch Church Libel" was most likely not Marlowe, but whoever signed it after the titular character of the playwright's massive hit *Tamburlaine the Great* (written and staged in "Part I" and "Part II") surely wanted the authorities to think that it was. For many who thrilled to his other great hit, *The Tragical History of the Life and Death of Dr. Faustus*, such impiety would have been believable. A bit of the Faustian clung to Marlowe's reputation, the playwright whose incantations were, according to some, capable of conjuring actual demons on the stolid wooden stage of the Rose (doubtful), while others figured him an atheist and a sodomite (less so), and a wicked genius of ill repute (certain).

The following day Marlowe's former roommate Thomas Kyd was arrested, a dramatist of similar contemporary renown whose *The Spanish Tragedy* competed with *Tamburlaine* as the most popular play of the period. Searching Kyd's lodgings, the authorities discovered a short, handwritten tract, lost to posterity, which contained numerous heretical claims, the chief of which denied the divinity of Christ. Under duress of torture, Kyd claimed that the manuscript had been written by Marlowe and attested to a number of other impious affirmations made by his friend. Nor were Kyd's confessions, perhaps procured by crushed thumb and extracted tooth, the only ones offered, for an associate of Marlowe's named Richard Baines, a turn-coat Catholic priest who'd supposedly been involved in shady government work, enthusiastically offered the Privy Council details about their dissolute charge.

According to Baines, Marlowe had claimed that "all they that love not tobacco and boys are fools," that he shared his bed with Kyd (not a stretch for audiences who've seen his play *Edward II*), and that among other religious pronouncements had claimed that Moses "was but a juggler" and that "Christ was a bastard and his mother dishonest." Eight days after the threat was affixed to the front of the Dutch Church, the powerful Privy Council, the equivalent of an Elizabethan Department of State, released a warrant for Marlowe's arrest. On May 20, Marlowe turned himself in, but was released until a trial could be set. On the penultimate day of May, Marlowe was stabbed above the eye with a pocketknife by Ingram Frizer in what was described as a quarrel over a tavern bill. Virtually nothing about the circumstances surrounding Marlowe's death have ever quite added up to biographers, and more than four centuries later the sense remains that the playwright's murder was more a political assassination than mere drunken brawl gone bad, but there are a multitude of hypotheses, of varying degrees of believability, as to the who and the why of the whole imbroglio.[3]

During the height of the English Renaissance, Marlowe's Faustus rejected the superficiality of dead empiricism; at the high-water mark of the Reformation, he disparaged the inanities of empty faith. When Marlowe's play begins, after the chorus has delivered its perfunctory prologue, we visit the good doctor in his study, having mastered every variety of earthly understanding. In monologue, the necromancer implores himself to "Settle thy studies, Faustus, and begin / To sound the depth of that thou wilt profess." Marlowe proceeds to offer an antidoxology, a wicked statement of faith's absence. Faust admits that "Sweet Analytics, 'tis thou hast ravis'd me!" but he has abandoned the schoolman's desire to "live and die in Aristotle's works," for the art of the syllogism, the desire to discover the valid but not the true (or better yet the secret) is an empty vocation. "Is, to dispute well, logic's chiefest end?" asks Faust, "Affords this art no greater miracle?" Farewell to Aristotelian science, along with medicine, and jurisprudence, and religion.

Both secular and sacred knowledge are disparaged as
meaningless, as the parsing of shadows on a cave wall.
What Faustus rather desires is a journey to the source itself, for conjuring spirits capable of taking him into the
sunlight, into the world of the forms. The closest the zealous heretic Marlowe comes to offering a cracked creed is in
Faust's declaration that:

> This metaphysics of magicians,
> And necromantic books are heavenly;
> Lines, circles, scenes, letters, and characters;
> Ay, these are those that Faustus most desires.
> O, what a world of profit and delight,
> Of power, of honour, of omnipotence,
> Is promis'd to the studious artisan!
> All things that move between quiet poles
> Shall be at my command: emperors and kings
> Are but obeyed in their several provinces,
> Nor can they raise the wind, or rend the clouds;
> But his dominion that exceeds in this,
> Stretcheth as far as doth the mind of man;
> A sound magician is a mighty god:
> Here, Faustus, tire thy brains to gain a deity.

Even without the benefit of a close reading, Faust's monologue is a remarkable one. Clearly a description of the wizard's powers, but not just that, for Marlowe equally gives
shape to the vocation of the *writer*.

The "studious artisan" who moves things at his command, who can raise the wind and rend the clouds—this is an ability of the artist able to envision alternative worlds and to create them in pure thought, who can compel men called actors to perform those words. In describing those "necromantic books," Marlowe is also simply describing *literature*. If magic books are composed of "Lines . . . scenes, letters, and characters," so are all books. Faust's paean to books seems to particularly describe *dramatic* works, for what is the play in which he's a character other that a work composed of poetic *lines*, organized into *scenes*, and performed by *characters*. If the enchantments of the wizard stretch as far as the mind of man, than the only limiting factor to his omnipotence would be the extent of his creative brilliance. God may have created man, but Marlowe reminds us that writers can also create gods. If a sound magician is a mighty god, how much more so the writer? Emperors and kings may have profane authority on earth, but he who crafted the Emperor Tamburlaine and King Edward II reminds us through his other creation that it is writers and artists who hold sacred abilities. What the playwright admits to us in this monologue is that writers are themselves magicians, and that Faustus is Marlowe. After Faust has rejected knowledge and faith, there is but one thing left, the most transcendent and sacred of things—imagination.

Nothing of genuine treasure is gained, however, without selling your soul, or at least an aspect of it. For

Marlowe's death was as mysterious and torrid as his life, this Cambridge-educated son of a Canterbury cobbler who through sheer force of demonic intelligence made himself into the greatest playwright of the very beginnings of the English theater. Entire academic careers have been staked in explicating what exactly the poet really believed.[4] A biography that was at least rumored to be replete with espionage, torture, sodomy, and blasphemy. Since that night in 1593 there has been a suspicion that whatever the ultimate reason for Marlowe's assassination, it had to do with work that he did on behalf of the queen's government. That Marlowe was involved in state espionage is fairly well substantiated, not least by extant financial records that show him to have lived far beyond his means while a masters student at Cambridge. He was awarded his degree despite being absent from campus for long swaths of time.

There were, additionally, suspicions that Marlowe planned to attend the Catholic seminary at Rheims in France, an institution founded for expatriated English recusants to become priests, which during the Elizabethan period would be a little like if a star Harvard pupil were to finish their studies at the Leningrad State University during the height of the Cold War. It's known with certainty that Marlowe was only passed through Cambridge because of the intervention of the Privy Council, who sent a letter to the university rectors attesting to the young man's role in "matters touching the benefit of this country." Naturally it's been assumed that Marlowe worked as an agent in France on behalf of the Privy Council, especially because of the playwright's known associations with the son of Sir Francis Walsingham, who was periodically Elizabeth's Secretary of State, and more importantly her fearsome "spymaster," notorious for approving the torture of Catholic agitators.

Because his life—at least what can be pieced together from scant record, rumor, and innuendo—is far more interesting than Shakespeare's, that bourgeois burgher of Stratford, an assortment of kooks since the Victorian era have proffered Marlowe as the actual author of the Bard's thirty-nine plays. Marlowe isn't the author of *Hamlet*, *King Lear*, and *Othello*, but it could be the creator of Dr. Faustus had a higher batting average, though with only six plays to his name and dead by the age of twenty-nine he had less opportunity to establish the repute of a Shakespeare. Head-to-head though, if we're being honest about it, Shakespeare's folio includes a few duds. I'd happily trade *Pericles* or *Timon of Athens* for just one act of an undiscovered Marlovian play.

Of the six plays written by Marlowe, their chronology of composition uncertain but including *Dido, the Queen of Carthage*, *The Jew of Malta*, *Edward the Second*, the two parts of *Tamburlaine*, *Dr. Faustus*, and *The Massacre at Paris*, it's arguably only the final script that's not pure fire, and that's because the foul papers which survive are almost certainly not the playwright's original, but a reconstitution made from an actor's memory after their performance. Combined with a number of exemplary lyric poems and some translations, especially some scurrilous renderings of Ovid's erotic verse, and Marlowe's reputation as both brilliant and dangerous is well earned. He is the Rolling Stones to Shakespeare's Beatles; Martin Scorsese to the Bard's Steven Spielberg; Brooklyn to his Manhattan. A dangerous man rumored to have been a member of a secret society known as the School of Night, which counted among its members the astronomer and explorer Thomas Harriot as well as Walter Raleigh, and who would meet by moonlight to abjure God. The sort of man you can't help but still talk about more than four centuries later.

Central to these six plays—disparate in plot, character, and setting—is Marlowe's great obsession of heresy. No author before, and few since, have so fully committed to interrogating doctrine in the manner in which Marlowe had, not with the syllogism of the schoolman but the heteroglossia of the poet. Each one of the plays written by Marlowe takes an aspect of belief or a particular religious tradition and with withering critique literally dramatizes its undoing. Each of his three most important plays—*The Jew of Malta*, *Tamburlaine the Great*, and *Dr. Faustus*—deconstruct the three major Abrahamic monotheisms, with Marlowe respectively turning his attention to Judaism, Islam, and Christianity.

The Jew of Malta, which has been accurately chastised for the antisemitic caricature of its central character Barabas, is also a damning mockery of Christianity and monotheism more generally, as well as being an unlikely hilarious play (in no small part due to the character of a dead monk being dragged across the stage in a strangely successful attempt at convincing others that he's still alive). More importantly, *The Jew of Malta* expresses a nascent form of freethought, the beginnings of the potent atheism which Marlowe was in the vanguard of, even if it wasn't quite yet intellectually a possibility at large. In the play's prologue, his character Machiavel—based on the infamous Italian political philosopher—claims that he does "count religion but a childish toy, / And hold there is no sin but ignorance." Part of what makes Marlowe so fascinating is that he was allowed to express blasphemous ideas on stage, and that none of their performances was censored by the Stationers' Register, whose responsibility that would have been.

Similarly, *Tamburlaine* questions the idea of divine sanction for evil, with Marlowe's memorable protagonist Timur, based on the fourteenth-century Tajik general and nephew of Genghis Kahn, bragging that "In vain, I see, men worship Mahomet: / My sword hath sent millions of Turks to hell, / Slew all his priests, his kinsmen, and his friends, / And yet I live untouch'd by Mahomet." Later on Tamburlaine burns a Qur'an before a gathering of captured mullahs (a scene that even if pantomimed has been found understandably objectionable to present-day audiences). For sixteenth-century critics of Marlowe, the Islamophobia was not a problem, but there was a sense that impugning the religion of Muhammad may have implied a broader impugning of all religion. Even more arrestingly,

Tamburlaine the Great: Part II does end with its anti-hero dying shortly after he used the Qur'an for kindling, raising the even more uncomfortable possibility that Marlowe was cheekily showing a preference for Allah over Christ (at least in the play).

Neither *The Jew of Malta* nor *Tamburlaine the Great* have proven as enduring, as intoxicating, as fascinating, as engaging, as troubling, as mysterious as *Dr. Faustus*. By far the most important treatment of Faust in the English language, Marlowe's vision has only ever been credibly supplanted by that of Goethe, and then only partially. As with its creator, what the play is really stating and how we're to understand its doomed namesake is ambiguous. Partially this is due to a complicated textual history of *Dr. Faustus*, a work that exists in two versions rather uncreatively named "Text A" and "Text B." Both are posthumous printings, the former published in 1604, more than a decade after its author's murder and the latter in 1616. The Devil is always in the details: 1604's Text A includes thirty-six lines absent from 1616's Text B, while Text B includes 676 lines absent from Text A.

Text B includes several scenes of comic interlude (such as when Faustus makes himself invisible and kicks the pope in the ass), but in my estimation it loses some of the chilling minimalism of the earlier work. As with the historical Faustus, there is the issue of authenticity—which one is the "real" play? Were those later additions made by a creative printer putting some fat on the bones of Text A? Were they based in performance, perhaps improvisations of the brilliant actor Edward Alleyn, an uncharacteristically tall man in that nutrient-deficient age, who would strut and preen and shout about the stage, all to make the role of Dr. Faustus his own? Or were they genuine different drafts of Marlowe? The earlier version displays an enchanting parsimony, a skeletal narrative that evokes the great Modernist drama of the twentieth century, while the later edition's comic scenes can, at least to me, feel more like vaudeville than anything else. Still, the particulars remain familiar from its German source material, the story still about the foolish sorcerer who sells his soul to Satan through the intermediary of Mephistopheles and acquires the abilities of incantation and conjuration. A script, in short, that had everything.

Secular drama had only existed for a generation by the time Marlowe was writing. Before the flowering of drama which marked the Elizabethan and then the Jacobean eras, theater was only slightly askew from religious ritual. This was the Medieval inheritance of the great miracle and morality plays, where in massively orchestrated arrangements of stages the various labor guilds were responsible for performing in intricate cycles that moved through both biblical narrative and hagiography, so that acting itself was charged with a bit of the sacramental.[5] We must contend with the strange reality that during the annual Holy Week staging of biblical tales by the northern English populace throughout the Middle Ages, common people pretended to be divine figures; a blacksmith could be the Archangel Michael, a fisherman St. Peter, and a carpenter Christ.

Something was uncomfortably Eucharistic in such theater—certainly there was to the Protestant Reformers who rejected it—for as wafer and wine can transubstantiate into flesh and blood, so too does pretending to be God imply something of being possessed by Him. To act is to incarnate.[6] Which is to say that for those who watched the Corpus Christi cycle in York, or in Wakefield, or Chester, there was a sense in which this *wasn't entirely pretend.* Arguably the rise of commercial theater, which supplanted the old sacred mystery plays, was a method for both Protestantism and commerce to separate the divine from drama. Impossible to ever fully exorcize either Satan or the Lord, however, for the mere act of performance still contains traces of holiness, and if Protestantism's intent was to take the theater out of the church it ironically only served to make the theater into a church. Even for Protestants, especially when it came to plays like *Dr. Faustus,* in which the incantations uttered on stage engendered a terror about them *not being pretend.*

—

Envision yourself standing with the groundlings that late afternoon in the winter of 1592 when *Dr. Faustus* premiered, waiting for the curtain to rise on this play by that crowd-pleaser behind *Tamburlaine the Great.* Crowded in among your fellow Londoners in the dirt-floor and sawdust covered environs of the open-air theater and there are the sounds of the Thames beyond the half-timbered lath and plaster walls, the tide coming in and out, the singing of the boatmen ferrying women and men to Bankside for an evening far away from the Puritanical clutches of the city fathers. An odor of wood smoke and offal, gamey perspiration and shit, silt and ash permeates the crowd anticipating the play, a miasma seemingly as thick as the polluted Thames itself. Throughout the wider district of Newington Butts there are more sounds and smells—the roaring bears from the baiting pits competing with the theaters for attention and expendable cash, fighting from the taverns and inns, laughter and moans from the brothels. A chill wind blows in from the river at a time when it was still frigid enough to regularly freeze over, rustling the heavy thatched roofing of the Rose.

Hawkers come through the impatient audience, selling oranges and ale, oysters and gingerbread. Dusk's final squibs would filter through the spindly filaments of late autumn's naked tree branches as candles were lit upon the stage, and finally Edward Alleyn, the prodigious, booming, and incandescent Edward Alleyn, appears as if in his library. "Settle thy studies . . . and begin / To sound the depth of that thou wilt profess," Alleyn says. Over the course of the play, these first people to hear Marlowe's words in performance would see the Good and Bad Angel in halo and horns; they'd witness the mottled clown's antics, a pubescent boy dressed in drag as beautiful Helen, and they'd see Mephistopheles disguised in his Franciscan cowl.

At a performance in Exeter, they would, apparently, see something else as well—"one devil too many amongst them." This is according to an author listed only as "G. J. R.," writing shortly after the premier of *Dr. Faustus,* claiming that during one of the scenes of conjurations there was one additional figure on stage than actors in the ensemble, Marlowe's Latin incantations achieving what Alleyn could only pretend to do. Similarly, in 1633 the Puritan demagogue and anti-theatrical agitator William Prynne would note in his massive tome *Histriomastix* that to the "great amazement both of the Actors and Spectators" there appeared a "visible apparition of the Devill on the stage," claiming that the truth of this account can be attested to by "many now alive, who well remember it." What seems to us as superstition and credulity marks the enchantments of the theater, the residue of the sacramental and the strange anxiety which accompanied fiction, this elaborate construction of illusions with so much verisimilitude that it's almost believable that a demon could be pulled from the ether.

So popular was Marlowe's *Dr. Faustus* that he existed in variation as a mainstay on the Renaissance stage. Barnabe Barnes's 1607 *The Devil's Charter* has a demonic contract at its narrative center, in its plot about the infamous Roderigo Borgia selling his soul to Satan's auxiliary Astaroth so as to become the infernal Pope Alexander VI. Drawing upon stories (scurrilous, apocryphal, and some real) that Alexander VI was in an incestuous relationship with his daughter Lucrezia or that he hosted an orgy with Roman prostitutes within St. Peter's remembered as the "banquet of chestnuts," Barnes's play is prosaic Reformation-era anti-Catholic agitprop, of little interest other than to historians and literary scholars, mostly lacking in the same subtleties that are so engaging in Marlowe's play. Most crucially, Alexander VI simply sells his soul for power—that old banquet of chestnuts—so that the philosophical considerations that Marlowe makes about creation and imagination, illusion and reality, are totally exorcized.

By contrast, Robert Greene, a university-educated wit like Marlowe and an avid explorer of London's criminal and bohemian underworlds, returned to the story of the brazen head in *Friar Bacon and Friar Bungay,* believed to have been written sometime after *Dr. Faustus.* Staging the legends of the Medieval monk Roger Bacon's feared brazen head, the penultimate scene sees the contraption cryptically utter "Times is, time was, time is past" before shattering on the floor. Whether well-written as with Greene or trash as with Barnes, all these plays largely adhere to the misanthropic vision of Marlowe. The dictates of grim Calvinism had filtered through the wider culture. "The most perfect expression of the Reformation is the legend of Faust" writes Culianu in *Eros and Magic in the Renaissance.* True, Bacon may repent in Greene's play, but his assistant is dragged to hell.

During our own melancholic time, it can be easy to look back at the beginning of modernity and imagine unbridled intellectual excitement, in which *progress* finally seemed a possibility, in faith, culture, science—but the reality was rather different. Optimism was largely eschewed in this beautiful but cynical age, all verities from the structure of the solar system to the map of the world had shifted; the possibilities of salvation were no different. Protestants had dispensed with holy water and crucifixes, incense and the ringing of bells. Whether anybody ever really knew that they were saved was ambiguous, and the result was a void that we're still in the darkness of.

Dr. Faustus, especially because of its two contradictory iterations, manifests this anxiety. For scholars of Marlowe, one of the most interesting differences between the versions separated by twelve years is the replacement of "can" with "will." In reference to the ultimate destination of Faust's soul, Text A says that it's "Never too late, if Faustus can repent," while that second-to-last word is changed to "will" in the 1616 printing. The difference between "can" and "will" is massive; religious wars have been fought on that difference. The replacement of this one word shifts the entire theological orientation of *Dr. Faustus.*

With "can," there is the connotation that Faust is not able to alter his own trajectory, that his fate is predestined, and that nothing the sorcerer does of his own free will can change this. By contrast, "will" makes the question of the necromancer's redemption one within his own purview, there is the possibility of choice, that Faust could save himself if he so desired. This shift may have been due to the changing sectarian affiliations within the English Church; while Marlowe was alive, and when Text A was printed, the unforgiving dictates of Calvinism were ascendant, with its slightly nihilistic affirmation that every individual's salvation or damnation wasn't just known by God, but chosen by Him as well, before the universe itself was even created. By 1616, however, the Calvinists were being censured by the more traditional-minded bishops being instated by the new king, adherents of another Reformed theology known as Arminianism. Which of the two is more in keeping with Marlowe's own beliefs—whether he was a Calvinist or an Arminian, a Protestant or a crypto-Catholic, or perhaps truly an atheist—is impossible to know.

What is incontrovertible is that whether it's possible for Faust to truly repent or not, he doesn't. The play's most overwhelming anxiety concerns its preoccupation with illusion, with the vocation of the writer as a new priest. If the Marlovian ethos is that storytelling itself is literal magic and the author the mage of this imaginative learning, then there is a profound danger in these skills. Insomuch as *Dr. Faustus* is about heresy, it's really about illusion, and only incidentally about how the latter can inculcate the former. "Was this the face that launch'd a thousand ships / And burnt the topless towers of Ilium" Faust asks Helen of Troy. But no, it's not the face that launched a thousand ships, regardless of how full and red her lips are, or how flaxen her hair is. This is a succubus made to appear as Helen. "Have I not made blind Homer sing to me?" says Faust. Again, no, that was not the blind Greek bard strumming his lyre, but another demon made to trick and cajole.

Whatever Marlowe's own religious sympathies, there is a profoundly Protestant anxiety in *Doctor Faustus,* a fear of the idol that's made to move and speak, of the artfully constructed lie which turns us away from the true and the good. In such a culture it's believable that the audience may have thought that a demon had been made manifest upon that stage at the Rose. Prynne is reticent in description, but could this demon have been one of those Boschian nightmares, a green and red and brown behemoth covered in sores and ulcerated anuses, twisted and chapped horns arising from his scabbed body, rows of sharp, broken, and glinting fangs in his hell mouth? Or, was the extra demon just a fading shadow, a brief interlude in the flickering candlelight, as subtle as hot breath in your ear? Maybe the extra demon just looked like another one of the players, for the most obvious devil in the play is the one which appears as our own reflection. Regardless, it's the demons of our mind, the myths and chimeras conjured by our thoughts, hell which "Stretcheth as far as doth the mind of man" that should be the most feared. To the Protestant, after all, we're saved by faith and damned by its opposite. As with the kingdom of the mind, "hell hath no limits, nor is circumscrib'd / In one self place," says Mephistopheles, "but where we are is hell / And where hell is, there must we ever be."

———

Now, picture yourself again, nineteen years later, standing with the groundlings that late morning in the summer of 1611 when *The Tempest* premiered. The last play by Marlowe's greatest student and the rare plot which was truly original. Drawing not from Greek or Roman myth, British history, or continental romance, Shakespeare derived his tale of the exiled Milanese magician Prospero and his shipwrecked countrymen from the power of his own conjuring, and perhaps from accounts he would have heard from his drinking partner Strachey in the Mermaid Tavern, the latter drunkenly recalling the Virginia-bound ship the *Sea Adventurer* dashed upon the shoals of Bermuda. For a few hours you would have watched this completely unfamiliar story of Prospero's exoneration, which veers perilously close to revenge, of his beautiful daughter Miranda and her love for Prince Ferdinand, of the boozy basement antics of Stephano and Trinculo, of the machinations of state with Alonso, Sebastian, Gonzalo, and Antonio, and of course the base ogre Caliban and the spritely neuter spirit Ariel. Rather than the spring air off the Thames, you feel the warm trade winds of the Caribbean, the sawdust of the Globe's floor transformed into the white-sand beaches of the isle, the thatched roof of the theater appearing as if the furry stones of coconut trees, and the withered oranges hawked by the concession men tasting as fresh, succulent mangoes.

Then, with the happy ending of *The Tempest*—a

salvation denied to Faustus—Shakespeare reveals his own magic, shows us the art of illusion, and exonerates the author as sorcerer. "These our actors," says Prospero, as tradition has it played by Shakespeare himself, "were all spirits and / Are melted into air, into thin air." The characters are denuded, returned to their status as mere performers, men as real and fleshy and material as anyone in the audience. Gone is the tropical wind and Caribbean sand, the coconuts and the mangoes. "And like the baseless fabric of this vision, / The cloud capped towers, the gorgeous palaces, / The solemn temples, the great globe itself, / Yea, all which it inherit, shall dissolve."

Just as those towers of Ilium were a trick, so too were the descriptions of the towers on Prospero's isle; even the great Globe Theater itself but a reverie, though a pleasant one. Hell might not be circumscribed, it may have no limits, but neither does that circular globe. *The Tempest* is Shakespeare's answer to *Doctor Faustus,* Prospero arriving to grant some consolation to his forerunner. "We are such stuff / As dreams are made on," intones Prospero, "and our little life / Is rounded with a sleep." No heaven or hell then, just the pleasant slumber of the twin deaths before we were born and after we depart this life. In between the power of illusion, the magic of fiction, wherein great sorcerers can conjure both the most frightening and most beautiful tableaus, where the world can be created, destroyed, and remade again, and finally where Faustus himself might finally find a bit of salvation.

CHAPTER SIX

GOING UPSTAIRS,
COMING DOWNSTAIRS:
ON WITCHES' SABBATHS
AND BLACK MASSES

All the wild witches, those most noble ladies,
For all their broom-sticks and their tears,
Their angry tears, are gone.
—William Butler Yeats, "The Wild Swans at Coole" (1919)

A year before the Wall Street crash plummeted the United States into the Great Depression, in the sylvan hamlet of Stewartstown, Pennsylvania three men led by John Blymire forced their way onto the farmstead of Nelson Rehmeyer, hit him on the head, strangled him, mutilated his body, and then set the corpse on fire before burning down his black, wooden house, all because they believed that he was a witch who'd hexed the three of them. This was a landscape which the Pennsylvanian poet Stephen Vincent Benét in his epic *John Brown's Body* described as a "Country of broad-backed horses, stone houses, and long green meadows." Spruces, beeches, and oaks, fed by the Delaware and Lehigh, the Susquehanna and Schuylkill, the Monongahela and Ohio, across the undulating ripple of the Allegheny Mountains, the Poconos, the northern Appalachians. Here where the soil was the blackest it would be anywhere north of the Mason-Dixon Line, this Commonwealth was founded as a religious utopia where all were free to exercise their faith.

For three centuries the Pennsylvania Dutch, though most were of German origin, practiced a multitude of faiths, mostly low church and dissenting Anabaptist. Among the Pennsylvania Dutch there developed folk magic variously known as *powwow* or *Braucherei*. Ritual practices included the casting of spells, the manufacture of protective amulets, the brewing of potions and tinctures. Magic for farmers to protect livestock and crops, abate fevers and heal wounds. As with most European folk spells, those who were adept at powwow considered it "good magic," and the women and men initiated into its secrets were also faithful Lutherans, Calvinists, and Moravians (the "Plain Dutch" of the Anabaptist Mennonites and Amish abstained). Yet as with other folk traditions, there were wicked practitioners as well.[1]

Blymire and Rehmeyer were powwowers, but the former became convinced that the latter had placed a powerful curse on him. Another practitioner of hexing named

Nellie Noll, but locally called "The Witch of Marietta," told Blymire that he must steal Rehmeyer's grimoire, a popular book from 1820 entitled *Pow-Wows; or, the Long Lost Friend* by John George Hohman, and a lock of his hair, and bury both some eight feet in the ground to break the hex. *The Long Lost Friend* is far from a nefarious book; it contains wisdom on among other subjects the brewing of beer, the deworming of cattle, and the treatment of diarrhea. This is in contrast to another popular grimoire, an eighteenth-century German text entitled the *Sixth and Seventh Books of Moses* which contained demonological material and is associated with the more infernal adepts of powwow (also a popular title in Caribbean voudon and African American hoodoo).[2]

Yet despite its gentler subject matter, the physical book of *The Long Lost Friend* itself was magical—enchanted with supernatural power, as it said right on the title page— and Rehmeyer's copy would have to be separated from him if the hex was to be broken. "You horseman and footman, whom I have conjured at this time, you may pass on in the name of Jesus Christ, through the word of God and the will of Christ" wrote Hohman, "ride ye on now and pass." All spells loosened, all bindings broken, all hexes lifted. The spruces, beeches, and oaks were naked that stark November evening, thin skeletal arms reaching up toward dark clouds when those three men set off to Rehmeyer's farm, silhouetted by the moon, past barns with the abstract, geometric circular designs known as hex symbols with their shapes of primary red, blue, and green arranged into double-headed birds or flowers.

Things got away from Blymire's control after they arrived; their attempt to break the hex ended up with Rehmeyer dead and doused in kerosene. Here are some other things that happened in 1928: the existence of DNA was indirectly proven, the first transatlantic television signal was broadcast, Charles Lindberg received the medal of honor, Margaret Mead published *Coming of Age in Samoa,* and congressional approval for constructing the Hoover Dam was passed. That an impromptu extrajudicial witch trial happened less than a hundred miles from Philadelphia the same year that Mickey Mouse appeared in *Steam Boat Willie* may seem shocking, but such irrational beliefs are only ever repressed, never eliminated.

Describing a similarly late instance of violence against somebody believed to be a witch, when a young woman was burnt to death in the rural south of Ireland in 1895 by her own family, Angela Bourke writes in *The Burning of Bridget Cleary: A True Story* that "Such incidents aroused horror and revulsion, but their perpetrators were usually treated leniently by the courts, which recognized the component of 'superstition' in their actions. Here, as elsewhere, 'superstition' means a system of reasoning which was alien to those in power." Such would be the case in Pennsylvania, where even after authorities arrested, charged, tried, and convicted Blymire and his coconspirators the sentences were shockingly lenient for men who had brutally murdered somebody, with all three released after only a few years (though none was known to have committed a crime again).

Obviously, a different result from during the height of the early modern witch trials in the sixteenth and seventeenth centuries when hundreds of thousands, maybe more, were executed on charges of having entered into union with the Devil. That, ironically, was an interlude as well, for during the Middle Ages the attitude toward witchcraft was surprisingly lackadaisical, the vast variety of folk healing and conjuration that would later be impugned during the Reformation and Counter-Reformation largely tolerated, with the real heresy being not the practice of witchcraft but the belief that it was possible at all.

As his defense attorneys would argue, Blymire may have considered both himself and the man whom he murdered to be witches, but this was merely evidence of his mental illness, as he'd been in and out of the state mental hospital in Harrisburg. Less a vestige of a Medieval past, Blymire was a remnant of the convulsions of modernity, of when the witch as an archetype spectacularly ruptured into being and enacted hideous violence before being once again explained away, this time by medicine.[3] Ecstatics and mystics, prophets and visionaries who were once persecuted would in modernity be pathologized and shunted away into hospitals rather than being burnt at the stake; as were those accused of witchcraft, the witch herself a potent fantasy of developing modernity. By the twentieth century someone like Blymire was no longer understood by the legal system as a font of supernatural forces, but as a schizophrenic. Which isn't to say that Rehmeyer's murder didn't initiate a witch-hunt of a sort—it did—even if the only witch to be burnt was Rehmeyer himself. This witch-hunt happened in Pennsylvania's major cities and her capital, a fear of so-called backwoods primitivism and superstition, with the police investigating every cold case as a "hex murder" and local school boards developing curriculum to discourage belief in powwow. Persecution of a type, promulgated not by priests and ministers but by politicians and bureaucrats, but in one important regard of a continuum with previous witch trials, for both were aspects of the centuries-long *depaganization* of Western culture.

Powwowers in Pennsylvania, the *benandanti* in Italy, the *sorginak* in the Basque country, *brujeria* in Latin America, the *noaidi* in Lapland, *oungan* and *mambo* in Voudon, *babalawos* in Santeria, *cunningfolk* in England— *witches*. A wealth of religious practices long categorized as "folk religion" have been slurred as something else when they come up against the organized strictures of a church hierarchy. Many of these traditions exist or existed organically within Christianity, as a supplemental wisdom and tradition based in an awareness of the natural world and the body, as well as the spirit-realm. Scholarship is apt to be as reductionist as the inquisitor (though less violent), so that it's a mistake, for example, to see a seamless connection between the benandanti of Friuli—the "Good

Walkers"—who believed that they used a witchcraft of benevolence to aid Christ in spiritual night-battles that occurred in nocturnal visions and the cunningfolk of England who applied herbal tinctures to illness or caste spells and divinations.

Still, the benandanti and the cunningfolk are perpendicular to the official religion, and both had their practitioners persecuted as witches, even while these same women and men oftentimes claimed that they were battling against witches themselves (as indeed Blymire had claimed in the twentieth century). For example, consider one Battista Moduco, interrogated by the Inquisition in Friuli in 1580, who openly claimed that "I go with the . . . [good witches] to fight four times a year, that is during the Ember Days, at night; I go invisibly in spirit and the body remains behind; we go forth in the service of Christ, and the witches of the devil." The reality is that as rich, varied, and dynamic as many of these traditions were (and are), they bore little similarity to witchcraft as it's been filtered through the wider culture, even if the lurid fantasy of a coven was originally based in a misinterpretation and slander against such beliefs.

The benandanti were self-admitted witches, as were the powwowers, but they were good witches.[4] Theirs was not an impious gathering, their goal was neither blasphemy nor heresy—in fact the opposite. Yet when most people envision a coven what they often imagine is less using herbs and flowers to treat indigestion or dropsy and more the scene depicted by the Spanish painter Francisco Goya in his 1798 composition *Witches' Sabbath* at the Lazaro Galdiano Museum in Madrid. Goya was obsessed with covens, and often revisited that subject and other demonic themes, most spectacularly in his "black paintings," private murals painted on the walls of his home.

In *Witches' Sabbath*, the imagery is familiar, if no less disturbing. Around a dozen women meet underneath a crescent moon in a rocky wilderness, a cloud of bats circling above. The women, in white and blue and yellow cloaks, some with exposed breasts or backs, are mostly withered, skeletal and elderly, the much maligned and feared *crones* of the witchcraft legends, though there are a few younger women as well. Misogynistic thinking, which was always central in the fear of witches, castigated women for either being not sexually desirable enough or too sexually desirable. Two of the crones each hold up an infant for sacrifice, one of the babies malnourished and skeletal, the offering a pantomime of the Eucharist. In the center of this circle? Is he to whom this hellish offering is being made—the massive bipedal goat man often known as Baphomet, a creature with slit-pupiled eyes glowing yellow, a hoof held out in damned benediction underneath his gargantuan, curved horns garlanded with fresh oak leaves. The Faustian bargain in its most brutal and horrifying manifestation.

When Goya painted *Witches' Sabbath*, most of the official panic about covens was in the distant past, but subterranean fears have a way of erupting now and again.[5] The "witch" is a curious and bifurcated metaphor for irrational-ism, for in their own figure they represent the homage to-ward chthonic and hellish forces, but they also represent the irrationalism of the witch-hunter, ironically willing to com-mit gross evil in a battle to eliminate evil. Always attuned to how the so-called rationalism of the Enlightenment subli-mated darker urges and beliefs, Goya was fascinated by the image of a Witches' Sabbath, and in this work and others he gives a visual language to that fantastical gathering of women signing their souls away to the damned being.

This is the connection to the Faust mythos, why witches must be understood as elements in that broader legend of the diabolical contract. Like Faust, witches called upon the Devil through arcane rituals; like Faust, they ex-changed their souls for occult powers. Any presumed dif-ference between the urbane, sophisticated, and educated Dr. Faust and the women accused of witchcraft has more to do with the vagaries of class and gender than it does with any appreciable difference between the two types of story. Examine the claim of the Italian Ambrosian priest Francesco Maria Guazzo who in his 1608 witch-hunting manual *Compendium Maleficarum* would explain how the sabbath was defined by the "pact formed between a witch and the devil" where this contract "consists of a sol-emn vow of fidelity and homage made, in the presence of witnesses, to the devil visible present in some bodily form." Not just evocative of the Faustian bargain, but explicitly the same thing.

At the center of much of the frenzied paranoia about witches was the setting of the sabbath, a cruel inversion of Christian worship which notably has little actual corollary among those adepts across the wide range of folk magic. What must be remembered is that the *coven* is called such for they are in *covenant* with Satan; the Witches' Sabbath may be a demonic ritual, but it's also an act of exchange, of betrothal, of contractual obligation. An initiate into witchcraft enters into such a bargain for gain, as any Faustian figure does—for wealth, power, knowledge. That witchcraft isn't commonly thought of as Faustian may be attributed to the vagaries of class and gender, a separation between the high culture character of the necromancer and the low culture figure of the witch, but both were in communion with the Devil.

Just as the Faustus narrative evolved during the Medieval into the Renaissance periods, so too did the character of the witch, and especially the setting of her sabbath in which she was supposed to acquire her damned abilities. As iconic as the parchment upon which Faustus scribbles his signature is the Witches' Sabbath. There is something Dionysian in the gathering of a witches' coven, of turning the world upside down and subverting the commandments of piety and faith.[6] Women at a sabbath are positively bestial, and the entire spirit of the coven is propelled by those caprine energies so aptly expressed in the looming image of Goya's Baphomet. Accounts of such rituals have tropes in common—those who've entered into a compact with

Satan and their initiates will meet late at night, in isolated and wild places. They may manifest their magical abilities, including levitating upon broom sticks, calling upon animal familiars, or transforming themselves into such creatures (black cats have long been favorites). Child sacrifice was often involved, so that ointments and potions could be made from the rendered fat of murdered children, a type of perverse anti-communion.[7] Finally, neophytes in the witch cult would be asked to enter their names into the Devil's book—an unmistakably Faustian conceit—and often to perform sexual acts with the goat-man Satan, including anilingus (the act of eating Lucifer's asshole is termed *osculum infame*, something important to know).

These colorful details are partially derived from a single source, one of the most catastrophic volumes to ever be written, a prurient guide to witch-hunting penned by the Dominican inquisitor Heinrich Kramer in 1486 to which much material was added by his fellow brethren Jacob Sprenger in 1519 and that was entitled *Malleus Maleficarum*—The Hammer of the Witches. Kramer and Sprenger's book was responsible for reformulating the conception of the witch from the vague but tolerated folk healers of the Middle Ages into the manifestation of pure Satanic evil and then into the dimly remembered phantoms of a superstitious past which they are today. A direct line goes from *Malleus Maleficarum* and its authors' fevered invention of the Witches' Sabbath to Goya's painting. Also, a direct line to the pillory and pyres, the rack and the river in which mostly women were humiliated, burnt, crushed, and drowned in the travesty of the witch trials which took thousands, hundreds of thousands, according to some maybe even millions of lives during the early modern period. An embodiment of the dangers of narrative, of how the Faust myth itself could metastasize.

As Hitler's *Mein Kampf* is to antisemitism, so is the *Malleus Maleficarum* to misogyny, and as the former is to the Holocaust, so is the latter to the witch trials. "What else is a woman but a foe to friendship, an inescapable punishment, a necessary evil, a natural temptation, a desirable calamity, a domestic danger, a delectable detriment, an evil of nature, painted with fair colors," write Kramer and Sprenger, declaring that "all wickedness is but little to the wickedness of a woman." Perhaps grossly embellishing magical folk practices, Kramer and Sprenger in some sense "invented" the witch as she's been passed down to posterity (though fair to note that the phrase "Witches' Sabbath" does not appear anywhere in the *Malleus Maleficarum*), concocting the myth of the organized, diabolical, Faustian sorority of those in league with Satan, seemingly hidden within every hamlet and town from the Straits of Gibraltar to the Bosporus, from the lemon groves of Sicily to the coldest reaches of Lapland.

The wicked accounts of the witch trials are an example of the ways in which the stories we tell ourselves can have horrific consequences. Kramer and Sprenger's *Malleus Maleficarum*, Guazzo's *Compendium Maleficarum*, King

James I's 1597 *Daemonologie*, the so-called "Witchfinder General" Matthew Hopkins's 1647 *The Discovery of Witches*, and a hundred other guides like them—these were the Faustian contracts by which thousands of human beings were persecuted, the false certainty of religious zealotry manifesting in the unspeakable violence that drove many Europeans to insanity.[8] From such guides came the conceit that witches could become invisible or transform into animals, that they rode on broomsticks and sacrificed infants, that they could be identified by having a "Devil's mark" found on their nude bodies. Belief in witches, insomuch as the idea that some people naturally have an affinity to practice magic, may be omnipresent and universal, but the slander that this involved a signature in the Devil's book was a novelty with hideous implications. Here are the ramifications of that belief:

> **Petronilla de Meath**—Flogged and burned at the stake, 1324 in County Kilkenny, Ireland. First known victim in the British Isles of the witch trials, accused by the Bishop of Ossory of having, among other things, "placed the intestines and internal organs of cocks, worms, and nails cut from the dead bodies" inside of the skull of a criminal, along with "hairs from the buttocks and clothes of boys who died before being baptized," all to ferment a potion used to summon an incubus. Accusations were

rendered by the husband of Alice Kyteler, the noblewoman for whom de Meath was a servant. Kyteler was the primary defendant but escaped to the continent with her life.

Sibilla Zanni and Pierina de' Bugatis—Burned at the stake, 1390 in Milan, Italy. Both were executed on orders of the Inquisition after having admitted, under torture, that they were part of a cult dedicated to the worship of a mysterious goddess named Madonna Oriente, who was the locus of an underground feminist religion.

Matteuccia de Francesco—Burned at the stake, 1428 in Perugia, Italy. Initial charges seem to be related to de Francesco's being a sex worker but transformed into lurid claims of her having been a sorceress capable of conjuration.

Guirandana de Lay—Burned at the stake, 1461 in Jaca, Spain. An unmarried woman who worked as a traditional folk healer and was accused by neighbors of being involved in the production of infernal potions used in diabolical ritual.

Agnes Waterhouse—Hanged, 1566 in Essex, England. Among the first women to be executed following Parliament's 1562 passage of an act against witchcraft. She was accused by a twelve-year-old neighbor of having terrorized her with an animal familiar that appeared as a horned, baboon-faced speaking dog which threatened to "thrust his knife to my heart but he would make me die." Also admitted under torture to possessing a shape-shifting feline familiar named Satan.

Thomas Doughty—Beheaded, 1578 in Porto San Julian, Argentina. Explorer and compatriot of Sir Francis Drake who was part of the latter's expedition to circumnavigate the globe. Ran afoul of Drake, who accused him of treason and witchcraft, with Doughty executed on the deck of *The Swan* in a forlorn bay along the Patagonian wilderness. According to another sailor, before the execution both Drake and Doughty supped for the last time, "as cheerfully, in sobriety, as ever in their lives they had done aforetime, each cheering up the other, and taking leave, by drinking each to other, as if some journey only had been in hand."

Ursula Kemp—Hanged, 1582 in Chelmsford, England. A local cunningwoman who was accused of making potions. Her conviction was based on the prosecution forcing her eight-year-old son to testify against her, with the young boy claiming that his mother was the master of four animal familiars in the form of two cats, a lamb, and a toad.

Dietrich Flade—Burned at the stake along with 368 other people, 1589 in Trier, Germany. A judge who helped to oversee witch trials in Trier, Flade would ultimately be accused of sorcery and find himself upon the same scaffolds, a victim in one of the largest such trials in Germany, a country riven by sectarianism and particularly pronounced in its violence to those accused of having sold their souls at the Sabbath.

Agnes Sampson—Garroted and burned at the stake along with seventy other people, 1591 in Edinburgh, Scotland. Sampson was a popular folk healer implicated in a fantastic plot to supposedly use magic to commit regicide, the object of this imagined conspiracy being James VI of Scotland (the future James I of England). Central to this plot was an image of the king gifted to Sampson by the Devil, who arrived in the "likeness of a Black man." James, who had a reputation for being learned but also superstitious, was greatly influenced by the mass executions related to the plot, incorporating elements from those trials into his own witch hunting manual (which in turn partially inspired Shakespeare's *Macbeth*).

Merga Bien—Burned at the stake along with 250 other people, 1603 in Fulda, Germany. Many accused witches came from marginal positions in society—the poor, the mentally ill, spinsters, the widowed—but not all. Bien was the heiress from two different husbands who'd preceded her in death, but any wealth she'd accumulated did little to protect her once she'd been accused. Despite being pregnant, Bien was burnt at the stake when after torture she'd "confessed" that the fetus in her womb was the Devil's progeny.

Isobel Gowdie—Most likely executed, 1662 in Auldearn, Scotland. A low-status peasant woman who along with her husband supported herself through weaving, Gowdie offered up four remarkable confessions related to

her interactions with the demon and fairy
realms. Academics have theorized that she
may have been psychotic, or perhaps under
the influence of ergot poisoning, a toxic and
hallucinogenic fungus that appeared in rye
throughout northern Europe. Regardless,
Gowdie's confessions were offered without
torture, that practice having been made illegal
(unlike the execution of witches). Whatever the
provenance of her own claims, Gowdie made
all sorts of remarkable assertions, such as her
ability to shape-shift into a rabbit with Satan's
intervention when she chanted the following
bit of doggerel "I shall go into a hare, / With
sorrow and sych and meickle care; / And I shall
go into the Devil's name, / Ay while I come
home again."

Barbara Kollerin—Burned at the stake, 1675
in Salzburg, Austria. Arrested for petty theft,
during torturous interrogation Kollerin was
made to claim that her twenty-year-old son,
Paul, had entered into a pact with the Devil,
and that he led a gang of vagabond children,
beggars, and vagrants in crimes assisted by
magical intervention. A staggering 139 people
would be tortured, decapitated, or burned alive
as a result of such accusations, the most being

children or adolescents whom we'd consider homeless today, the youngest no more than ten years old.

Malin Mastdotter—Burned at the stake, 1676 in Stockholm, Sweden. A Finnish midwife, Mastdotter was implicated by her nineteen-year-old daughter who claimed that her "mother had always had a bad language, cursed and used ugly words, particularly on great holy days." Ultimately the accusations became more incredible, with witnesses claiming that Mastdotter was able to manifest a giant, horned, caprine devil in the courtroom itself, invisible to everybody but those standing in accusation. On the pyre, authorities tied a bag of gunpowder about her head as an act of mercy.

Elizabeth Proctor—Hanged, 1692 in Salem, Massachusetts. Among the nineteen people executed for witchcraft in Salem, Proctor's husband John was at the center of the hysteria whereby the Puritan fathers of this New England town believed that the Devil was corrupting its youth. The most famous of witch trials in colonial America, if not all early modern history, Salem was not remarkable for being particularly cruel so much as for

being so late, as the mass hysteria associated
with demonic pacts and magic in Europe had
already begun to subside.

Nelson Rehmeyer—Strangled and burned to
death, 1928 in York County, Pennsylvania.
The perpetrator, as has been established, also
claimed to be a witch.

A painfully incomplete and arbitrary list of the thousands of people executed during those gloaming years, a
mere sixteen people out of what's most likely around sixty
thousand dead.[9] Outside of historical journals and a hand-
ful of plaques, their voices are silent, their faces forgotten,
their names unuttered. As always, the novelistic impres-
sions of such a monstrous crime—the terror, pain, and
grief that attended the victims—lay beyond the veil of history. Furthermore, obviously, the vast bulk of women and
men (around 85 percent of the murdered were the former)
are anonymous, merely numbers in a ledger rather than
human beings in all their goodness and wickedness, our
cosmic complexity immolated upon the green wood pyres
of an age which was supposed to be a Renaissance.

The best sense we can get of the horror, shame, em-
barrassment, and pain, is from works like the minister
James Carmichael's 1591 pamphlet *News from Scotland*,
proudly describing Agnes Sampson brought before the king

at Holyrood palace (where the British monarchy still vacations), having "had all her hair shaven off, in each part of her body, and her head constricted with a rope . . . being a pain most grievous, which she continued almost an hour, during which time she would not confess anything until the Devil's mark was found upon her privates." And so it was, another human betrayed by a mole, or their madness, or an angry husband, child, neighbor.

In 1634, there was another trial in Loudun, France. At the Ursuline convent, several of the nuns had become possessed by demons, expressing their conditions with screamed obscenities, shrieked heresies, moaned blasphemies, and an assortment of barks, growls, and yelps, as well as shouted expressions in ancient tongues. During investigations, several of the nuns accused the appearance of these demons due to the machinations of the Jesuit priest Father Urbain Grandier. A 1627 engraving of Grandier shows a man who is dissimilar to the hags and crones persecuted in those contemporaneous witch trials. In his cassock and with his stylish, neat vandyke beard, the curly-haired Grandier looks more the raconteur and libertine than he does the witch, though according to the Mother Superior, Jean des Agnes, that's exactly what he was. Charged and tried for witchcraft (it seems that Grandier had run afoul of some powerful people, including Cardinal Richelieu), and an actual, physical Faustian contract was produced.

Still extant, the contract says that in exchange for annually trampling the sacraments, molesting the transubstantiated Eucharist and defiling relics and crucifixes, Grandier will be granted the "love of women, the flower of virgins, the respect of monarchs, honors, lusts and powers." Nor does the contract eschew naming who Grandier has entered into covenant with, for this is a pact with "the influential Lucifer, the young Satan, Beelzebub, Levithan, Elimi, and Astaroth," each of their autographs indicated with various hermetic symbols, alongside the Jesuit's signature. Whether that contract appeared to be in the handwriting of the Mother Superior was incidental; Grandier was tortured with red-hot spikes, and then he too was burned at the stake.

If most witches were poor, Grandier was wealthy; those condemned in the bulk of the persecutions were marginalized and powerless, but this Jesuit was well-connected and powerful; most witches were women, but the priest was a man. Another difference in this preternaturally Faustian tale are the ways in which the accusations so clearly map onto a narrative worthy of Marlowe rather than the inchoate and bizarre dream-logic of witch persecutions, with those delirious accounts of women turning into toads or flying through the sky.

Something about the possessions at Loudun was far more aesthetic in a sense, a story which is less folktale than conscious literature.[10] In some ways the Loudun crisis was both indicative of something old and new, for it harkened to the witch trials then still ongoing as well as the rise of a fantastic new fear that would come to supplement and in some cases replace the Witches' Sabbath in the nightmares of the public—that of the Black Mass.[11] Grandier may have died as a witch, but the narrative accoutrement of the sorcerer which surrounds his persona evokes the legend of the Black Mass, the inverted Satanic mockery of the Catholic Eucharist, which began as legitimate anxiety in the early modern period and then transitioned into mere satire, a titillating story for decadent writers.[12]

The first thing to acknowledge are the similarities between accounts of the Witches' Sabbath and of the Black Mass. They both describe nocturnal rituals supplicating Satan that are connected to the practice of the dark arts and which demand the defilement of the sacraments. Despite those similarities, the Black Mass differs in some important respects. The Black Mass is more regimented, it follows a script meant to mimic the actual Mass, and though it blasphemes, magic may not become visible. Most crucially, the imagined Witches' Sabbath was an exercise largely of the working class while the Black Mass was a trifle of the upper classes, and the former was almost certainly mythic while the latter has been documented.

Maybe even more crucially than that, thousands died accused of the fantasy of the Sabbath, but, Grandier notwithstanding, very few would be condemned for the Black Mass. Nobody today believes that the Witches' Sabbath as described by the Inquisitors happened, even if the Church was actively persecuting residual (non-Satanic) pagan cults. By contrast, at least as early as the eighteenth century, the Black Mass was practiced by some as an act of impiety, protest, or mockery, the secular age manifesting the Witches' Sabbath into reality after all of those spurious accusations, thus distinguishing it as an aesthetic act rather than a ritual one. Black Masses were in the repertoire of the cursed priest Etienne Guibourg in the seventeenth-century Sun King's court, the cleric preparing the damned Eucharist for the mistress of Louis XIV, as well as featured in the pornographic writings of the Marquis de Sade a hundred years later, in the profane "Hell Fire Clubs" of Georgian England where rakes like Sir Francis Dashwood mocked Catholic ritual at demonic orgies and at the Hollywood parties of the twentieth-century grifter and "Pope" of the Church of Satan Anton LaVey. "In nominee magni dei nostri Satanas, introibo ad altare Domini Inferi"—"In the name of our God, Satan Lucifer of the most high"—begins LaVey's ungrammatical missal, but as belief in Satan became more pose than fear, the Black Mass moved into the realm of performance art rather than socially punished blasphemy, even while the Faustian pact remained, the selling of one's soul ever a possibility whether during an age of faith or doubt.

As with the Witches' Sabbath, a Black Mass inspires disturbing imagery. The Satanic priest in his dark vestments in front of the diabolical congregation, perhaps an inverted crucifix, a naked and lithe woman beside the altar, a Eucharist not of wine but already of blood, the affixation of red pentagrams upon the tabernacle, the Latin invocation of the Dark One. A decadent affair, but an aesthetic one as well. As the Witches' Sabbath became the Black Mass, it transitioned from heresy to the avant-garde. This was the Black Mass as fixed in the reading public's mind by the French Symbolist writer Joris-Karl Huysmans, who in his 1891 potboiler *The Damned,* about a scholar of the Medieval serial killer Gilles de Rais who discovers that Satanism is real and still secretly practiced in the underground of Paris, describes such an event in the final scene. As much as an artistic manifesto as an ethical rumination, Huysmans declares that "imagination is the only good thing which heaven vouchsafes to the skeptic and pessimist, alarmed by the eternal abjectness of life."

Interpreted generously, Huysmans' is a declaration of freedom, though a freedom which irrevocably slides into nihilism. You can see such hollowness in the six minutes of the 1928 French pornographic film *Messe Noire,* ostensibly a real video of a Satanic initiate at a ritualistic orgy, but which is also unmistakably a record of rote, joyless, and mechanical sucking and fucking. In a scene from the film there is a line of naked women, dead-eyed, staring at the flickering camera in Manichean black and white, human beings reduced to mere flesh. What both the Sabbath and the Mass shared in their sacred profanations was the wisdom which does deference to these things of darkness in this world, and that in struggling to completely eradicate evil the persecutor will only transform themselves into that which they imagine they're fighting. *Messe Noire,* an account by the Prince of this Fallen World, released in that last decadent year before the markets would crash—those anonymous performers preserved on celluloid are not so different from John Blymire, resident of a place seemingly distant but really just around the corner, who that same year decided to murder his neighbor.

CHAPTER SEVEN

FAUST IS AN ARTIST:
CHRISTOPH HAIZMANN AND
THE INFERNAL PAINTING

Don't paint the Devil on the wall, or he will appear.
—Traditional Hungarian proverb

Christoph Haizmann's entire cursed artistic career—the crux of his *entire infernal life* for that matter—is rendered in oil of green and patina of brown upon a votive triptych he painted sometime between 1677 and 1678 after he sold his soul to Satan in exchange for creative immortality, that autobiographical composition narrating both his inexcusable damnation and his miraculous salvation. The original, made in a psychotic fever by a hand that also signed the Devil's parchment, is lamentably gone, long victim to negligence and entropy. The version that's visible today is a copy made by the monks of Neustadt an der Mettau in Bavaria in 1714, some fourteen years after Haizmann had died while reposing at their monastery, the tortured artist finally at peace. Since it's a copy it's impossible to really gauge Haizmann's talent; the painting is passable but hardly brilliant, though Satan had promised the artist immortality, not brilliance, and at least in monograph footnotes and psychology journals he has endured with a type of infamy.

From left to right Haizmann's triptych takes as its subjects his own infernal contract and his eventual salvation due to the intercession of the Virgin Mary, the Mother of God called upon again to help an unfortunate Faustian figure who has sold more than he possessed in his storehouse. On the left of the composition there is a young Haizmann, upon his knee, looking up at Satan who appears as a bourgeois, Bavarian burgher attended by his barking and jumping familiar, a small black dog. Beneath this scene, Haizmann helpfully includes a transcription of their contract, whereby the artist offered to serve the Devil for nine years, during which he'd be able to work as a painter, after which both body and soul would be pulled to hell. The first contract was signed in ink; as if to make the deal more official, a second was proffered to be marked in his blood.

That later deliberation is depicted by Haizmann on the far-right of the triptych, where now the older and more successful painter wears the garb of a respectable gentleman (starched collar and all), while the Devil appears in his true form, a fearsome red beast with clawed feet and a set of pendulous breasts hanging from his scaled and horned body, though he still walks with a cane. In the center of the triptych, there is a grey classical arch, rendered so smooth that it appears to be made out of ivory, and underneath its keystone there is an explosion of orange and yellow and red flames, the Devil now transformed into a flying crimson dragon compelled to heave both contracts into the fire, for unconsumed and unburned within the conflagration is the Queen of Heaven herself, regal and robed in her golden crown, a line of four black-clad priests and Haizmann on bended knee praying before the sanctified presentation.

Again, the painting itself is not particularly good, whether the deficit was with Haizmann or his monastic copyist impossible to know, but that does little to make the scene any less disquieting, this account from an apparently diseased consciousness who believed that his soul had been consigned to the Devil for the period of several years. Tortured by his overwhelming desire to be a great artist and the grief at his father's death, Haizmann was prone to attacks of convulsion and glossolalia, fits of shrieking and screaming, hallucination and psychosis. By the late seventeenth century, the fear of witches was in decline and though Haizmann was treated several times by an exorcist, the painter was more ill than damned. Certainly that's how the Haizmann case would be understood today. "The states of possession correspond to our neuroses," wrote Haizmann's most famous psychoanalyst, none other than Sigmund Freud, who considered the historical case in his 1923 paper "A Seventeenth-Century Demonological Neurosis." Freud continues by arguing that Haizmann's demons must be understood "as having arisen in the patient's internal life, where they have their abode." For the psychiatrist, the red-papped Devil was a surrogate combination of both Haizmann's mother and father, a projection of the painter's grief and guilt. Today, when the ethics of diagnosing long-dead individuals from profoundly different times and cultures is a bit more refined, there is still the unavoidable sense that the visions so painfully experienced by Haizmann are the products of an ill consciousness, of a schizophrenic mind. Which, despite the dearth of evidence beyond some monastic records, is probably true. And yet, those paintings—amateurish though they may be—make us less certain.

Among the vocations of the Faustian personage—wizards and witches, necromancers and sorcerers, even writers and scientists—the artist remains the most predisposed to the infernal. Remember the historical Faust's invocation of sumptuous feasts as pulled from the ether, then gaze upon a still life by Caravaggio or Francisco de Zurbarán, bright yellow lemons whose pebbly skin and dappled condensation is merely an illusion of oil set off against the void of the canvas's black; or, a bunch of overripe green grapes sitting in a wicker basket appearing fresh though they were painted several centuries ago. Tell me that there isn't a bit of the sulfurous about artists. Especially with the new verisimilitude made possible by advances in Renaissance art, the techniques of linear perspective and trompe l'oeil, oblique projection and chiaroscuro, which seemed to preserve reality.

By the time Haizmann was painting, artists had already been separated from the craftsmen they were understood to be during the Middle Ages (admittedly exalted craftsmen). In the maw of secularism there developed a burgeoning aesthetic ideology of "art for art's sake" that replaced the old verities of divinity, in which a new image of the artist as priest couldn't help but emerge.[1] Such a view finds its origin in biographers like Giorgio Vasari, who in his sixteenth-century *Lives of the Most Excellent Painters, Sculptors, and Architects* established a myth of the artistic genius that endures even today, but as perhaps intuited by Haizmann, the Faustian imperative was equally fit for understanding the skill required to generate vistas and tableaus, illusions pulled from nothingness (of course the Bavarian's problem was that he wasn't very good).

One artist who *was* good is Michelangelo.[2] Looking at *The Last Judgment*, Michelangelo's massive fresco behind the altar in the Vatican's Sistine Chapel, is like viewing the Book of Revelation as it happens, the artist's talents implying a certain Faustian excess even if there is nothing untoward in the artist's reputation (or at least as regards diabolical contracts). A tumult of angels and demons, the souls of the saved and those of the condemned, all tumbling in the ecstasy of this universe's finality. At the bottom of the composition are those who are beyond salvation, the damned being pulled by demons into Hell. A fleshy, elderly donkey-eared man is encircled by a serpent, the head of the viper gnawing at his shriveled cock. This is Minos, one of the classical Greek judges of the underworld; Michelangelo used as this demonic being's model the Cardinal Biagio da Cesena, the cleric having dared to criticize the master's inclusion of naked figures as unbecoming of Rome. To the left of Cardinal Minos are a number of devilish interlocutors; a clawed and green-tinged man with a rodentlike cleft palette, a wild-eyed red figure with buck-teeth and ass's ears, behind da Cesena's shoulder a creature that looks as if its entire face is made of rocky protuberances, grey tumors crowding out its twisted and cruel features. Just as we're told Faust was capable of making demons manifest, here comes Michelangelo to actually do it.

Goethe, writing in 1786, some several decades before his version of Faust, claimed that "No one who has not seen the Sistine Chapel can have a clear idea of what a human being can achieve," confessing that he was so engrossed by the work of "Michelangelo that even Nature makes no appeal to me, for my vision is so small compared with his." A telling admission, for though the pious Michelangelo (profane though his personal life may have been) would have blanched at my comparison of him to Faust, Goethe's acknowledgment of how the phantasmagorias of the painter exceed those of even nature—of God's compositions—is a statement of what's so infernal about creative art in the first place.

Just as a wizard can conjure immaculate illusions, so too does the artist, and the cult of genius which began to accrue about such men during the Renaissance was explicitly Faustian, even if this wasn't always conscious. Faustian not least because we expect our geniuses to have a bit of insanity about them, to see them not as dutiful and professional craftsmen, but as fundamentally condemned sinners who in fact damn themselves for the benefit of beauty. Such is the tale of Caravaggio, the drunken hustler, the petty criminal, the sodomitical murderer who was said to have either withered away from syphilis or was killed in a vendetta in 1610, but who three years before that ignominious death was also capable of rendering in exquisite perfection the body of Christ, of conjuring Jesus strapped to the column before His flagellation, an inner divine light radiating from his being into the shadows. A powerful magician, this devil capable of conjuring God.

Vasari writes that this "beautiful creation the world supplied the first model, while the original teacher was that divine intelligence which has not only made us superior to the other animals, but like God Himself, if I may venture to say it." Venture to say it Vasari did, and it was a statement of orthodox humanism, this unbridled optimism about humanity's capabilities of self-invention and self-creation, of being able to ascend that ladder toward the angels, toward the Lord. A consummate Humanistic faith, as well as a consummate Faustian one, especially insomuch as the latter is merely the darker variation on the former. At the core of both the artistic and Faustian imperatives is the desire to replicate Genesis, of humanity being able to do what God did, to improve upon it.

Look at the 1621 marble *The Rape of Proserpina* as executed by the Baroque sculptor Gian Lorenzo Bernini, Michelangelo and Caravaggio's fellow countryman taking as his subject that horrific story about the fair maiden absconded with toward Hades. As with all of Bernini's sculptures, the breathing, perspiring, radiating white of the marble is as stone turned to flesh. Even in our current epoch of photography and computer simulated imagery there is a type of reality-beyond-reality evidenced by the statue. Periodically popular on social media is a detail of Pluto's muscular hand grasping at the soft skin of Persephone, each one of the rapist's fingers leaving an ever-so-slight indentation into the flesh of her thigh as she is carried off to the underworld. Incandescent skill and technique for such an ugly theme, yet despite Bernini's subject it's difficult not to see each one of Pluto's digits grasp the marble of Persephone as if living skin and not inert stone quarried from Carrara.

De Cesena's quibble about nudity in the Vatican's murals, or the Protestant reformer John Calvin's iconoclastic fury at representative art, and even Plato's ancient complaint about the way in which art lies are of a piece, all are an understanding of what's unsettling about representation which is perfectly executed.[3] To accomplish Genesis anew, but on humanity's terms, is forever the hubristic desire of the truly inspired artist. The desire to supplant God, to replace Him.[4]

Naturally the Faust legend has occasionally been a topic of some painterly consideration. The Dutch master Rembrandt made an etching of the wizard in 1652, depicting the learned mage in cross-hatched black-and-white wearing his robes within a heavily curtained study, a glowing alchemical symbol bedecked in esoteric letters emerging from his window. The overall effect of the rather barebones illustration is slightly spooky; the correct interpretation of what exactly Rembrandt meant remains elusive. Tradition has offered the identity of this sorcerer as being Faust, though no scene such as this corresponds to either Marlowe's texts or the German origin story that Rembrandt was more likely to have been familiar with. Then there is the proper reading of the theurgical cipher floating above the window, the hermetic letters glowing in this disk not easily corresponding to anything which any scholar has ever been able to definitively interpret, the mystery of what any of this means still enduring. Is it Mephistopheles? The Devil? God? Something else entirely?

By the time the French artist Eugene Delacroix took on the subject in his 1828 painting *Mephistopheles Approaches Faust in his Study,* there were decades of Goethe's Romantic treatment of the legend to influence how an artist might envision such a scene. Delacroix had already illustrated an edition of the Goethe version, but in his more recent study he enlivened the scene with a bit of colorful detail, from the crimson hose clinging to the Demon's calf and Mephistopheles arriving disguised as a dandyish scholar-gentleman, to the woven light blue thread of the tablecloth in Faust's study. In his black cloak and cap, Faust appears stern and doctrinaire, not unlike dour John Calvin.

More interesting than Delacroix's composition is a painting by the German illustrator Moritz Retzsch made a decade later, often entitled *The Chess Players* or *Checkmate,* which brings a sumptuous color to bear. Evocative of Faust without referencing a scene in either Marlowe or Goethe, Retzsch prefigures the famous scene from Ingmar Bergman's *The Seventh Seal* in which a Knight plays a game of chess against Death for the former's life. In the Retzsch painting another respectable-looking Devil in green robe and feathered cap sits atop a throne decorated with gryphons and skulls, glowering across the chessboard at his adversary, a young and beautiful Faustian everyman in black tunic and red shirt, seemingly lost in thought. Strategy isn't the man's forte, for as the Devil's black pieces aggressively move across the board we see that perilously few of them have been taken while a whole host of the white pawns, bishops, knights, and rooks are in Satan's possession. In the middle floats Faust's Guardian Angel, who despite her worrying expression has not interceded to prevent the inevitable loss. In an 1837 article about

Retzsch, *The Saturday Magazine* considers the shine of the
white-and-black board, the cruel expression of Satan, the
befuddled concentration of Faust, and asks "What witchcraft has the artist used?" Indeed.

Among my favorite artistic treatments of the Faust legend is yet another nineteenth-century piece, the gloriously
evocative and upsetting *The Vision of Faust* painted by
Luis Ricardo Falero in 1878, a work which is also sometimes understandably listed as *Witches Going to their
Sabbath*. Within this slightly gauche and exploitative painting is a summation of all the great Faustian themes—of
the connections between death and sexuality, of the fee-
ble and unearned confidences of man, and this particular
man's foolish desire for power. Most of all, of the ways
in which visions, illusions, fantasies, and art can enrap-
ture the imagination, at least for a time. The Spanish-born
painter, celebrated during his lifetime for the care and attention he gave mythological and fantastic subjects, presents a coven of a dozen witches contorting and writhing in
mid-air. Most are beautiful, nude and nubile women, their
black and auburn hair wind-blown, bare breasts and but-
tocks framed by the grey midnight clouds on a Walpurgis
Night. One wild woman with glowing red eyes straddles a
flying black goat, another seems to writhe in orgasm as she
balances gingerly on a flying broomstick. In the center of
the painting, toward the bottom, is a withered crone with
hooked nose and wart-covered chin, gaunt and scowling,
who orchestrates the movement of these woman. Behind

her is a purple, skeletal figure, a flying cadaver with eyes still in its lidless sockets, a corpuscular creature pointing with one bony finger toward the crone and with its other hand grasping the tail of a potbellied green reptilian demon that looks a little like an iguana. The opposite side of the painting depicts Ricardo's titular character, a hairy and obese naked Faust, the bearded and aged scholar tumbling alongside these women and looking not unlike the artist who created him.

The eroticism of *The Vision of Faust* is obvious, no doubt there is more than a bit of titillation intended in these images lovingly and immaculately rendered, for Ricardo was known for painting naked buxom women, nor is it the last time he inserted such figures in a specifically Faustian vision, revisiting the sexual dreams of the wizard in a different painting only two years later. Yet the slightly dumpy male in the composition may evidence more understanding of ironic masculine frailty than would first be assumed. What makes the painting so fascinating is that Ricardo specifically takes as his subject the visions of Faust. None of this is "real," this is Faust's dream, his fantasy, his nightmare. For that matter, none of the actual painting is itself "real," all of it a masterful illusion. The nature of art is that it merely represents, that it's at a remove from reality regardless of how expertly or inexpertly accomplished. A lesser creation according to those iconoclastic scolds, and yet Ricardo's maidens shall never age and wither like the crone, who herself shall never die and decompose, so that even the flying cadaver will forever be in that state, never turning to dust and ash. An eternity captured by this canvas, a type of magic, a creation which can pretend to be greater than God's, for a time at least, until flames or water, or just entropy, take this painting. Faust may be the one experiencing the vision, but it is Ricardo who has made it possible.

If proficiency in illusion is one correspondence between the Faustian and artistic genius, another is the cacophonous clamber of Hell, for as Caravaggio's dissolute example demonstrates, we ascribe to our creative prodigies a certain hallow-eyed haunting, a possession from something beyond their rational faculties and the danger which that embodies. To live beautifully and die young. The Dionysian thrums through artistic creation, chthonic energies that can't always be reduced to sensible explanation. Mysteriousness still imbues artistic creation, even if it's digitally manufactured, for the origin of ideas and concepts, images and words, dreams and fantasies, still seems to be from a country slightly beyond the horizon. "The muse and the angel come from outside us," wrote the Spanish poet Federico García Lorca, "the angel gives light and the muse gives form . . . but one must awaken the demon in the remotest mansions of the blood."

Now, I must be honest and admit that the word "demon" in that quotation is strictly speaking inaccurate; the word which Lorca used was "duende," as the title of the piece from which I've drawn that excerpt is a work of sublime literary criticism entitled *Theory and Play of the Duende*. A duende, in Spanish folklore, is more an imp, an elf, a fairy, than it is a Devil per se, though it shares with those other examples a sense of the ominous, a prickling of danger. Lorca borrowed the duende as his symbol for all that is irrational in creation, all that is absurd, illogical, and at times portentous. Certainly Lorca was familiar with the importance of danger—of the death-drive, really—which was at the heart of his most beloved of art-forms, from flamenco to bull-fighting, this freedom fighter who would be executed by the Francoists in Granada. For our purposes, there is enough of the Faustian about the act of artistic inspiration, of the creator fully giving themselves over to this force of the duende, that the slight mistranslation of "demon" can, at least partially, be justified. "All that has dark sound has duende," wrote Lorca, and though he wrote of poetry and dance, music and theater, the plastic arts can have more than a smidge of that obsidian aura as well.

Lorca writes of "the roots that cling to the mire that we all know, that we all ignore . . . the mysterious power that everyone feels but no philosopher can explain," this inscrutable origin of the creative act. Those enraptured to the idea of skill can explain art by recourse to technique and proficiency, training and education, while those of a sociological bent will examine the role that culture and economics play in evaluating what counts as brilliant art, indeed what counts as art at all. And yet anyone enraptured by the flow of the creative act, whether the concentrating painter with tongue between lips applying one more dab of oil to her composition, or the violinist in a reverie, improvising notes which seem borrowed from a different realm, or the writer unleashing a torrent of words that come from somewhere beyond biography or cerebral cortex, all of them understand that the act of creation isn't quite intentional or conscious. Something mysterious still haunts the creative act, and neither science nor cultural studies can totally exorcize it, but as in the Devil's contract, it often comes at a cost.

For Lorca's contemporaries, the Surrealists and the Dadaists, avant-garde movements that reveled in the Dionysian aspects of art, the irrational core of creation was obvious, and whether from God or demon, duende or muse, they tried different methods to inculcate inspiration and to draw upon that strange *something* that's born from a dimension we're not usually privy to. Automatic drawing was one such technique, the turning off of conscious faculties as much as possible when creating art, the result being some compositions of surprising skill, even if the person who rendered it may have had no idea what the final would be. Occasionally these automatic drawings would be inspired by the use of spirit-mediums or Ouija boards, the artist attempting to connect with that same force which Haizmann believed himself indebted to.

In the nineteenth century, Spiritualist artists like Georgiana Houghton, Anna Mary Howitt, and most famously Hilma af Klint produced splotches of color and beams of radiance in paint that were a beautiful abstraction which prefigured modern art, but which they claimed came from the unconscious influence of the spirit realm, a confession of the deep and irrational nature of inspiration that permeates creativity, whether acknowledged or not. André Breton, in his 1924 *The Surrealist Manifesto,* described his aesthetic goal as being "Psychic automatism in its pure state, by which one proposes to express . . . the actual functioning of thought . . . in the absence of any control exercised by reason, exempt from any aesthetic or moral concern." Surrealist André Masson in 1921, among the greatest of automatic artists, emptied his mind and let his pen-gripped hand roam free upon the paper, creating three wild, androgynous Pan-like figures, nude beings with wild tendrils of twisting hair, horned heads, and caprine beards. Two years later, Masson produced a mass squiggle of black lines, curved and organic, but here and there figuration arises out of the chaos of abstraction—something that looks like a hand, a face.[5] Mind and soul emptied in reverie, the image that entered Masson's consciousness in 1938 as the world faced immolation was a hideous, snarled, being that appeared as if an animal sutured together from different parts, a demonic minotaur who looked not unlike the Canaanite demon Moloch who devoured the innocent, a painting appropriately entitled *The Labyrinth.*

My reasoning could lead to the conclusion that all inspiration has something demonic about it, that creativity is by its nature Faustian. I acknowledge degrees of difference, lest I accidentally fall into the thinking of the Puritan scold, but I suggest that, to varying degrees, the horned god does influence a bit of anything as mysterious as creation. Which is why pushed to its most extreme, its most all-consuming and obsessive, the vocation of the artist takes on the gloss of madness, to the point where a Haizmann could believe he'd actually sold his soul to the Devil. Witness a painting known as *The Anguished Man*, made by an anonymous artist and infamous in certain sundry corners of the internet, which depicts a red, abstracted figure who looks as if he may be made from flames, or is perhaps a flayed and scabbed-over human. His mouth is agape as a black void, his eyes are similarly a nothingness. According to the owner, an Englishmen from Cumbria named Sean Robinson, he inherited the painting from his grandmother in 2010, the work kept in her attic for decades. Even without a proper identification of who produced the horrifying image, Robinson's grandmother claimed that she had heard that the artist had mixed the red paint with his own blood, before killing himself.

Shortly after Robinson came into possession of his piece, he reported strange occurrences in his home, knocks and bumps, screams and shrieks, the afterimages at the corner of his vision of faceless figures. I've no idea, or the means, to verify if any of that is true. What I can confirm is that I'm unable to look at a reproduction of the picture for more than a second or two, that it disquiets me deeply, that whatever its provenance or the truth of its story, at a deep level I certainly would never wish to be in possession of the painting. A damned artist producing a cursed picture. Something about *The Anguished Man* recalls to me the lurid blood-red images of Haizmann, who though his own amateurish work is admittedly less disturbing still has that intimate connection to evil, to the extent that somebody might go to acquire the pure, nihilistic freedom of being able to make the world again according to their own individual and idiosyncratic aims. When skeptics examine the horned, bearded, pot-bellied figure with webbed feet and clawed hands at the corner of one of Haizmann's paintings they see not a picture of Satan, but a self-portrait of the artist's own tortured psyche, and perhaps they're right. Yet when I look at *The Anguished Man*, whatever artist painted it and whenever it was made, part of me feels that I'm seeing is evidence of a creator who went as far as he could to that other side and returned briefly to depict the horror he witnessed there.

CHAPTER EIGHT

A ROMANTIC HELL:
GOETHE SAVES FAUST

Am I a god? Light fills my mind.
—Johann Wilhelm von Goethe, *Faust: Part I* (1808)

On a cool October 2nd in 1808, through the court-yard and underneath the red-tiled mansard roof of the Medieval complex known as the Electoral Mainz Lieutenancy at the center of the small German town of Erfurt, the most brilliant man in the world made his way into the reception-room of the world's most powerful man. This was the same year that the first part of Johann Wolfgang von Goethe's great life-long masterpiece *Faust: A Tragedy* was published after decades of writing; also the

same year that the Thuringian town of Erfurt passed from
Prussian control to French. And so, in the Baroque par-
lor of the former governor's residence—a room of heavy
wood and buttressed ceilings, intricate German murals
and the finest French crystal chandeliers—Goethe first met
Napoleon Bonaparte.

By this point, Goethe was the most famous poet in
the world, the sixty-one-year-old author, artist, scientist,
and statesman having already penned such seminal works
of German literature as the Sturm und Drang exemplar
Wilhelm Meister's Apprenticeship, the historical play *Götz
von Berlichingen*, and the epic *Prometheus*. A polymath,
Goethe was also known for his scientific writings on biology, optics, and geology, having been the administer of
mines in Weimar before being given directorship of the
national theater, and *The Metamorphosis of Plants* studied as fervently as his poetry. But most of all, Goethe was
revered and reviled as the author of the scandalous *The
Sorrows of Young Werther*, with scores of young suicides
throughout Europe following its 1774 printing who were
supposedly influenced by the final decision of the novel's
namesake. "I am indeed a wanderer, a pilgrim on earth,"
says Werther, "But are you anything more?"

Such sentiments would effectively inaugurate the
Romantic movement, a coterie of thinkers who questioned
Enlightenment rationality by rather embracing a cult of
feeling. Napoleon, obviously, had no less of an impressive
curriculum vitae. By the time of their meeting, the Emperor

had already conquered much of Italy, Egypt, Spain, and Portugal, and been crowned in Notre Dame by the pope as the Emperor of France. A Romantic hero *par excellence*. At the Electoral Mainz Lieutenancy, Napoleon signals Goethe to approach. "I remain standing in front of him at a suitable distance. After looking at me for a moment, he says to me: 'You are a man,'" remembered Goethe. Either would have been forgiven for assuming that the other wasn't.

Goethe and Napoleon cut Faustian figures, the first a scholar of inconceivable learning, arguably the last of the Renaissance men capable of knowing all that could be known, and the latter the general who briefly conquered the world. At the Erfurt governor's mansion they met for around an hour, the two exchanging small talk in which they debated realism in novels and Napoleon disdained Goethe's admiration for Shakespeare. Combined with the fortuitous publication of the first part of *Faust*, the Erfurt meeting is the sort of biographical coincidence which is only too appealing to the essayist who wishes that he was a novelist.

In imagining these two great men of the nineteenth century meeting in such a resplendent rococo setting—Goethe with his stolid, granitoid features in the plain, black frock of a German academic and the diminutive Napoleon in his uniform the color of the French tricolor—there are the intimations more of parable than of mundane biography. The king and his wiseman—fairytale more than history. The two dominated their age, Goethe the prophet of Romantic feeling, while Napoleon spread French Republican ideals at the point of the bayonet. And yet between the two of them, neither Napoleon nor Goethe equal the depth of the legendary character of Faust, for if the general exalted power and the scholar venerated knowledge, then the necromancer combined those desires in one personality. Goethe's Faust surpassed even his creator, because more than just knowledge and power, what he desired was *experience* in all its multitudinous complexity.

"I want frenzied excitements, gratifications that are painful," Faust tells Mephistopheles, "Love and hatred violently mixed." The work of Goethe's entire life, his Faustian drama, is dedicated to the Romantic desire for experience and energy, fullness and feeling, in which what is created is not a separate work of art but the life itself. As in Marlowe and his predecessors, Faust is a cloistered scholar who signs a contract with Mephistopheles for his eternal soul, but what Goethe's Faust wants in exchange is rather different. This Faust thirsts for "Anguish that enlivens, inspiriting trouble . . . From now on my wish is to undergo / All that men everywhere undergo, their whole portion, / Make mine their heights and depths, their weal and woe, / Everything human encompass in my single person, / And so enlarge my one self to embrace theirs, all."

It's as if the classical poet Terence's humanistic injunction to let nothing which is human be foreign to us was pushed to its utter extreme; what Faust envisions is being transformed into a singularity of all people, a monad reflecting all our species's baroque glories and degradation within a single life. This zeal, this love for experience, is what saves Goethe's Faust. Which makes the sorcerer a messianic suffering servant, at least for his own salvation.[1] For Goethe, and the Romantics in his stead, the very act of living became a form of art, a type of incantation. Living in all its complexities understood as magic.

—

Faust is a tremendously baroque text, with the first part published in 1808 after decades of work and the second in 1832 a year after Goethe died. To the bare scaffolding of the legend as recounted in Speyer, Goethe creates a splendiferous, majestic, and most of all massive drama in which the wizard is no longer mere cipher, but now a fully realized human character with interiority. "In me there are two souls," says Faust, "and their / Division tears my life in two." Among the most significant alterations is the inclusion of Faust's romantic interest, the pious and pure maiden Gretchen, who at the conclusion of Goethe's first part incalculably suffers because of the scholar's hubris. Described as a fresh-faced and innocent *fraulein*, she is tricked into believing the aged scholar to be a young paramour, who seduces her, impregnates her, and then is unable to save her from prison after she commits infanticide. Wailing for her demon-lover, Gretchen's downfall has all the pathos of Greek tragedy.

At over twelve thousand lines, a full performance of both parts would take around twenty-one hours, hence the debates surrounding whether the author actually intended it to be performed. Certainly the stage directions would make standard blocking difficult—Mephistopheles taken to Faust's study in the form of an animal familiar (in this case the world's grumpiest black poodle), who then transmogrifies into a poor student; a host of gibbering, talking apes attending to a witch; and notably a conclave between God and the play's most famous demon in heaven. Mephistopheles, in Goethe's version, is simultaneously more malevolent and less uncannily mysterious than in Marlowe, a chaos demon suitably matched to the good doctor. That wager in heaven is only one of the numerous instances in which Goethe embellishes the legend, as God and Mephistopheles decide to enact a bet about the temptation of Faust, a conscious and perceptive allusion to the biblical book of Job.

Such a wager is paralleled by one that attends the contract between Mephistopheles and Faust, for in signing over his soul, the latter includes the caveat that if "Ever you see me loll at ease, / Then it's all yours, you can have it, my life! / If ever you fool me with flatteries / Into feeling satisfied with myself, / Or tempt me with visions of luxuries, / That's it, the last day that I breathe this air, / I'll bet you!" Faust wagers his own capacity for life, his own energy, his own vibrancy. Tempted not by territory or treasure, power or pleasure, Faust rather has faith in his own power to withstand the most sublime, transcendent, and ecstatic of moments. As he tells Mephistopheles, should the demon ever conjure a moment—a single second—so powerful that Faust would desire it to continue indefinitely, then the sorcerer's soul should belong to hell. What's ironic is that when just such a moment arrives, its intensity is precisely that which warrant's Faust's salvation. "I'll show you things no man has seen before," says Mephistopheles. And he did.

Like Dante's *The Divine Comedy*, Milton's *Paradise Lost*, and James Joyce's *Ulysses*, Goethe's *Faust* is a maximalist enterprise, a work containing its own cosmos. If Marlowe roughly followed the Aristotelian unities of time and place, Goethe exploded the structure of drama, creating a work which seems to encompass both eternity and infinity. Ranging from locations as personal as Faust's study and the Auerbach *rathskeller* to the heavenly environs of the cosmos, the play fuses the macro and the micro, the cosmological and the quantum, into a single unity.[2] Seemingly much more is at stake than the soul of a mere man.[3] For Goethe's Faust, the ultimate purpose isn't to elevate himself above our physical world, but rather to fuse with it, to become its incomparable master.

If Goethe was the last of the Renaissance men, he was also the first of the moderns. By casting aside the foolish chimeras of faith which reigned during the Middle Ages but also the rationality which so obsessed his Enlightenment antecedents, while tethering scientific and technological progress to the realm of emotion and feeling, he prefigured modernity—in some of its darkest aspects. More crucially, his fictional Faust was like the homunculus created in the play's second part, a tiny avatar of a greater truth, of the coming epoch. Faust is not the representative man, but he is the representative *modern* man.

Now, the prophet of that modernity, as well as its midwife, amanuensis, engineer, and tutor, is clearly Mephistopheles. The Devil implores Faust—*he implores us*:

> No limits restrain you, do just as you like,
> A little taste here, a nibble, a lick,
> You see something there, snatch it up on
>   the run.
> Let all that you do with gusto be done,
> Only don't be bashful, wade right in.

As for the origins of Goethe's vision, scholars don't believe that he was familiar with Spiess's original, though Marlowe's play was an obvious source. More than the Elizabethan dramatist even, Goethe drew from childhood memories of Faustian puppet shows in Frankfurt, marionettes wearing the black smock of the scholar and little horned Mephistopheles painted a vulvic red, dangling from strings like souls being held over the firmament of perdition. Young Goethe had a visceral fascination with these puppet shows, an infernal Punch-and-Judy in which performers drew from the legend as it had permeated German culture for centuries.

This elevation of the low culture puppet show into something as grandiose as *Faust* was characteristic of the Romanticism for which Goethe became the central inspiration (even as he distanced or disdained many of those writers inspired by him). For German Romantics like Goethe and his good friend Friedrich Schiller, there was a primitive, collective, primordial genius belonging to the masses, to the folk, and that this rough brilliance could be distilled into the pure spirit of great art.[4] All of this helped to establish a cult of feeling which, whether it was something he desired or not, Goethe had conjured.[5] Romanticism is threaded with certain contradictions; a deep, almost reactionary conservatism valorizing tradition combined with a desire for radical change, an egalitarianism among the people but an elitism among the artists themselves. Most notably, Romanticism inculcated a zeal for revolution and liberation (which reached a head in the international movements of 1848), but also a deeply pernicious nationalism which at its most toxic bloomed into the blood-and-soil horrors of the twentieth century.

As part of this fascination with the ostensible wisdom of the peasantry, there was an enthusiasm for the collection and categorization of folktales, a monumental effort of fieldwork and classification which stands as a landmark of nineteenth-century philology. William Thoms in England, Thomas Crofton Croker in Ireland, Andrew Lang in Scotland, Francis James Child in the United States, and obviously Goethe's contemporaneous countrymen the linguists Jacob and Wilhelm Grimm all brought rigor and methodology to the collection of folktales, but also a deep desire to uncover the intrinsic, elemental, and singular collective genius of their individual nationalities.

Across the canon of folktales the Devil's hoofprints make a clear path, and blood from the contracts he signed can be found smeared on the sundry pages of their anthologies. By the twentieth century, a vogue for mathematical structure accompanied the writings of many folklorists, so that the narrative of the Devil's contract could be reduced to its bare essentials. For example, in the *Motif-Index of Folk Literature* compiled by Stith Thompson in 1928, the archetypal legend "Man sells soul to devil" is given the taxonomic number of M211. In identifying the motif, Thompson strips the story of Faustus to its first element, a skeleton that has undergird thousands of different permutations, across centuries and continents. Despite its minimalism, however, Thompson's five-word description of that basic plot already has enough detail to chill us— "Man sells soul to devil."

In the selling of one's soul there is a perversion of freedom, the conscious abdication of one's human uniqueness in exchange for *something*. It's with that *something* that the legend demonstrates its profound flexibility, providing an understanding of what people are willing to part with to gain something more valuable than their humanity. Often these folktales have a deep understanding of the darkness of the psyche and of existence itself; they are arguably just as, if not more, disturbing than the canonical Faustian bargains.

In the German fairy tale most often referred to as "The Girl Without Hands," there is a story every bit as unsettling as its name would foretell. Collected and recorded by the Brothers Grimm in their improbably titled 1812 collection *Children's and Household Stories*, the story concerns a mysterious stranger—understood to be the Devil—who arrives at the homestead of a poor miller. The Devil tells the miller that he will give him great riches in exchange for what happens to be standing behind the house. Unbeknownst to the miller, his daughter is behind the house at that very moment—he had assumed it was just the apple tree which the stranger was bargaining for—so he readily agrees. As in the story of Pluto and Persephone, Satan arrives three years later to collect the blameless girl, who remains a paragon of virginal innocence. Because of her goodness, the Devil is undeserving of the girl, but he threatens to abduct the father unless they amputate the daughter's hands. Father and daughter agree and as Satan leaves with those clean appendages the girl is left crying onto her stumps.

This weird and upsetting story, written by collective voices and edited by the process of centuries, reflects a far more disturbing understanding of reality than either Marlowe or Goethe evidence. While both writers countenance an understanding of cosmic justice, and in the latter case even of forgiveness and salvation, "The Girl Without

Hands" takes place in a reality in which the innocent are tricked and punished, where misfortune is capricious and there is no justification as to why evil befalls some and not others. It's a world that much more obviously matches the real one.

Another story recorded by the Grimms is about a destitute soldier during a war's conclusion. The Devil arrives disguised and tells the soldier, who is starving and homeless, that if the latter agrees not to bathe, cut his hair, or clip his nails for several years, then in exchange he will be given a green coat whose pockets will always be replenished with gold. If he should ever break those commandments, then to Hell would the soldier's soul be spirited. For the duration of his sentence, the soldier travels through the devastated countryside, distributing treasure and requesting prayers from those whom he encounters. Encrusted with filth, with long tendrils of matted, greasy hair hanging in front of his pockmarked and pustule-laden face, the soldier comes to an inn maintained by an impoverished old man who agrees to house the filthy vagrant. With gratitude in his heart, the soldier pays the old man's debts and saves him from prison. The innkeeper promises the soldier the hand of one of his daughters in marriage, but the two oldest are revolted by the disgusting itinerant and they refuse, leaving only the most dutiful, youngest of the girls to agree. After the sentence has expired and the soldier has fulfilled his contract with the Devil, that perfidious Prince returns and tenderly bathes the man, clips his nails and cuts his hair. The soldier is as if a Nazirite who has survived the desert, an anchorite returned to the city. Arriving back at the inn, the soldier's nuptials to the youngest daughter are fulfilled and the couple are now able to live in the comfort and security from the final treasures saved from the green jacket. The two other daughters, realizing their error, both kill themselves. After the suicide, the Devil knocks on the door of the soldier late one night, standing in the entrance to his sumptuous, new home, to inform his former business partner that Hell was able to acquire two souls for the price of one.

—

Far more famous stories situate the bargain as the denouement; both the agreement which Ariel makes with Ursula the sea-witch in Hans Christian Andersen's *The Little Mermaid* and the infernal contract made with the withered, hunchbacked, hideous dwarf Rumpelstiltskin in the Grimm's tale are clear variations. There is tremendous diversity in these tales, all categorizable under that broad umbrella of "Man sells soul to Devil," numbered as M211 and put away in a drawer of the Stith-Thompson classification system.

Common to many of the stories are the way in which the Devil faithfully adheres to the letter of the law but not its spirit, how verbal dexterity can be deployed by humans and Satan to either affirm a contract or deny it, and in some tales (though not the ones that I've recounted) the possibility of people being victorious against the cloven-hoofed one, of being more talented in the skills of wit and duplicity.[6] Like a prism, Goethe's *Faust* took the white light of that folklore, the accumulated wisdom of thousands of women and men over the centuries who refined these tales, and then broke them into the rainbow of subsequent literary treatments of the legend.

Regardless of the seeming universality of the Devil's contract, the Faust legend's cultural history can be divided into the period before and after Goethe. Not even Marlowe was as influential in disseminating the theme, for Goethe made the Faustian bargain a fit subject for tragedy, having drawn from the compendium of folklore and transformed the tale into something considered Literature with a capital L. Obviously Mephistophelean themes were popular in potboiling Gothic page-turners, exploitative works from the Englishmen Matthew Lewis's 1796 *The Monk* to the American George Lippard's 1845 *The Quaker City, or the Monks of Monk Hall*, but more enduring books also bear the burning imprint of the Faustian signature. As modernity continued its disenchantments of the world, the figure of the Faustian wizard would come to be replaced by a new character type—the mad scientist. But as in Marlowe and Goethe, this new variety of person was still really just the same thing—an obscured and secret artist.

Only seven years after the publication of Goethe's first part of *Faust,* the greatest English Romantic novel would appear, Mary Shelley's *Frankenstein; or, the Modern*

Prometheus. Shelley's book is often interpreted as an allegory of the dangers of unfettered science and technology. *Frankenstein* concerns the creation of a being composed of sutured together corpse fragments then animated by electricity. A monster not of magic, but of science.[7] By stripping *Frankenstein* of demons and incantations and giving over her narrative to biology rather than theurgy, Shelley birthed the mad scientist.

That the book is so often described as the first science-fiction novel doesn't mean that concern with science is necessarily at its core, however. *Frankenstein* itself evidences that the novel is "about" something else, even. Victor Frankenstein writes that he wished to "procure the whole works of [the medieval alchemist Cornelius] Agrippa and afterwards of Paracelsus and Albertus Magnus," two similarly occult writers. The doctor explains that he "read and studied the wild fancies of these writers with delight; they appeared to me treasures known to few besides myself," acknowledging this, though magic had been eclipsed, and that his fellow students are ignorant of those worthies.

Frankenstein later embraces (unclear) scientific methods, but the aura of the sacred permeates his experimentations. He exclaims that he had a "contempt for the uses of modern natural philosophy" and felt that it was "very different, when the masters of science sought immortality and power." Those desires were "grand," while Frankenstein bemoans that "now the scene was changed."[8] Meanwhile, Shelley reflects on the conception of that monster, writing that "frightful would be the effect of any human endeavor to mock the stupendous mechanism of the Creator of the world," later describing the title character as a fellow "artist," and the monster as his "odious handiwork," thus revealing an interpretive truth—*Frankenstein* is about the writing of *Frankenstein*.

The creation of this monstrous being, cobbled from the dead, and itself a representation of creative inspiration, makes plain that *Frankenstein* is a Faustian work, prefigured in part by the creation of a homunculus in the second part of Goethe's tragedy. Like all the English Romantics, Shelley couldn't resist working in the vein of Goethe, writing of the German's work that he constituted a "more divine being that I had ever beheld or imagined . . . calculated to fill me with wonder."

Shelley's partial secularization of the Faust legend in the form of the mad scientist would endure in Victorian literature and beyond. When Robert Louis Stevenson penned his 1886 classic the *Strange Case of Dr. Jekyll and Mr. Hyde*, that infamous tale about the duality of man made clear by alchemical means, it bore the hallmarks of the Faustian imprimatur despite being ostensibly a "scientific" story. "All human beings, as we meet them," writes Stevenson, "are comingled out of good and evil." The bestial Mr. Hyde emerges from the countenance of the dignified Dr. Jekyll, but they're the same man, of course. Hyde arguably serves a similar function as Mephistopheles does in the Faust legend, both conjured by esoteric means, and guiding their charges to perdition. With Stevenson, Mephistopheles has been relegated into an aspect of Faust's consciousness, the first example of the psychoanalytical projection of the Devil's contract. Commenting on his own novella *The Picture of Dorian Gray*, the immaculate Irish aesthete Oscar Wilde claimed that "in every first novel the hero is the author as Christ or Faust," and that is true in every life lived as a work of art.

There is no Wilde, no Stevenson, no Shelley without Goethe, without this new Faust who isn't just an artist creating a representation of reality, but an entirely self-created being living his life to its fullest experience as a variety of art. For this Faust, the work of life is an aesthetic act, a work of conjuration. This was the crux of his wager with Mephistopheles, that should he ever encounter a moment so filled with exuberance and power that he'd wish for it to continue indefinitely then the Devil would have charge to drag him to hell. But by the Romantic postulates of Goethe himself, it's precisely being able to live within the eternity of that second, the infinity of that moment, which earns the soul its redemption.

By the fifth and final act of the second part of *Faust*, the wizard has become incalculably powerful, in the service of the Holy Roman Emperor and arguably a monarch in his own right, using his magic to transform the sea into land toward which his domains grow. Having accumulated so much wealth and power, land and prestige, Faust is finally graced with a realization of how these works of self-creation were made for the betterment of his fellow man, that his ever-progressive striving was in desire to establish a utopia for those of us who shared the world with him for a while. So blissful are these ruminations, as Faust realizes the nature of his restless striving, that he wishes he could extend such a second just a bit longer, just a bit toward eternity. That is when it would seem Mephistopheles could finally make his claim, yet "Who strives always to the utmost, / For him there is salvation."

A chorus of angels spirits the soul of Faust toward heaven, repelling Mephistopheles and his demon hordes with a volley of burning rose petals while in the astral realms the wizard finally receives his benediction from the "Eternal Feminine" in the form of the Virgin Mary and other biblical women, as well as from his own beloved Gretchen, who has forgiven him. "Freedom and life are earned by those alone," writes Goethe, "Who conquer them anew each day."

The legacy of the Romantic Faust was as the most highly regarded, widely read, and fully venerated work of German literature ever produced. Even while Goethe himself had a proper Romantic's suspicion of Enlightenment rationality, he shared in the progressive fantasy of that age's myths of human perfectibility, of individual self-creation. His Faust is such an individualist that he's able to effectively save himself through his own intercession, by his own experiences, and by proxy his creations have rendered themselves sacred. As George Santayana would claim of

Goethe in *Three Philosophical Poets,* the play formulated a "philosophy of life" whereby he who "strives strays, yet in that straying finds his salvation," the entire work existing to "touch the heart, to bewilder the mind with a carnival of images, to amuse, to thrill, to humanize." Contemporaries questioned Goethe's piety, for surely he wasn't an orthodox Christian, but if the poet possessed an inviolate faith it was this—humanity's striving ability to walk in truth and beauty, regardless of the reasons by which those things speak and sing.

When an aged man, Goethe would remark in a letter that "I saw Mozart as a seven-year-old boy . . . I was fourteen years old, and I can clearly remember the little man in his wig with his sword," the supernatural prodigy performing *Allegro for Keyboard in C Major.* Such talent, such skill, such perfection. Goethe would carry that strange, beautiful, and terrible memory of the child Mozart's ability to generate pure melody, rightly understanding that there are things made by humans that can't be explained by recourse to paltry logic and disappointing reason. Nor can they always be explained by recourse to God, either. "Wolfgang is quite extraordinarily jolly," wrote the prodigy's father about that same concert, "but also naughty."

Mozart and Goethe would become touchstones of German culture, European culture, Western culture. Manifestations of genius and goodness, the common currency of a cosmopolitan inheritance. In his own writings, even though he was conservative, Goethe rejoiced in the brotherhood of humanity and the communion of nations, yet every human is divided, every concept contains within it its negation, and all of us can be both jolly and naughty. The twentieth-century German philosopher Walter Benjamin would astutely note in his "Theses on the Philosophy of History," surely with works such as Goethe's *Faust* and Mozart's music in mind, that there is "no document of civilization which is not at the same time a document of barbarism." For any work, even beautiful works, are at the expense of someone, or can be used to justify atrocity. If Mephistopheles has tutored humanity in anything, it's in how the urge toward destruction can be hidden within our own impulses.

Romantic individualism, Romantic feeling, Romantic emotion—there is something liberatory in those dictums, the opportunity for self-redemption. But the initiate often ignores the possibility of the rank nihilism implicit in those things; they can be as misguided as the sorcerer when he began his incantations. Returning to *Faust*, before the sorcerer's salvation, he commands that Mephistopheles remove from Faust's now copious landholdings an innocent, elderly couple named Baucis and Philemon whose simple existence happens to be complicating his attempts to remake the world as he sees fit. And so, Mephistopheles murders them. If life is lived not as a life but as a work of art, then the author can make other humans mere ancillary characters, capable of being written out of the script as needed, a wicked act of instrumentalization.

Goethe's translator Martin Greenberg notes a disturbing premonition in the text concerning Baucis and Philemon, explaining how when Faust asks Mephistopheles to deal with the couple, he wishes to "open up space for millions in which to work and live," the German original containing the word *Lebensraum*, literally "living space." That was infamously the same word used by Nazi Germany to justify its brutal expansion into eastern Europe, with the genocidal elimination of Jews and others as if they were Baucis and Philemon burnt to death in their cottage. Greenberg writes that Goethe's language has hidden within it the logic of "slave labor gangs, slave laborers dying in the dark, resettled populations, innocents burned alive," asking if this is the language of "uncanny anticipation? Or a fortuitous conjunction of elements already there?"

A toxic element in Goethe's individualism and humanism which easily metastasizes into something else. By another one of those aforementioned novelistic coincidences that occur in history occasionally, the Erfurt Governor's Mansion where Napoleon and Goethe had once met would be converted to a different purpose a century-and-a-half later. By then, the building had become the local headquarters of the Gestapo, scholarly Goethe now replaced by packs of Nazi officers in their polished black leather boots and their military caps affixed with the Death's Head skull-and-crossbones. Claiming to be the inheritors of a great civilization, such men would spend the morning and afternoons tabulating lists of people to be shot, of women and men to be deported, then gassed, and finally immolated, while in the evening they would retire to their houses and apartments where perhaps they'd put *Allegro for Keyboard in C Major* on the phonograph while cracking open a dog-eared and underlined copy of Goethe's *Faust*, laboring under the illusion that such superficial things might still make them somehow worthy to be called human.

CHAPTER NINE

MELODIES OF DAMNATION: FAUST IS A MUSICIAN AND COMPOSER

Why should the Devil get all the good tunes,
The booze and the neon and Saturday night,
The swaying in darkness, the lovers like spoons?
Why should the Devil get all the good tunes?
—A. E. Stallings, "Triolet on a Line Apocryphally
Attributed to Martin Luther" (2005)

Following a concert at the Wisconsin Lutheran College in January of 2014, the first chair violinist of the Milwaukee Symphony Orchestra was tasered and badly beaten in a university parking lot, the two assailants stealing his priceless three-century-old Stradivarius on which Satan had once composed a sonata for the Venetian musician Giuseppe Tartini. The Lipinski Stradivarius, as it's known after one of its former owners, was crafted in the Milanese workshop of Antonio Stradivari, lovingly carved from spruce and maple, stained red with iron, madder root, and cochineal varnish derived from the smashed bodies of thousands of the scaled insects which give the color its name, the instrument dyed a sanguineous, oxygenated red. First purchased by Tartini, who was a failure at being a Franciscan monk but a genius at composing baroque music, the bow of the violin would be cradled in the hands of countless musicians from the eighteenth century until today, from mysterious Venice, elegant Dresden and Leipzig, cosmopolitan London and Amsterdam, energetic New York and Havana. Appropriately enough the most celebrated work ever written for the instrument—Tartini's *Violin Sonata in G minor*, better known as the *Devil's Trill Sonata*—was as energetic, cosmopolitan, elegant, and mysterious as any of those places. The Lipinski's abode was found to be an attic in Bay View, Milwaukee, where the pilfered instrument was recovered by the FBI, Interpol, and the local PD. For the criminal who masterminded the job, it was a "dream theft"; he and his accomplice were charged with assault, robbery, and possession of marijuana; the violin was returned, the violinist resumed his vocation.

The Lipinski Stradivarius was not the one on which Tartini would have heard Satan compose the fifteen-minute *Devil's Trill Sonata*; though both the piece and the instrument have a provenance of 1713, it would be two years later that the composer would tenderly cradle the Stradivarius in his hands and to the best of his human ability attempt to transcribe the Dark One's eerie and melancholy work.

"One night, in the year 1713 I dreamed I had made a pact with the devil," Tartini told the occult-minded astronomer Jérôme Lalande, as recounted in the latter's travelogue *Journey of a Frenchman in Italy,* published in 1769, a year before the violinist died. "Among other things, I gave him my violin to see if he could play. How great was my astonishment on hearing a sonata so wonderful and so beautiful, played with such great art and intelligence, as I had never even conceived in my boldest flights of fantasy." In a caricature from 1824 by the French painter Louis-Léopold Boilly entitled *Tartini's Dream*, the composer is thin, tall, and Roman-nosed, reclining in bliss underneath crisp white sheets in his billowy night clothes and cap, eyes closed in reverie as he appears to conduct the musician perched at the foot of his bed, a feral, naked blue-grey devil with the face and wings of a bat, fanged and horned, a tail flicking underneath his crossed legs, while with an intense eye the Devil grasps the Italian's violin and performs the sonata. So warm is Boilly's drawing that Tartini and his master could be as student and mentor; so intimate that they could be lovers.

Satan's sonata delivered that night in 1713 heavily featured the characteristic trills of Baroque music, those rapidly fluctuating pairs of notes giving the slightest intimation of greater discordance beneath the seeming harmony, even while the work itself prefigures the clean grace of classical music, though through all of it thrums a faded elegance that sounds, at least to my untutored ear, almost modern.

The Devil is a brilliant composer—Tartini tells Lalande that the composition left him "enraptured, transported, enchanted"—and the Italian vainly tries to note down what he can remember upon awakening, though it will take two years and the Stradivarius to approach an approximation of the original nocturnal concert.

As ultimately rendered by Tartini, the fifteen-minute-long composition was one which the violinist judged as different enough from the Devil's original that he considered destroying his instrument and abandoning music, but confessed that it would not be "possible for me live without the enjoyment it affords me." No matter how great that gulf may have been—perhaps Tartini's is merely an extreme humility before the glint of his master's jaundiced yellow eye—the germinating seed of *Violin Sonata in G minor* remains largely the original notes as performed by the Prince of Darkness.

Mournful yet frenetic, playful yet ominous, beautiful but infernal. Caressing the ruddy flesh of his violin, Tartini was able to make it quiver, make it pulsate with those notes of the Devil. For what Lucifer has sometimes lacked in painting and the plastic arts, it is commonly agreed that he exults at the musical, that in the arrangement of notes and rests, the exuberance of performance, the genius of melody, harmony, and most of all rhythm, Satan is a true master. Perhaps Tartini's tale was merely a bit of entertainment concocted for the credulous Lalande, or a random firing of a neuron while unconscious. Whether or not the

Devil manifested, Tartini was among the first of a type to be recorded: the composer, musician, or performer who enters into a contract with Satan to gain a bit of Hell's musical beauty, the paradoxically cursed purveyor of what's indisputably our most heavenly form.

—

There are many people who don't read, or those who don't appreciate art, but there are infinitesimally few who don't like at least some sort of music, who don't nod their head or tap their foot at least occasionally.[1]

So elemental, so primal, so universal, there's an ecstatic reality to music, the way it can move past conscious intention, deep into the intrinsic part of the mind, of the soul. If there be magic, music seems an obvious example of it, which is why it's always been so associated with conjuration and incantation. Examining the pebbled, jagged, white-bone of the Neanderthal flute, it's easy to envision some Paleolithic shaman draped in reindeer furs playing whatever the earliest melody may have been, a hymnal dirge in conjuration of the Great Horned Deity, perhaps.[2] The Faustian prerogative inscribed in song from the very beginning is why those continual tales of devilish contract in exchange for prodigious talents ala Tartini are so common. Only politics—maybe sports—are as capable of the orgiastic frenzy made possible by music.

Consider the riot that broke out at the premier of Igor

Stravinsky's *Rite of Spring* in 1913 at Paris's Champs-Elysees Theatre when the ordinarily decorous audience couldn't countenance the pagan discordance of that masterpiece, or recall the faces of the screaming adolescents crowded into Shea Stadium to hear the Beatles play songs off of *Help* in 1965, then tell me that music doesn't have magic about it, a whiff of the infernal. Nobody has ever reacted in such a way at a lecture or poetry reading, so the answer to the question of why the Devil gets all the good tunes is posed in its asking. Scripture notes of Lucifer's role in Heaven before his fall that the "workmanship of thy tabrets and of thy pipes was prepared in thee in the day that thou wast created" (Ezekiel 28:13); even the Lord granted the power of the angelic choirs to the Devil. Music is Dionysian, it is chthonic, it is Luciferian—that's precisely why it's so lovely.

Composers are aware of this lineage, if the canon of music about the Faustian bargain is an indication. Drawing from Marlowe, Goethe, and folktale, the legend appears repeatedly throughout classical music. At least four nineteenth-century operas—the genre best equipped to stage the pyrotechnics the story requires—were directly based in Goethe's *Faust* or some variation thereof. The Italian pianist and composer Ferruccio Busoni's posthumous German-language *Doktor Faust* (1925) is a characteristically bombastic production, the basso of the necromancer first thundering among the plush-red velvet seats and crystal chandeliers of the rococo resplendence of the opera house two decades before it would be largely destroyed in an Allied bombing campaign. "Nothing is proven, and nothing is provable" says Busoni's Faust, a succinct statement of the tyrant's preferred epistemology in the infernal century during which this work was composed. Arrigo Boito, a Paduan Teutonophile, directly translated Goethe's German into Italian for his libretto *Mefistofele*, first performed within the neoclassical splendor of Milan's La Scala to largely unfavorable reviews, domestic critics disdaining the Wagnerian excess of the piece as incommensurate with the dignity of opera in the country where it was invented. *Mefistofele* was written by Boito in response to the French composer Charles Gounod's opera of a decade earlier simply entitled *Faust,* which the Italian composer dismissed as frivolous and superficial. An odd accusation against this more enduring work, written by a man who had trained for the priesthood and is most famous as the composer of the "Ave Maria." With an understanding of music as Faustian vocation, Gounod's Mephistopheles instructs his charge "Let me tell you that with Satan / One must sing another tune."

Among the greatest of adaptations of Goethe is the French composer Hector Berlioz's *The Damnation of Faust*, a propulsive and regenerative imagining of the tale which premiered at Paris's Opera-Comique in 1846. "I am the Spirit of Life," says Berlioz's Mephistopheles, "and it is I that console. / I will give you everything, happiness, pleasure, / All that the most ardent desire can dream of," all the thumping, thrumming, strumming rhythm that courses through existence from Heaven to Hell.

Nothing *about* Faust can compare to something *by* Faust, which is why the productions of Busoni and others are less evocative than that fifteen minutes by Tartini. The former are interpretations of a play by Goethe, itself a secondhand version of a tale by Marlowe, who was merely copying the Spiess pamphlet, which may or may not be based in reality. Tartini, on the other hand, gives us the source of such dark things, his music a conduit to the damned. To listen to it is an eerie, otherworldly, unsettling experience, partially because it's a beautiful piece of music, maybe all the more so for those jarring moments when it's not (just more evidence of its ultimate provenance).

———

Niccolò Paganini was as prodigious at the violin as his fellow countryman Tartini, born a few decades after that master had passed on into hell. A contemporary of Goethe, Paganini had to make his own accommodations to the princes of this world, the drunken, whoring, gambling Genoan offering his services as a musical tutor to the brother-in-law of Napoleon after the French invaded and occupied northern Italy, a job from which he first gained his fame. A critic writing in 1837 for *Blackwood's Edinburgh Magazine* described Paganini as a "tall, gaunt figure, his long fleshless fingers, his wild eager and wan visage, his thin grey locks falling over his shoulders, and his singular smile sometimes bitter and convulsive, always strange, made up an aspect which approached nearly to the spectral." Because of his exemplary skill with a bow, Paganini was long rumored by concertgoers to have entered into an infernal bargain, and his compositions were similarly assumed to have had Satanic origins.

Paganini would bounce his bow off the bridge of the violin, plucking and hitting the purposefully mistuned strings because he knew disharmony was sometimes truer than its opposite, bending and swaying with wild gesticulations, arms akimbo, hair disheveled, eyes shut so that the audience couldn't see his possessed eyes. Spectators timed him—Paganini was able to play around twelve notes a second, a creature who moved with determined efficacy, known as the "Rubber Man" by admirers and called the Devil's violinist for good reason. Because he just preceded recording technology, Paganini must remain forever mute to us, but based in the reactions he engendered, it seems that his performances were incantatory. His surviving compositions recall Tartini in the balance of beauty and the shriek and squeal of the strings, sounding not unlike the women's screams that were claimed to be heard from within the chamber of Paganini's violin as he played; that clash of electricity as if the lightning bolts that some listeners said they saw striking at his hands as he played.

In his consummate *24 Caprices for Solo Violin*, there may not be screams, per se, but in its often-frantic speed, its staccato plucking, its often uncanny, eerie, but none-theless gorgeous melody, there is a sense of the demonic. Music capable of either saving or damning, the most celestial of the arts but the one also prepared and preserved in heaven for Lucifer. "Variation upon variation, but which variation leads to salvation and which to damnation?" he asks in the American dramatist Don Nigro's contemporary play *Paganini*. "Music is a question for which there is no answer." Upon his deathbed in 1840, his earthly body wracked by syphilis, tuberculosis, and larynx cancer, the final act of Niccolò Paganini was to dismiss the priest who'd come to administer the last rites, leaving only his music. As God concludes in Nigro's play, "The saved and the damned are the same."

Listening to either Tartini or Paganini, there is an evocative quality to the violin's sound—its tone, its speed, its playfulness—which reminds me of a particular genre, though I lack the music theory or history to fairly make this judgment beyond a gut feeling. That's to say that both Italians sound to me as if they're performing *gypsy music*. Of course the accurate phraseology here is the music of the Romani people, the massive diaspora of women and men who left Rajasthan, India more than a millennia ago and migrated westward into Europe, forever denied their own homeland, spurned, abused, persecuted, and also emulated by the people of Hungary and Romania, Poland and Russia, Italy and Spain, France and England. If this still-persecuted minority calls themselves the Roma, or the

Sinti, or the Travelers, then for much of European history they were erroneously the gypsies—exoticized, orientalized, sexualized, demonized. Marked by their darker skin as obvious outsiders within the countries that they settled, the oft-migratory Roma were associated with necromancy, divination, conjuration, incantation, and, notably, music. The stereotype maintained that within the colorful gypsy caravans of dozens of wagons were musicians of incomparable brilliance, untutored and unschooled but somehow conduits of a transcendent talent, something unearthly and devilish. Casting fortunes, reading Tarot, preparing potions and tinctures, well into the nineteenth century (when they were still legally enslaved in much of eastern Europe), the Roma were the locus of fears, and they paid a heavy price for the bigotries of those among whom they settled.[3]

As the concept of a secular "Europe" developed from the remains of Christendom, the Roma were often configured as the ultimate Other to white civilization, as a sable and exotic race permanently unconstrained by borders and forced to wander the earth (not unlike the Jews). Not just in spite of those libels, but often because of them, the Romani became the progenitors of much of Western folk music, the peoples of the continent expressing themselves through syncopation, harmony, and phrasing as heard in Turkish taverna music, Greek bouzouki tunes, Italian tarantella's shouting-and-clapping, mournful Jewish klezmer, florid Spanish flamenco, lush French manouche, sensual

Argentinian tango, even in the stolid songs of the Irish pub. A Faustian bargain even in the very evolution of Western European music, as the talents and vision of the oppressed are taken and cannibalistically absorbed into the folk culture of the various nationalities of the continent, the beginnings of that heist apparent in the bohemian phrasing of Tartini and Paganini.

Across the Atlantic, the United States didn't originate taverna, bouzouki, tarantella, flamenco, or tango, but it is the land of ragtime, jazz, rock and roll, gospel, soul, hip-hop, and more than anything else the blues. The locus of cultural appropriation may have shifted, but the process was similar and the results no less infernal for the people robbed of their music while being left in bondage. American popular culture is one long deal with the Devil, certainly in the manner by which America commodified, exploited, and outright stole the contributions of Black Americans, but also the horrific history of the transatlantic slave trade which made this vibrant and new syncretic culture possible.

The most distinctive American genre, to which the alternating quartertone and semitone of the blue note are as distinctive as Romani trills, may derive from the call-and-response lyrics, the nasal intonation, the twelve-bar expression of the traditional music performed by griots in places like Dakar and Timbuktu, but it was the demonic nightmare of the United States that inculcated the music. And when speaking of American culture's blue note Faustian contracts, one location must be mentioned—the crossroads of U.S. Highways 61 and 49, in Clarksdale, Mississippi not far from the Delta, where legend made manifest the painful tale which defined this nation.

———

All that remains of Robert Johnson—master of the Mississippi Delta Blues and spiritual progenitor of rock and roll—are three blurry photographs and twenty-nine songs, some of them recorded in a makeshift studio at the Gunter Hotel in San Antonio, Texas in 1936 over the course of a few days, for which he was paid $300 with no royalties. "Me and the Devil Blues," "Hell Hound on My Trail," "Cross Road Blues"—many of Johnson's tracks refer to the central legend of his talent, that following the scorn of audiences at roadhouses and dive bars who mocked his mediocre technique, he traveled down to that intersection in Clarksdale to make an exchange. In the faith of the Wolof and Igbo people of West Africa from where the musician's ancestors could have come generations before, it was affirmed that at such liminal crossings the trickster god Legba can be conjured. Johnson sold his soul to Satan in exchange for the talent and brilliance that would be incandescent and alien to practice of any ordinary human. When Rolling Stones guitarist Keith Richards (also familiar with tunes imparted through dreams and devilish negotiations) first heard a recording of Johnson, he assumed it was two men playing rather than one, because such sounds coming from a single instrument just didn't make sense.

There are no recordings of Johnson before said contract, so it's impossible to know the veracity of the claims about his rapid ascension in skill, though based on listening to any of those twenty-nine songs (fifty-nine recordings over all, but there are several versions of the same track) it's easy to see why many heard something supernatural in his abilities. He is capable of making the guitar sing and shout, shriek and scream, the low mumble whine of his lyrics about damnation and hell in cursed duet with his instrument. Of the three verified photographs of Johnson, the most famous is a studio portrait of the man as thin and gaunt as Paganini, wearing a dapper double-breasted pinstriped suit, smart black wingtips, and an angled fedora, legs tightly crossed while he caresses his guitar, the long and thin fingers of his left hand demonstrating some complicated fingering on the fretboard[4]

Johnson's smile is simultaneously mischievous and exhausted, his eyes are those that you'd expect from a man who'd been down to the crossroads. "I got to keep movin', I got to keep movin' / Blues fallin' down like hail, blues fallin' down like hail . . . And the days keep on worryin' me / There's a hellhound on my trail, hellhound on my trail, / Hellhound on my trail." An unappreciated aspect of the repetition in twelve-bar blues, the distinctive lyrical innovation of that genre's prosody, is the way in which it mimics incantation, those cryptic phrases recurring like a ritual chant. A personal apocalypticism haunts Johnson's lyrics, in "Hell Hound on My Trail" the wind rises and the leaves tremble, for the great theme of the hour or so of revolutionary music which was pressed into acetate on a warm San Antonio night is Johnson's own troubled negotiations, the curse of inspiration and the ever-present shadow of the Devil in the life of the tortured creator.

Romance obviously accrues to his name, so much so that he's not the only bluesmen to have supposedly made this bargain, nor even the only one with that surname to have done so, for his distant cousin Tommy Johnson was also have said to have taken a trip to the crossroads.[5] At the same time, and there's always a same time, legends have a manner of metastasizing far beyond the reality and a man of twenty-nine brilliant songs and three blurry photographs is as appropriate an unknown cipher as any to which such tales can be applied. Besides, even if the actual Johnson's own interest in the occult has been vastly overstated, a bit of hokum extended to credulous reporters and researchers as marketing alone has to be appreciated, if not more generously interpreted as its own manner of artistic self-creation, an aspect of the mythos which ties together all of the songs as if a narrative frame-tale.

Because the story of Johnson down by the Clarksdale crossroads is undeniably evocative. Envision twitchy, nervous, anxious young Johnson, working all day as a sharecropper with blue-note dreams, coming to the crossroads on a sweltering Mississippi night, the full moon visible through the clouds like a candle viewed through cotton, waiting for Legba, or Satan, to arrive.

There he comes, slowly walking across the rail tracks that bisect Dockery Plantation, or the Hazlehurst grave-yard, or at the intersection of Highways 8 and 1 in Rosedale (for there is no consistency in this story). Satan walks stiffly but with confidence, slowly but with purpose, a tall and broad and large Black man in jeans and plaid work-shirt, toothpick between his lips, mirrored sunglasses conceal-ing his eyes. As he approaches Johnson, who stands a bit straighter, who tries to not look like he is shaking, the Devil wordlessly puts out his hands, and the aspiring bluesman knows that this creature wants his guitar. Handing over the beloved instrument to the Devil, Johnson watches as his tutor adjusts the tuning pegs, presses some of the strings on the fingerboard, and strums a few chords, competing with the cacophonous keening of the cicadas in the night. Only a few minutes pass before Satan hands the guitar back to Johnson, nodding his head with a perfunctory motion, then turning back the way he came, toward the woods of sweetgum, shortleaf pine, and white oak that line the edge of the town, with the now greatest bluesman in the world still standing at the crossroads, intuitively understanding that a detail of his contract was that he wouldn't live be-yond the age of twenty-seven.

"Early this mornin' / When you knocked upon my door . . . And I said 'Hello Satan,' / I believe it's time to go," sings Johnson, a man seemingly conversant with the hidden things. This is an American myth, a modern myth, traces of the supernatural about a man who, nonetheless, was real—you can even see a photograph of him. "You may bury my body / Down by the highway side . . . So my old evil spirit / Can get a Greyhound bus and ride." As it would come to pass, Johnson would be twenty-seven when he died—his revelatory career as an itinerant bluesman playing on streetcorners and gin-jukes, hardscrabble road-houses and dingy bars a short one—poisoned with strych-nine-spiked whisky by the jealous husband of a woman whom the musician had been flirting with. It has long been said that when the crossroads' demon came to claim his charge that the death was convulsive and excruciating.

There is, to be sure, the taint of condescension in the tale, whereby the blues man's genius can only be attained through supernatural means, a myth that is appealing obvi-ously for many white fans of the genre interested more in hoodoo than music theory.[6] That's if read literally, though, and the Devil is far more subtle than that. Whatever hap-pened at the crossroads is more than mere legend, a creepy story repeated over whisky in the back of some old blues club or recounted by a white fan waxing poetic about the Delta he has never seen. Johnson's is a parable, an arche-type, an allegory, a story about the dangers in all such pos-sessed performance, in all such devilish inspiration.

A numerology to Johnson's tale, foaming at the mouth and shaking before he collapses in death at that young age, for he was the first to die at twenty-seven but not the last. Brian Jones, guitarist for the demon-intoxicated Rolling Stones, found face-down in his pool at Cotchford Farm manor in 1969; that voodoo child Jimi Hendrix, drunk on cheap wine and stoned on barbiturates, asphyxiating on his own vomit at London's Samarkand Hotel in 1970; the pained blues crooner Janis Joplin found in the shambles of her room at the Landmark Motor Hotel in Los Angeles, her system thrumming with booze and spunk, the year 1970; the Lizard King, Mr. Mojo Rising, Jim Morrison bloated and water-logged in his bathtub at the Rue Beautreillis in the 4th arrondissement, dead from a fatal speedball, in 1971; dirty-blond Kurt Cobain wandering misty Seattle for days before he did it in 1994, long terrified of having "sold out," placing a shotgun in his mouth and pulling the trigger with his toe, the corpse discovered a few days later by the electrician in the rock star's rustic Lake Washington Boulevard home, it being better to burn out than fade away—every single one of them twenty-seven.

More than all the demonic accoutrement that is associated with rock music, that grandiose child of the blues, more than the tales of heavy metal bacchanalian Satanic excess, or even of rock stars like Jimmy Plant, David Bowie, or Bob Dylan selling their souls to the Devil—the last of whom confirmed to Ed Bradley on *60 Minutes* that he'd been to the crossroads—this confounding death gematria is Johnson's Faustian legacy. Whatever happened in Clarksdale, there is an intimation that it wasn't just

Johnson who sold his soul, but an entire nation, a brilliance appropriated from America's historically most disenfranchised group, refined in the smithy of individual pain, suffering, and excess, followed by a trail of those who died long before they needed to. Much wealth was accumulated but not often by the people who died for that music.

CHAPTER TEN

MEPHISTOPHELES
IS AMERICAN:
FAUSTIAN CONTRACTS IN
THE UNITED STATES

The Devil—had he fidelity
Would be the best friend—
Because he has ability—
But Devils cannot mend—
Perfidy is the virtue
That would but he resign
The Devil—without question
Were thoroughly divine
—Emily Dickinson, "Poem 1479" (c. 1855–1865)

Salem remains the same grey and drizzly town the color of the north Atlantic which it was when Roger Conant arrived as a representative of the Massachusetts Bay Colony in 1626. Obviously Salem is not *exactly* the same, now it's not a Puritan settlement but rather a North Shore exurb of Boston catering to tourists with a macabre bent, though despite the vagaries of climate change, on a lashing and rainy October afternoon when

the New England sun seems to commit suicide, it's hard
not to imbibe a bit of Salem's pleasant melancholy, the forlorn yearning that is felt deep in the intestines for such a
town's rough beauty. Look beyond the predictable scatter-
ing of Dunkin' Donuts and the confusing roundabouts, the
decaying Stop 'n Shop and the Market Basket, for Salem's
origins remain where they were.

Still a relatively small town, Salem is like many coastal
Massachusetts locales defined by the preponderance of
rough-hewn, wooden-joisted, peak-gabled, half-timbered
dwellings from the seventeenth-century, a place settled
three years after Shakespeare's first folio was printed and
that austerely wears its long history as a Puritan wears his
black coat and hat. Like so many places in the far east, in
the earliest of regions to be settled by the English, Salem's
history can be bewildering to those of us from newer locales. The wooden timbered homes of the Federal Street
District built from trees amid which the Lenape use to live,
the red-brick Custom House built in 1819, even Nathaniel
Hawthorne's House of the Seven Gables with its vaguely
menacing, black, wood visage. History as thick as fog running in off the Massachusetts Bay in November, as seemingly eternal as a New England winter. Unscientifically
speaking, there is a sense in which New England seems
more Old England than the rest of the United States, that
the American experiment may have started upon the frigid
and rocky shoals of Massachusetts, but that the future
always lie toward the setting of the sun. Salem, though,

prefigures and manifests America as it was and the United States as it has become, because there is no comprehending the latter without the former.

If you should visit today, which makes a charming afternoon trip, you can spend a few contemplative moments at the Salem Witch Trials Memorial. In a town long equivalent with the sprouting of irrationality and hate which led to the state-sanctioned murder of nineteen people accused of having sold their souls to the Devil, the memorial strikes an appropriately solemn tone. A granite wall surrounds a parcel of land that could be a churchyard, with cantilevered stone benches set into the rock at even spaces and dedicated to every one of the victims, their names and dates of execution engraved above each seat. It took three centuries for a memorial to be dedicated, the commemoration marked with a speech given by the Auschwitz survivor and Nobel Peace Prize winner Elie Wiesel in which he wisely intoned that there remain "many Salems," the speaker himself introduced by the playwright Arthur Miller whose heavy-handed but still indispensable allegory *The Crucible* largely remains most Americans' introduction to these events.

"A fire, a fire is burning!" says Miller through the character of John Procter, whom the playwright made the protagonist of *The Crucible* and thus its most enduring victim. "I hear the boot of Lucifer, I see his filthy face! And it is my face, and yours!" shouts Proctor. For as much remains a bit stuffy about *The Crucible*, not least of which the chauvinism of Marilyn Monroe's husband making the hero of his play Proctor, despite his being one of only five men out of the nineteen executed in an atrocity largely aimed at women, it remains a work with something to say about the ambiguities of Faustian bargains. Despite the pentagram trinkets left by Neo-Pagans and the purple votive candles placed by Wiccans at the memorial, it's doubtful that any of the condemned would have considered themselves witches, which was part of the point of the cryptic irrationality of the trials. When visiting in 2017, walking beneath the naked locust trees of a damp October, I heard a tinny noise emanating from around the corner. A recorded advertisement, spooky Halloween music and all, imploring visitors to come to a wax museum of Salem horrors, the travesty reduced to kitsch, a most American process.

There was an eruption of madness starting in 1692, when two hundred women and men were accused of conspiring with the Devil, thirty were found guilty, and nineteen were executed. A popular misapprehension has it that those accused of witchcraft—of having written their names in the Devil's book and entered into Faustian covenant with Satan—were burnt at the stake, but none of them were. They were hanged and in a few memorable instances pressed to death. Not to debate the relative merits of different methods of barbarity, but the fantasies of autos de fé and green-wood pyres in the Massachusetts chill perhaps indicates a desire to relegate the whole sordid affair to some distant Medieval past, as an archaic holdover not indicative of nascent American modernity. But much of what happened in Salem can be attributed to some enduring American afflictions. Outsiders in the community, such as the Irish Catholic indentured servant Ann Glover and the Barbadian enslaved woman Tituba, were accused of witchcraft, one of the ways in which women—feared for their agency and sexuality—became the locus of patriarchal rage; Glover was hanged, while Tituba's case was dismissed.[1]

Consider upon the scaffold Bridget Bishop, Sarah Good, Rebecca Nurse, Elizabeth Howe, Susannah Martin, Sarah Wildes, Martha Carrier, Martha Corey, Mary Eastey, Mary Parker, Alice Parker, Ann Pudeator, Margaret Scott, and Elizabeth Proctor, wife of John, pardoned only because she was pregnant. Not only by misogyny, the Salem madness was seeded by the nature of the Puritan project, the theft of land which was not theirs, on which they pretended to establish their religious utopia. For the earliest generation of colonists America was an Eden, a land where The Fall had not happened, but for the Puritans this paradise was in a howling wilderness, a place where Satan had established his throne. "Go tell Mankind, that there are Devils and Witches" wrote the Puritan divine Cotton Mather in his 1689 *Memorable Providences, Relating to Witchcrafts and Possessions*, "and that though those night-birds least appear where the Day-light of the Gospel comes . . . not only in the Wigwams of Indians, where the pagan Powaws often raise their masters, in the shapes of bears and snakes and fires, but the House of Christians" as well.

However, the only Faustian contract in Salem—or Boston—or Plymouth—or Jamestown, Philadelphia, Charlestown, Savanah or New Amsterdam—was the town charter. America itself was a Faustian bargain, but the bloody ink on the parchment was not from the bodies of those who signed it, rather that of those killed and enslaved to establish this apocalyptic kingdom. The Salem dead were a sacrifice to religious nihilism, of Calvinism taken to its conclusion, and an intimation of the nation which was to be birthed from the Puritan example. Thomas Maule, a Quaker of Salem whose real sect was almost as despised by the Puritans as the imagined witches, noted with disdain that the accusers and the prosecution in the town believed that the "Devil hath a visible Book of natural paper, and with the natural Blood of mens natural Bodies, they subscribe to this natural Book." According to Maule, the Devil was at work in Salem, but not in the literal manner which the town leaders believed, rather he was working through those same leaders.

These were men—ostensibly stolid, sober, and dependable men—who made their case through a recourse to empirical reasoning. By calling upon all manner of evidence—physical and spectral—from pins left in bobbins and the delusions or fantasies of children who claimed to see their neighbors cavorting with Old Scratch—the leaders of Salem impugned hundreds as having affixed their name within the infernal book, but there is no such volume, at least not in any literal sense. Were Salem some vestige of a pre-modern time, it would be less unusual, but the judges drew upon their own rigorous scientific reasoning to reach their verdict, making this a trial that's as much of the Enlightenment as it is any projected Medieval past. More than Torquemada's cells, Salem prefigures the gulag and the concentration camp. The Devil cleverly ruled from the bench in this circumstance.

Mather in his 1693 account *On Witchcraft* intoned "Since the Devil is come down in great wrath upon us, let not us in our great wrath against one another provide a Lodging for him," except that's obviously what happened. By contrast, as Proctor knowingly says in Miller's play, there are still Faustian contracts aplenty, none less than that whereby the Puritan leaders deigned themselves to be holy at the sacrificial expense of their fellow citizens, trading the lives of the innocent for the satisfactions of righteous insanity. Nor does Proctor—a man who is after all guilty of adultery, though not of fraternizing with the Devil—spare himself, for he understands that we're all a bit of that party, and that we know it. Faust's story is all of ours. Give it to Proctor, who'd fallen away from Massachusetts's established church, as having a better understanding of guilt and total depravity than the Calvinists who reigned in Salem.[2]

What must be remembered about the Puritans is that these were a people for whom the Devil was very much real. They heard him dragging his clanking chains through the dirt cow-paths in the dead of night, they smelled his gamey odor of offal and fucking when they had impure thoughts, they saw him in their peripheral vision dressed as a fine gentleman smiling in the back of the white clapboard Congregationalist church or in the public meeting hall. Perhaps a manifested guilt at building their city on a hill upon a foundation of bones, in the cemeteries of those they killed. As a perverse irony, Protestants had magnified their belief in Satan's sovereign power, but their staunch iconoclasm made it impossible for them to soothe their consciousnesses in the manner a Catholic might have. No holy water or relics, crucifixes or icons to dispel the Devil, who could only be met on his own terms, the rest of us left naked and terrified before the ultimate.

Calvinists are riven by a type of madness, for if the zealous Catholic penitents must manifest their anxiety in the still estimably physical rituals of continual prayers of the rosary or supplications before the Stations of the Cross, such scrupulosity for the Puritan is wholly more mental, the nagging suspicion that you've not been made elect by the Lord for salvation, but that unlike the Romish believers whom you've defined yourself in opposition to, nothing of your own merit can be done to prevent your hellfire future. "The God that holds you over the pit of hell, much as one holds a spider, or some loathsome insect over the fire, abhors you," thundered Jonathan Edwards to a congregation in Enfield, Connecticut in 1741, "his wrath towards you burns like fire; he looks upon you as worthy of nothing else, but to be caste into the fire . . . you are ten thousand times more abominable in his eyes, than the most hateful

venomous serpent is in ours."[3] These were theocrats in colonial Massachusetts, they were most austere, stern, doctrinaire, and frigid, but what exactly would they have to
do with our contemporary maximalist, excessive, and orgiastic nation?

Everything, I'd argue. Calvinism posited the existence
of an elect of justified sinners; of men and women chosen
by God for salvation, and though nothing done through the
individual merit of works can ensure salvation, there were
certain clues that an individual soul could expect to go upward rather than down upon death, chiefly the favor of the
Lord as granted in the form of material prosperity. Where
Medieval Catholicism and other forms of Protestantism
emphasized a certain spiritual glory in being impoverished,
the Calvinist saw the rich believer as being favored by God,
and the hungry, destitute, and homeless as being cursed
by that same deity. In this way, the human predicament
as understood by the Puritans was both depressingly and
startlingly modern, even post-modern.

For the pious of New England, the metaphysical individual stood alone, because whatever communitarian associations connected people with one another, the soul itself
was naked before the Lord—a pure, solitary, atomistic
thing. Interiority was emphasized, a type of hyper-attenu-
ated consciousness that could veer from neurotic to narcissistic. Edwards's infamous sermon "Sinners in the Hands
of an Angry God," with its deity that sounds like Satan to
me, was delivered during the series of revivals known as the

First Great Awakening because the grandchildren of that
first generation increasingly found it impossible to countenance the draconian psychological torture of Calvinism,
the sheer nihilism of this theology which judged us worthy
of eternal torture before we were even born.[4]

As could be predicted, women and men left the church,
but since nobody can ever truly dispel the traces of the faith
in which they were raised (even the absence of faith is a
faith), the United States became an upside-down Calvinist
hell, a nation that's both repudiation and consummation
of those dark visions. Rather than fearing and worshiping
Calvin's God, we've rechristened Him the Invisible Hand.
Obvious in Salem, both then and now, in that settlement
which was named for peace but which remains synonymous with violence, where today you can visit tourist traps
selling the atrocity.

Only a people as repressed and sin-obsessed as the
Puritans could conjure such Faustian fantasies, could mistake the Devil for God. In its compromises and contracts,
its negotiations and nightmares, America is the Faustian
Republic. More than beginning in the Pilgrim's Plymouth,
Puritan Boston, or Cavalier Jamestown, America began in
Salem and a direct spiritual route links that Massachusetts
hamlet to Wall Street and Capitol Hill, Silicon Valley and
Hollywood, Los Alamos and Las Vegas, for what all share
is a stated commitment to rationality, to logic, to produc-
tivity, to utilitarianism, to liberty, all to mask something
much darker. Because, as Leslie Fiedler argues in his classic

Love and Death in the American Novel, the prototypical American from the revolutionary Founders of the United States onward "defines himself by denying the Calvinist . . . theology of his world," even as the archetypal rugged individualist transubstantiates into a "Faustian man [who] needs that theology to create the tensions of his life; he is a blasphemer and blasphemy is the sign of the secret though tormented believer."

The social economy of the Puritans would, by contemporary Reaganite standards, seem positively socialistic, but once God and the Devil are subtracted from cosmology the contract concerning mutual charity and welfare becomes null and void. That's Fiedler's point, that a Calvinist atheist is a dangerous thing, because they've preserved the iron cage of reformed theology while emptying it of its already minimal enchantments. The path from John Winthrop's exhortation in his 1630 sermon "A Model of Christian Charity," wherein he said that "We must delight in each other, make other's conditions our own, rejoice together, mourn together, labor and suffer together, always having before our eyes our commission and community," and Margaret Thatcher's declaration that "There is no such thing as society," involves draining Calvinism of all that pesky God and Devil talk, leaving behind the justification without the sin.[5]

—

Mark Twain imagines what this God would look like in
the Satan which he depicts in his unfinished novel *The
Mysterious Stranger*, a faux-Medieval fabulism written as
he became increasingly cynical and despondent, especially
about his nation, which oppressed workers at home and
promoted bloody imperialism abroad. "There is no God,
no universe, no human race, no earthly life, no heaven, no
hell," says Satan. "It is all a Dream, a grotesque and foolish
dream. Nothing exists but you." Supply-side epistemology,
the metaphysic of the libertarian. From impious Calvinism
was derived a nation of little Fausts who've retained their
belief in election but abandoned any sense of the sacred.

Nathaniel Hawthorne, that stolid son of Massachusetts,
understood that dark core of Calvinism well. Direct descendant of Judge John Hathorne who had sat on the
bench during the witch trials, Hawthorne had opted to alter the spelling of his name to differentiate himself, yet he
was a good enough believer in original sin to know that a
mere "w" can't erase such wickedness. "Young Goodman
Brown," Hawthorne's short, gothic tale first published in
1835, is the sort of sin-drenched tale that could only be written by somebody both recovering from his own Calvinist
inheritance while being aware of the dark contradictions
hidden in a steadfast faith which worships a god every bit
as malevolent as the Gnostic demiurge.

Hawthorne's titular character, a young seventeenth-
century Puritan of Salem, takes leave of his new wife Faith
for a nocturnal pilgrimage through the dense, howling

wilderness surrounding the settlement, a "forest peopled with frightful sounds."[6] While making his sojourn, he encounters a man of about fifty years of age who looks curiously as if an older version of himself, carrying an ominous walking stick in the shape of a snake. As the two walk through the woods, the stranger tells Goodman that he is "well acquainted with your family . . . I helped your grandfather, the constable, when he lashed the Quaker woman so smartly through the streets of Salem; and it was I that brought your father a pitch-pine knot, kindled at my own hearth, to set fire to an Indian village," counting both men as "good friends."

Goodman is disturbed; he's a simple man of simple faith and was unaware of such family history. Later, Goodman espies the stranger conversing with a stalwart, elderly woman of the church, a Goody Cloyse who not only confirms the man as being the Devil, but joyfully greets him as an old friend. "'That old woman taught me my catechism,' said the younger man; and there was a world of meaning in this simple comment." Indeed, Hawthorne interprets the meaning of the story itself within that same story and its many ambiguities and ambivalences. In the context of the story, there is a "world of meaning" whereby a seemingly pious catechist was also a worshiper of Satan.

Finally, Goodman reaches the wooded spot to which his perambulations were subconsciously drawing him, a clearing in which he sees the gathered respectable of Salem, the ministers and deacons, the town fathers and the merchants, the faithful widows and the zealous newlyweds, all gathered to convene some sort of Witches' Sabbath. Faith, he will discover, is also there, for the two are to be baptized into a new covenant, genuflecting before a different Lord. Facing a stone altar lit by burning pines are the gathered faithful of Salem, along with the dissolute and the criminal, the known heretics and blasphemers, the savages and pagans, all "flashing forth, as it were, in a sheet of flame, the fiend worshippers . . . the smile of welcome gleamed darkly on every visage."

Approaching the shrouded figure that they worship, the assembled draw from a font emanating a red light, to baptize Faith in the blood of the innocent. Goodman screams out to his wife to resist such overtures, to blot out her name in the covenantal book before she has even signed it, but as soon as he shouts all of it vanishes as mere chimera, and the disoriented young man is alone in the dark and chill wood. So he returns to Salem, though as Hawthorne tells us Goodman was forever altered, unsure as to whether this vision was reality or mere phantasmagoria. He lives an unhappy lifetime, for as that prince said at his own ceremony, "Evil is the nature of mankind. Evil must be your only happiness. Welcome, again, my children, to the communion of your race."

Often, "Young Goodman Brown" is read as an impugning of Puritan sanctimony, of the no doubt hypocritical behavior of those divines. Then there are the readings that place Hawthorne in a long and fevered American tradition

that sees conspiratorial ritualism threaded throughout society, but that's to reduce the story to a Reddit post about
the Reptilians or the Illuminati. I wonder, though, if
there isn't something more subversive going on in "Young
Goodman Brown," if Hawthorne understood that the
Puritan dilemma was that they weren't hypocritical, they
weren't liars, they weren't unfaithful, but that the worship
of Calvin's god might look indistinguishable from bowing
before Satan.

———

A writer whose most famous work is often misattributed to
Hawthorne comprehended something similar, but as writ
through the national ethos of America. Stephen Vincent
Benét has the distinction of writing something so successful that it's attained the status of folklore, its author all
but forgotten. "The Devil and Daniel Webster," the 1937
story of a yeoman farmer in antebellum New Hampshire
who foolishly sells his soul to the Devil only to be defended
at trial by the brilliant orator and congressman Daniel
Webster is well-known in American popular culture, so
that many broadly know the story, but not the name of its
creator.

There's a reason for the success of this story about a
New England necromancer, and that's because many of
us intrinsically understand its unsettling moral—that
America has always been a Faustian bargain. In Benét's tale

Jabez Stone sold his soul to "Mr. Scratch" in exchange for material prosperity, and per the stipulations of their contract, after seven years the Devil arrives to collect his due. With no one else to turn to, Stone hires the great Webster to plead his case before a thoroughly "American jury . . . with the fires of hell still upon them," an infernal group that includes the libertine colonist Thomas Morton, the feared Wampanoag chief "King Philip" Metacomet, and Blackbeard the Pirate, with the court presided over by Judge Hathorne. With grand rhetoric, Webster convinces the jury that Stone's soul was never for sale in the first place, claiming that "no American citizen may be forced into the service of a foreign prince."

Ever the patriot, the historical Webster's doctrine of unionism above all else entailed its own Faustian negotiations, as with the Compromise of 1850 that he helped broker in Congress, which preserved the shaky foundations of the state at the cost of passing the Fugitive Slave Act and allowing Southern states to expand into new territories. Because of that, after the jury finds in Stone's favor, Mr. Scratch reads Webster's palm, predicting that the representative will be considered a traitor by his fellow northerners, while his sons will die in an apocalyptic civil war which all the representative's political concessions did nothing to prevent.

The joke is that Satan understands the national soul better than Webster does—"I am merely an honest

American like yourself," the Devil tells the congressman. We'd all do well to meditate upon Satan's courtroom testimony, wherein he reminds the reader that "When the first wrong was done to the first Indian, I was there. When the first slaver put out for the Congo, I stood on her deck . . . 'Tis true the North claims me for a Southerner and the South for a Northerner," though Lucifer precedes both, being the spirit of the nation whose "name is older in this country than yours." Benét's story argues that not only is American history a story of oppression—*but Satanic oppression at that*—should put a lie to the idea that so-called "identity politics" is something just dreamed up by liberal Ivy League faculty or progressive public-school boards. The other thing that must be remembered is that Benét's claim—that American prosperity, power, and privilege were born from the incomprehensible evils of slavery and genocide—is true.

When Benét conjures an image of Satan overseeing the arrival of the Spanish, and French, and Dutch, and English in the New World, it evokes the metaphysical evil of the genocide which defined European colonization; when he imagines Lucifer aboard a slave ship traversing the horrific Middle Passage, where as many as thirteen million Africans were kidnapped and almost two million died during the voyage, it's to understand that slavery wasn't just a political or even a moral issue, but a religious one. American wealth, power, and influence is directly attributable to not just historical injustices, but historical evils. Presidential committees and conservative pundits might not admit that, but our greatest poets and prophets always have.

American literature is not about Faust; it is written by Faust. A creed of freedom without responsibility, liberty without repercussion, of endless consumption, eternal paradise, and *pure, white innocence*. Faust is a prelapsarian, that is to say that he desires the freedom to self-create which was humanity's inheritance but for The Fall, so he conducts his life in a manner as if he's not indebted to his fellow humans, as if he's not part of society. These are the paradisical fantasies that could lead the seventeenth-century philosopher John Locke to intone in his *Second Treatise on Government* that "In the beginning, all the world was America." A fantasy and Faustian covenant that entailed the genocide of indigenous peoples and the enslavement of Africans, all while maintaining an illusory innocence (they maintain it still).

Our Puritan ancestors may have believed in the Devil, feared him, spurned him, even worshipped him, but it was left for later generations to make him real. "The fiend in his own shape is less hideous than when he rages in the breast of man," Hawthorne reminds us. Such is the tale of New Hampshire Brigadier General Jonathan Moulton, the "Yankee Faust." A hero of the Seven Years War and the American Revolution, Moulton challenged Satan by saying that his soul should belong to Hell if the Devil were ever able to completely fill a pair of boots with gold coins. Ever the industrious and cagey New Englander, Moulton placed his soleless boots over two holes in the floor above his root cellar, so that like water through a well or oil from a pump the wealth would flow uninterrupted.

The Brigadier General earned his sobriquet well, for the Faust in him may have challenged the Devil, but the Yankee is who would win. A desire which is the fundamental mythos of the United States; of limitless, consequence-free material plenty, all acquired with a friendly grin. Marlowe's Faust may be dragged to hell, but the American Faust beats the Devil and drinks his beer for free. Americans perfected a new type of Faust, the one who *wins,* for a while. At least that's the first part of that innocent tale, for it's the foolishness of an American to believe that he can ever really vanquish the Devil. Moulton grows rich on diabolical gold, but his punishment is that Satan returns and sets his house on fire. Our Faustian contract, for the wage of sin is that all of us shall perish in this warming, scorching, burning husk. No more profit, only dust and ash.

CHAPTER ELEVEN

THE DARKEST OF ARTS: TOTALITARIANISM IN THE FAUSTIAN CENTURY

Well, as everyone knows, once witchcraft gets
started, there's no stopping it.
—Mikhail Bulgakov, *The Master and Margarita* (c. 1928–1940)

In envisioning the location where the greatest German-language novel of the twentieth century was written, the details might include a half-timbered Bavarian house facing a charming cobble-stoned courtyard, a white-washed Alpine hunting lodge with Linden trees laid heavy with snow lining the front pathway, or an elegant apartment in a Bauhaus building in Berlin overlooking Potsdamer Platz or the Oderberger Strasse, the author fueled by copious quantities of espresso from Café Kranzler and Schoko-Sahne tarts. German history being what it is, especially in the twentieth century, none of these places describes where the most notable work in the language was penned, for rather than Cologne, Frankfurt, Hamburg or Berlin, Vienna or Graz, Zurich or Bern, Königsberg or Prague, Thomas Mann produced his *Doctor Faustus: The Life of the German Composer Adrian Leverkühn, as Told by a Friend* near the Pacific's lapping waves.

Far from the chill Baltic and North Sea, the most pertinent and powerful novel written in the tongue of Goethe was completed in that Kingdom of Perpetual Sunshine, California, not within a half-timbered house but in a gleaming white Modernist bungalow, all straight lines and shining walls, at 1550 San Remo Drive, in Pacific Palisades, Los Angeles, which, rather than with Mann's beloved Lindens, featured palm trees.[1] Here Mann spun his own enchantments in rightful condemnation of the culture which had made him possible. California would become the empire of illusions, so that *Doctor Faustus* appropriately has a bit of magic about it, a bit of conjuration. "There is a great deal of illusion in a work of art," says *Doctor Faustus*'s narrator Serenus Zeitblom, "one could go further and say that it is illusory in and of itself." Enchantments and myths are both the subject and the materials of all art, this set of the stage-play world; it includes the twelve-tone arrangements of notes which Leverkühn configures as if alchemical symbols and even Mann's novel itself. Illusions and fantasies are a dangerous thing, though; easy to become sentient in their own right, chthonic forces that when applied to the political realm can conjure malevolent deities.

Doctor Faustus, in the best tradition of Goethe, is not a simple book. A Modernist novel in the form of a nineteenth-century door-stopper, *Doctor Faustus* is structured as a biography of the brilliant composer Leverkühn as written by his childhood friend Zeitblom, who is an otherwise forgettable, middle-aged professor of classics, organizing his memories from previous decades at the same moment that Germany is disappearing into the Hitlerian singularity.[2] Ranging from the composer's 1885 birth in the fictional Kaisersaschern, a prototypically Medieval German hamlet, until his death in 1940, *Doctor Faustus* includes shockingly little story (several complicated sexual entanglements and a murder on a street car aside).

That's because true to being a philosophical novel of ideas, *Doctor Faustus* is structured as an intellectual biography, the account of an artist whose dramas are cerebral. Mann follows Leverkühn's development from aspiring Lutheran theologian to avant-garde composer, and then finally his descent into madness; his brain rotted from the syphilis he purposefully contracted to trigger the fits of artistic ecstasy he thought necessary to achieve inspiration. Cold and distant, but occasionally explosive and ecstatic, Leverkühn shares affinities with that other Teutonic syphilitic Friedrich Nietzsche with his declaration in *Ecce Homo* that "I am not a man! I am dynamite!"

Leverkühn demolishes the humanistic pieties of the

German musical tradition, embracing the atonal and
the discordant. His aim is to apotheosize the individual
(composer) by embracing a radical libertarian creative
freedom. When it comes to such genius, Zeitblom wor-
ries that the "demonic and irrational have a disquieting share in that radiant sphere" and how much more
so when that creative freedom—to demolish and build
according to artistic dictates—isn't limited to the individual, but writ across an entire nation, an entire culture? Zeitblom enumerates Leverkühn's gothic heaviness,
the haunting traces of Germany's past of flagellants and
zealots, mystics and fanatics. With his polite sense of op-
probrium, Zeitblom says that "our times are inclined,
I say, to return to such epochs and enthusiastically re-
peat symbolic actions that have something sinister about
them . . . burning books, for instance, and other deeds I
would rather not put into words."

Nothing is so simplistic or juvenile as characters that
match one-to-one with ideas or nations or historical per-
sonages; *Doctor Faustus* isn't a cipher and Mann isn't
George Orwell. Yet in some sense, even if Leverkühn isn't
supposed to be "Germany," Faustus remains a cautionary
tale about "Germanness," which also afflicts Zeitblom.
Leverkühn may be Nietzsche's dynamite, like the Nazi re-
gime then in the process of murdering six million Jews,
while Zeitblom is the good, liberal, humanistic professor,
but Mann conveys much in that clause, "deeds I would
rather not put into words." The good professor may

disdain Hitler, but he is quiet; he may find it distasteful that his own sons are employed by the Third Reich, yet his own life remains comfortable even while the gas chambers and crematoria operate. After all, Mann has his narrator note that when it comes to "skilled German technology," despite his supposed anti-fascism, "I cannot suppress a certain satisfaction at our ever-resourceful spirit of invention, at our nation's competence."

In keeping with the psychology of such repression, the novel's narrative is digressive, meandering, and labyrinthine; Zeitblom's voice is allusive, apologetic, and ambiguous. Frequently drawing attention to his own supposed deficiencies as a stylist, Zeitblom also repeatedly insists on his trustworthiness, which after 512 pages has the tendency to make us doubt his accuracy.[3] Doubts are replete in Mann's novel, for there is a general lack of the supernatural within *Doctor Faustus*, the Mephistophelean figure of Sammael arriving about halfway through the book and offering twenty-four years of creative genius in exchange for the composer's soul. The reality of Sammael's existence is uncertain, as it's argued that the shape-shifting demon (variously a scholar, a critic, and a pimp—not so different) is a delusion rendered by Leverkühn's tertiary syphilis, a chimera not of hell but of spirochetes.

For around forty pages, reproduced by Zeitblom as a letter by his friend, Leverkühn and Sammael dispute the nature of art, inspiration, agency, and ecstasy. In proper Protestant fashion, Leverkühn acknowledges having little choice in whether his soul is up for bargain. Much of the scene involves Leverkühn trying to dodge the great trickster's syllogisms, the tack of the Devil's argument as variable as his physical form. "You might hold me in esteem as a savant at least," Sammael says, "The Devil surely knows something of music."

Throughout their discourse, a recurring theme (as indeed throughout the entirety of *Doctor Faustus*) is the untamable presence of the demonic, in not just music, but all inspired arts. Among artists there may be a requirement to give the Devil his due deference, but there is also a need to make sure that the leash is kept tight. What Sammael presupposes, is that the gathering storms on Germany's horizon can't be explained by sociology or economics, mere history or psychology, but only by something numinous, mysterious, secret. "Believe me," Sammael says, "barbarism has a better understanding even of theology than does a culture that has fallen off," for what's soon arriving will break with the "Age itself, the cultural epoch, which is to say, the epoch of this culture . . . And dare a barbarism, a double barbarism, because it comes after humanitarianism, after every conceivable root-canal work and bourgeois refinement." Enlightenment politics denied the Devil's existence, the easier for him to sneak back into the hearts of man.

Doctor Faustus, a book which explicates the German spirit at the moment that nation was losing its soul, could have only been written in exile. It is a testament of the refugee, the émigré, the homeless, and the abandoned. Throughout the Palisades, a wealthy neighborhood of 75-degree days and perpetual light, clear air and cloudless nights, Mann was joined by a coterie of other German intellectuals and dissidents, luminaries such as the philosopher Theodor Adorno, the playwright Bertolt Brecht, his collaborator Kurt Weil, and composer Arnold Schoenberg, transforming this corner of Los Angeles with its hilly, winding cul-de-sacs into the intellectual capital of the German speaking world.

Indeed it was Schoenberg's compositional methods that Mann adapted for Leverkühn in *Doctor Faustus,* and the former music critic Adorno who helped tutor the author in the complexities of atonal composition. More than a sonata, symphony, or opera however, *Doctor Faustus* is a dirge, a mournful song about the eclipse of German culture, about the terrors and traumas that had driven men like Adorno, Schoenberg, and Mann to America. The route which led Mann from Germany to Switzerland then into Los Angeles is arguably the great theme of *Doctor Faustus,* a diagnosis of what can drive an entire culture insane. *Doctor Faustus* offers a sense of how the nation of Mozart and Beethoven, Kant and Goethe, became that of Dachau, Buchenwald, and Auschwitz.

Having been a former German nationalist who'd had his own intellectual dalliances with the right-wing following the Great War, Mann's analysis of the mass-appeal of something as rank as fascism is keener than mere economic reductionism, for he intuitively understood the power such mythic systems could have over otherwise ordinary people, the way in which an entire nation could become demonically possessed. In the persona of Zeitblom, Mann describes that "wild intoxication—for constantly yearning to be intoxicated, we drank freely, and under that illusory euphoria we have for years committed a plethora of disgraceful deeds."

Mann would write *Doctor Faustus* in his Pacific Palisades house not as *apologia* but as *mea culpa*, the loyal German turning his intellectual faculties toward his home nation, distilling its Faustian essence at the moment the Holocaust was reaching its cannibalistic apex.[4] Mann was foremost a cosmopolitan and a humanist who would eschew the dangers of noxious blood-and-soil provincialism, and *Doctor Faustus* is a searing admonition of Germany's embrace of unimaginable evil during the 1930s and '40s. In its portrayal of Adrian Leverkühn, Mann's penultimate novel marshals the accoutrements of German high culture to explain how a nation viewed as a paragon of urbane, sophisticated, and elegant values could descend into pure Satanic madness.

Zeitblom says that "popular myths, or better, myths trimmed for the masses, would be the vehicle of political action—fables, chimeras, phantasms that needed to have nothing whatever to do with truth, reason, or science in order to be productive nonetheless, to determine life and history, and thereby to prove themselves dynamic realities."

If fascism aestheticizes politics, as Walter Benjamin had claimed, then *Doctor Faustus* is an allegory of the dangers of illusion, of the way in which such enchantments can suddenly exert their own dark power over material circumstances. Fascism is the politics of the Faustian bargain, the national soul exchanged for fantasies of the Reich made great again, but finally, as Zeitblom mourns, "Germany is done for, or will be done for," as it must be—as it must be for any such nation so enticed.

Germany's greatest cultural contribution is the Faust legend from Hrotsvitha to Goethe, and so Mann's withering autopsy of what "drove a whole culture mad," in W. H. Auden's memorable phrase, should naturally return to the source material. If Benjamin is correct about the provenance of civilization, then it's to Faust that Mann would naturally turn to understand Hitler. As archetype, the legend explains the demonic powers of both Nazism and fascism more completely than any other method of analysis, not in the language of reason and argument, but rather that of emotion and barbarism which those ideologies are already fluent in.

———

Hitler's rise can be told as a tale of various coinciding Faustian bargains. To begin with, there were the capitulations and concessions given to Hitler and his National Socialists by the mainstream conservative political parties of Weimar Germany, men who believed that

Der Führer could be constrained and used to further their own political aims.[5] Like most conventional conservatives, they were elitists, nationalists, chauvinists, and racists, though not necessarily genocidal. As elitists, they found the buffoonery of a little man like Hitler contemptible, but they believed that his histrionics could be bottled, that he could be deployed as a creature capable of granting them power, but whom they'd steadfastly control. As distasteful as Hitler may have been to them, he was a tool for bashing liberals and labor unions, socialists and communists. They were felled by not taking Hitler seriously, by not understanding the demonic import of his claims. Nobody signs a contract with Satan and avoids hell.

Were the cynical calculations of German conservatives the only means by which Hitler would acquire absolute power, then the Nazis may very well have failed, but as Mann makes clear, the myopia and naivety of liberals is also a necessity, not least of all in their own overweening humanistic arrogance that refuses to acknowledge evil's reality, including in their own souls. Mann describes the good people who:

> voted the Social Democratic ticket at the polls,
> [but] were capable at the same time of seeing
> something demonic in the poverty of the little
> old lady who could not afford room above
> ground, capable of reaching for their children
> when she approached in order to defend them

from the witch's evil eye. And if such a woman were to be burned, which, with only slight changes in pretext, is hardly outside the realm of the conceivable these days, they would stand behind the barriers set up by the town council and gape, but presumably not revolt.

Even among those on the left who most vociferously fought Hitler's thugs through ballots and bullets, strikes and fists, there were occasional Faustian bargains, of the so-called "Red-Brown Alliance," the attractions of a communist and fascist union against liberalism and capitalism requiring some blood on the contract.

As it is, there's an actual example of just such a Faustian bargain—maybe a mutual Faustian bargain where both parties are necromancer and demon—in the infamous Molotov-Ribbentrop Pact of non-aggression signed between the German Reich and the Union of Soviet Socialist Republics on August 23rd, 1939 just more than a week before their dual invasion of Poland. Germany and the Soviet Union carved up the territories of eastern Europe while promising not to attack each other; Hitler betrayed that assurance, something Stalin refused to acknowledge until the Nazis were almost at Moscow, for what of the foolishness of a devil who trusts the devil?[6]

Centrists often characterize communism and fascism as touching points on an ideological horse-shoe, but this is a simplistic assertion that too often veers into anemic mutual equivalency. Yet the historical fact remains that Joseph Stalin—as Mephistophelean a figure as Hitler—was willing to sign such a Faustian bargain, and whatever role the Soviet Union may have played in defeating Germany, the Nazis were first enabled by Moscow. Furthermore, another historical fact remains—which was abundantly demonstrated by the members of international communist groups that had been adamantly pro-Soviet and anti-fascist before the pact but that were willing to excuse Stalin after such duplicity was revealed—even a utopian politics can make its own Faustian negotiations.

As Mann himself clarified in an interview with the U.S. military newspaper *Stars and Stripes* in 1947, while Nazism was always nothing more than "devilish nihilism," Soviet communism had sabotaged its utopian aims as it descended into Stalinism, a betrayal which he considered a genuine "tragedy." Truly the most Faustian of epochs, when those who marched under the banner of the hammer and sickle, ostensibly representing the international community of all workers regardless of race, could through convenience and greed embrace the flag of the swastika, a symbol of all that the communists opposed.

Examine the photographs taken on September 22, 1939, in the Polish city of Brest-Litovsk (now in Belarus), where the Wehrmacht and the Red Army held a joint military parade in honor of the former handing the town over to the latter. With streetlamps in Brest-Litovsk decorated in banners alternating between the swastika and the hammer and sickle, soldiers in General Heinz Guderian's Panzer Group 2 and Vasily Chuikov's 4th Army marched through the occupied city, posed for pictures together, and both armies solemnly stood for the lowering of the Soviet standard and the raising of the Reich's flag.

By the time some twenty-four million Soviet soldiers and civilians would perish in Hitler's horrific push toward the east, Stalin had expunged any memory of the brief Faustian collusion between the two regimes; after the hammer and sickle was raised over the smoldering ruins of Berlin's Reichstag in 1945, the USSR was only ever the hero in the "Great Patriotic War," for the nature of deals with the Devil is one of illusion and trickery. Regardless of the respective differences between Nazism and Stalinism, both understood themselves as being quasi-messianic, millennial faiths; as attempts to reinvent the human and to abolish history as such. Emerging from the war was a new word for a particular type of Faustian politics which imagines a control as complete as the necromancer's power—totalitarianism. As the German Jewish philosopher Hannah Arendt would explain in her study *The Origins of Totalitarianism*, this was a politics fit for conjuration and enchantments, where "everything was possible and . . . nothing was true."

———

If Mann's novel understood the Faustian spirit of fascism, than it was the Ukrainian writer Mikhail Bulgakov's satirical masterpiece *The Master and Margarita* which performed a similar literary maneuver upon Stalinism. The two books are dissimilar; Bulgakov is wickedly funny, while it's impossible to smile, much less laugh, through Mann's novel. Another rather stark difference is that if little happens in *Doctor Faustus,* seemingly *everything* happens in *The Master and Margarita*—men are transformed into conscious uniforms, bureaucrats break into musical song and dance, rubles into flying insects, and decapitated heads are reattached. What they both share, however, is an innate understanding of the demonic forces which can operate through politics, and in Bulgakov's case the way in which such energy can animate even an ideology which presumes itself to be rational, materialistic, atheistic. "Never ask for anything!" notes Bulgakov, familiar with the promises of Comrade Stalin who often censured and occasionally imprisoned the author, "Never for anything, and especially from those who are stronger than you."

Written in installments between 1928 when Stalin launched his first Five Year Plan and finished twelve years later mere months before Hitler would initiate Operation Barbarossa, *The Master and Margarita* would be for the duration of its author's life a secret book, a private volume, a clandestine novel. Distributed as *samizdat* in the years after Stalin's death, Bulgakov's novel would be published posthumously in the West in 1967, a record of the various capitulations and negotiations of Soviet citizens recorded from within the belly of the Beast itself. As a writer always willing to give the censor a challenge, such as in works like *A Young Doctor's Notebook* and *Heart of a Dog*, Bulgakov's greatest masterpiece had to be surreptitiously composed, lest the author's own words condemn him.

As its great theme, *The Master and Margarita* scorns the official Soviet religious position of atheism in a fabulist tale of Satan manifesting on a Moscow Walpurgis night as the elegant, sophisticated, and cosmopolitan Professor Woland. Strolling through the environs of the stylish Presnensky District with his companions—the hideous valet Koroviev, the demonically named assassin Azazello, Hella a vampiress, and an anthropomorphic black cat christened Behemoth—Woland descends upon the headquarters for the Soviet trade union for writers, Masolit. Arriving at Griboyedov House, where Masolit met, Woland provides enchantments and prophecies to try and convince the assembled (officially) atheistic writers that God exists, for the Lord has never had a more steadfast, loyal, and fervent believer than the Devil.

Professor Woland's claims are dismissed as mere tricks and madness, at least initially. Witchcraft, as Bulgakov makes clear, never stays repressed for long, as the magical ruptures in Moscow become harder to ignore. Unimpressed with the pieties of Marxism, just another heretical sect of Christianity, Woland dismisses Soviet utopianism as producing just more "people like any other people . . . they love money, but that has always been so." Whatever the vagaries of state-sanctioned dialectical materialism, the Devil's magic will always be stronger.

The Master and Margarita alternates between Moscow in the 1930s and first-century Judea in the form of what's later revealed to be a novel written by one of the members of Masolit, the titular "Master." His is a book which focuses on the persecution of Christ and his interactions with a not unsympathetic Pontius Pilate.[7] Like Bulgakov, the Master is persecuted for penning a manuscript that's so intimate with the particulars of faith that he is arrested by the secret police, consigned to an insane asylum, and finally must burn all the pages that he's written while abandoning his lover Margarita. However, as Bulgakov writes, "Manuscripts do not burn," for belief can't be fully sublimated or totally repressed, whether it's good or evil, wise or wicked.

Both novels, that of Bulgakov and of the Master, function not just as satires of austere Soviet orthodoxy, but as condemnations of the unfounded faith that either the Devil or God—those eternal twins—can ever be exorcized from the human heart. True to the vagaries of fiction's enchantments, there is a permeable interaction between Moscow and the Judea of the Master's novel; the apostle Matthew (who tries and fails to mercy kill Christ) is able to discourse with Woland; toward the end of the narrative, the Master even grants a degree of redemption to Pontius Pilate, who more than anything is only guilty of an awareness of human depravity. Margarita enters into covenant with Satan as a witch, only to be condemned, but is later saved from hell along with her lover, the two living out an eternity in the shade of a cherry tree in Limbo where the Master will finally complete his immolated novel. Bulgakov's plot is baroque and labyrinthine, a morass of characters and incidents that flit about as if Walpurgis specters.

At the conclusion everything dissipates into the ether, Moscow's authorities attributing such phantasmagorias to mass hypnosis. Mere hallucination, the majesty of Satan and the heat of Hell are dismissed as superstitious epiphenomenon. Therein lay the fatal flaw in the utopian delusions of the Soviet Union—not centralized planning, not economic determinism, or collective ownership over the means of production. All of that is debatable on its own merits, but the steadfast philosophical materialism of the project eliminated the numinous, a grave danger. Belief in human perfection proved the most dangerous of epiphenomenon, leading directly to the gulag. All of it allowed the Devil to sneak back in, perhaps with a thick black mustache, swept back hair, and a Georgian accent. "You pronounced your words as if you don't acknowledge the shadows, or the evil either," Woland says, but "Would you be so kind as to give a little thought to the question of what your good would be doing if evil did not exist, and how the earth would look if the shadows were to disappear from it?"

Totalitarianism posited a world that was nothing but specters, a grim Gehenna, a shadowy shoal. That such evil had no need for a Devil, that it was the product of human emotion and human aspiration and human desire—that was Satan's greatest lesson for the twentieth century. Like a proud parent, Mephistopheles must dab at moist eyes as Faust matures, content to learn that his wickedness can be found within his own stained soul. The most Faustian of political systems, totalitarianism demands the payment of freedom in exchange for the feeling of incomparable power; ironically the ultimate valorization of the individual, where every member of the party is as if a corpuscular atom in the great Leviathan of the dictator himself, whether he is the voice of the people or the avatar of the race. That is the great analytical failure of rational, bourgeois politics—whether left, liberal, or conservative—they're unable to recognize the threat of the fascist Devil because they can't recognize the Devil, they don't smell the sulfur or see his pointed-tooth sneer unless he's already clawing at their throats.

People who've idolatrized rationality can't understand the irrationality of the Faustian imperative until the machine guns have already been loaded, the ovens already tended. A horror of totalitarianism, whether in its right or left permutations, is how it emerged directly from the heady fermentation of Western culture, from Christianity and humanism, the Enlightenment and democracy, an inversion of stolid values, but one which required those values, nonetheless. "Freedom always has a propensity for dialectical reversal," says Leverkühn to Zeitblom, it "recognizes itself in restraint, finds fulfillment in subordinating itself to law, rule, coercion, system—finds fulfillment in them, but

that does not mean it ceases to be freedom." Leverkühn
is half-right here; he alludes to the infamous paradox of
tolerance whereby democratic values allow demonic forces
to operate unfettered until they crowd out democracy itself, but he's wrong that constrained freedom is such, for
the very concept is oxymoronic. Zeitblom chastises his
friend, saying that "in reality that is no freedom at all, no
more than a dictatorship . . . is still freedom," to which the
composer coldly responds "Are you so sure of that?" This
is the Faustian bargain offered to the true believer—that
for the price of their soul they will gain untold powers so
much greater than mere freedom, though the ultimate destination remains perdition, with millions of the innocent
dragged there as well.

CHAPTER TWELVE

MEPHISTOPHELES IN HOLLYWOOD: THE FAUSTIAN DESIRES OF ENTERTAINMENT

Wouldst thou like to live deliciously?
—Black Philip the Goat in Robert Eggers's *The Witch* (2015)

O n a cool summer evening in 2015, within the leafy environs of the Südwestkirchof Stahnsdorf Cemetery in Brandenburg around thirty miles outside of Berlin, by the dim light of the waning crescent moon, *someone* or *something* used *some implement* to pry open the heavy iron lid of horror director Friedrich Wilhelm Murnau's coffin, entombed eighty-four years earlier, and then detached his decomposed head from his skeleton's boney shoulders.

It's a desecration that is in keeping with Murnau's body of work, including such films as *Dr. Jekyll and Mr. Hyde*, *The Haunted Castle*, and *Journey into the Night*, most now as lost as their director's head. Almost a decade after its theft, the skull has yet to be retrieved, nor have authorities made any arrests. Not the first bit of travel that Murnau's remains have made, albeit in the past he accomplished the journey complete.

Germany's greatest director died in a Santa Barbara hospital in 1931, succumbing to injuries sustained in an automobile crash several days after his driver had swerved out of the way of a truck that had crossed over into the wrong lane on the sunny Pacific Coast Highway a few miles outside of L.A. "What I refer to is the fluid architecture of bodies with blood in their veins moving through mobile space," Murnau said of his own oeuvre in a premonition of his body being flung through a windshield. He described "the interplay of lines rising, falling, disappearing; the encounter of surfaces, stimulation and its opposite, calm; construction and collapse . . . the play of pure movement, vigorous and abundant," as if a debt being paid.

Following his death, Murnau was embalmed and shipped back to Brandenburg, though presumably not in a coffin filled with fresh earth as his greatest fictional creation, Count Orlok, had been. Murnau created the beak-nosed, pointy-eared, spindly-fingered, sharp-toothed Carpathian vampire in the 1922 film *Nosferatu*, after the estate of Bram Stoker refused to grant the director rights to the name "Dracula." With some foreshadowing of Murnau's own ultimate fate, a character in *Nosferatu* says "I am going far away to the land of robbers and ghosts," to which could be added demons as well.

Somebody alive right now must know the location of Murnau's head. The authorities, *Der Spiegel* reported, claimed that the granite relief of Murnau's mausoleum was coated in melted candle wax, evidence that grave-robbing occultists or Satanists had performed a ritual before they absconded with the skull. Apparently within the confines of that sepulcher, or at least within the ever-fanciful imaginations of law enforcement, there was yet another great reckoning within a small room. That original repatriation of Murnau's mortal remains to Brandenburg was appropriate, for it signified the reunification of body and soul, as only the former had really been in California for those five years, while Murnau's spirit— expressionist artist *perfekter Vollendung* and keen reader of Nietzsche and Arthur Schopenhauer—was always in Germany.

Murnau's *Nosferatu* had defined the visual idiom of German expressionist film, the startling contrasts between black and white, the uncanny disorientation of certain camera angles, the unusual perspectives—all in the service of a new variety of alchemy that trades not in oil of vitriol and quicksilver, but rather celluloid, as cinema would become the greatest magic of the young twentieth century.[1] Nonetheless, as the experimental director and closeted homosexual watched with wearied worry as the Nazi Party gained acolytes, antiseptic and artificial Hollywood came to seem preferable to Dionysian and decadent Weimar Berlin. With gothic aplomb, Murnau's great hero Schopenhauer would declaim in his 1851 *On the Sufferings of the World* that this "world could not have been the work of an all-loving being, but that of a devil, who had brought creatures into existence in order to delight in the sight of their sufferings." Sounding exactly like Marlowe's Mephistopheles, Schopenhauer concluded "For this world is Hell, and men are on the one hand the tormented souls and on the other the devils in it."

The title-card of Murnau's magnum opus asks of its titular monster's name "Does this word not sound like the midnight call of the Bird of Death? Do not utter it, or the images of life will fade—into pale shadows and ghostly dreams will rise from your heart and feed your blood." Orlok, as played by the brilliant and disturbing Max Schreck is iconic; Murnau's shot of the vampire's gaunt, corpuscular shadow coming up the steps as he nocturnally stalks his prey is one of the most celebrated scenes in horror cinema, the silhouette of the creature's long fingers adorned with sharpened nails appearing like the bars on Renfield's cage. It would be both an act of critical selfishness and interpretive malpractice to subsume Dracula under the mantle of Faust—there can be more than one such demonic creature, after all—though *Nosferatu*'s title card does evidence an admirably Mephistophelean position concerning reality and fantasy, and the dangers in confusing them.

We have an injunction against uttering incantations, an invocation of the chimeras of shadows and dreams, a warning about how blood shall pluck upon blood. However, as a product of the Teutonic soil and air, Murnau obviously took his turn at adapting that most German of legends in his 1926 *Faust,* which unlike most of his productions thankfully still survives. Drawing primarily from Goethe, with some Marlowe and older sources distributed throughout, Murnau's *Faustus* exists in five separately edited versions with two different scripts, one of which was by the German Nobel laureate Gerhart Hauptmann, though a less distinguished author's contribution was the one which was used by the distributor.[2] Perhaps as divine punishment, the producer would go bankrupt because of *Faustus,* which despite being a critical triumph was a financial disaster.[3] Maybe a contract that was worth it, because *Faust* was celebrated for breathtaking special effects, a movie of cinematic chiaroscuro where a glowing Devil appears out of the darkened mist, where Mephisto is rendered as looming over a Medieval German town with his bat-wings spread wide, the demon and the wizard briskly flying over a landscape of mountains, rivers, and small hamlets, while the diabolical contract is signed in glowing, bloody letters (an effect which took Murnau an entire day to film).

The broad contours of the movie are familiar; like Goethe, Murnau opens with a wager in heaven between the Devil and God, shades of Job's tribulations, except that if Mephisto successfully debases Faust, then the apocalypse will consume all of creation. There are other narrative novelties as well; this Mephisto entices Faust by giving him the ability to stave off a plague that is decimating his village, and the final scene of the film has the good doctor immolating himself alongside his beloved Gretchen who is being burned at the stake in punishment for a murder she is innocent of, the love of the wizard being enough to save the world from the Armageddon that would otherwise rightfully be Mephisto's purview.

Plot details are incidental, however, for the major Faustian theme remains the same—the demonic import of illusions, of being able to bend reality to your human will, of artistic inspiration and creation. "Do you want a woman, a card game, an orgy?" asks Mephisto, but it hardly matters, as now Faust has gained the ability to conjure something from nothing, the domain of God. "What you wish, I must fulfill it," says Mephisto, "Do you want the emperor's crown?"

As with all Faustian literature, the plot is thus self-referential, perhaps more so for a director of technical brilliance like Murnau, who conjured such miracles as if *he* were the wizard and not his title character. Along with the Soviet director Sergei Eisenstein and the American D. W. Griffith, Murnau is among the most consequential innovators of silent cinema. The first to use the camera to depict the perspective as seen by individual characters, the first to use the process of superimposition whereby two images overlap and thus convey what a character might be thinking, indeed the first to liberate the camera from its stationary position and *move* it about the set.

Like Copernicus nudging the earth along its rotation in the starry firmament, Murnau brought fluidity, change, and motion to film. Nearly a century later, *Faust* is still visually arresting, shocking even. In part this is because the artifice is obvious, for Murnau's film is not an example of *cinema verité*, but rather a carefully constructed dollhouse world generated by the god-director. In one scene using superim-position, which in its shades of light and dark appears as if a Gustave Doré print made flesh, the massive behorned and bestial Mephisto materializes behind a small Faust, who with his robes, long white beard, and clutched grimoire looks like a condemned Moses. Later in the film we see beautiful Gretchen in a veil, looking like a Medieval Virgin Mary. In another scene, we view behind the darkened sil-houette of Mephisto's head a glowing good angel framed by the caprine wings of the demon, a shocking contrast be-tween good and evil. To watch *Faust* is to witness a gothic illustration suddenly move, a magic trick worthy of a mage.

Faust would be the last of Murnau's German pictures before his move to Los Angeles, but as with *Nosferatu* which burnished his technical reputation but diminished his standing as a good investment, the former would be-come notorious for its role in bankrupting its producers.[4] Emil Jannings, the Swiss-born actor who played Mephisto as a round, roly-poly, nefarious, and nihilistic trickster, would come to his own dissolute Faustian ends. Acting opposite the icy brilliant Marlene Dietrich in Josef von Sternberg's *The Blue Angel*, Jannings would follow Murnau to Hollywood, winning the first Academy Award for Best Actor in von Sternberg's *The Last Command*, though the advent of sound ruined his American career as audiences found his thick German accent incomprehensible. Unlike Murnau and Dietrich, whose anti-fascist commitments were immaculate, Jannings had no trouble with complicity, returning to Germany and trading his actorly acumen for starring roles in several movies produced for the Reich.

Now Faustus rather than Mephistopheles, Jannings appeared in such films as Hans Steinhoff's 1935 *The Old and the Young King*, in a movie that extolled blind obedience to a leader, playing the eighteenth-century Prussian King Frederick William I; in Veit Harlan's 1937 *The Ruler*, about the owner of a munitions factory; and a historical slapstick comedy, *The Broken Jug*, supposedly a favorite of Hitler. Whatever the variable artistry of such films, they were still exercises in the way in which mass media could be put to certain incantatory purposes, for what was propaganda other than a variety of magic used to get people to do what you want them to do?[5] "The best propaganda is that which, as it were, works invisibly, penetrates the whole of life without the public having any knowledge of the propagandistic initiative," astutely wrote that rat-faced Nazi pustule Joseph Goebbels, Hitler's Minister of Propaganda who would confer the honor of *Staatsschauspieler*—"Artist of the State"—on Jannings. Here was an award that the actor could exhibit on his mantle alongside his Academy Award. In fact it was his little golden Oscar that Jannings would grab when the Americans occupied Germany, bringing it with him to vouch for his steadfast Yankeeness despite all the Nazi propaganda films he acted in, but the U.S. Army was unconvinced.

———

To make a film is to court the Faustian bargain, to claim for oneself a power which only rightfully belongs to God. There is an ugliness in such beauty, as the example of many Nazi propaganda films shows. Leni Riefenstahl's *Olympia* and *Triumph of the Will*, the former with its shots of athletic prowess and the later with its stunning opening scene of Hitler's airplane landing, are examples of how art is often not pure, how beauty can't exonerate everything, and how the all-encompassing vision of the director can often veer from the emotionally fascist to the actually fascist. "Director" and "dictator" only differ in a single phoneme, after all.

"I feel how inside of me word follows word and thought follows thought, growing to the last act of creation," wrote Goebbels in his 1929 novel *Michael,* a thinly veiled *roman a clef.* "Holy hour of bringing forth, you are pain and pleasure, and a longing for form, image, and essence . . . I am only the vessel that nature smilingly fills with new wine." Characteristically histrionic and lacking in any self-aware irony, Goebbels even sounds like Faust in his ejaculations, with his cankered fantasy of being a self-created god the same imperative which motivates the wizard in those permutations of the legend, but which also often motivates the most grandiose of film directors (and in the Minister of Propaganda's case, movie producer). Orson Welles, Alfred Hitchcock, Stanley Kubrick, Akira Kurosawa, Werner Herzog—F. W. Murnau. All have a reputation for being maximalists, for obsessive control and often cruelty against their stars, the *auteur* as Faustian figure. "Propaganda as such is neither good nor evil," Goebbels said at the 1934 Nuremberg Congress, "Its moral value is determined by the goals it seeks."

Both correct and ironic, it's true that film as a technology is neutral, that it can be put to the wicked uses of the Nazis, but also the sublime uses of Murnau. Even in the purest of motivations, though, a tinge of the Faustian persists in any of creation of this kind, the artistic prerogative to remake the world in our own image inevitably courting blasphemy, and sometimes unconsciously other evils as well. As unassailable as Murnau's own political convictions were, as a gay man and steadfast anti-Nazi, *Nosferatu* still disturbingly echoes some of the ugliest antisemitic imagery, even if that wasn't the director's intent.

There is an important lesson here—much as Faust's own incantations had a way of getting far beyond his own desires, so is artistic creation a spell that can have unintended consequences, and it's irrelevant if the one casting it may believe that she is in control. All art reflects the societies in which it is produced, working as handmaiden to culture, politics, and economics, even while a part of its soul may be transcendent. The films in which Jannings performed can't be separated from the spirit of the Faustian negotiations in which he made them, and Goebbels is distressingly correct that such movies must be read from the perspective of their goals. Berlin may have been defeated, but the utilitarian function of film to reshape a society's understanding of itself, to further certain goals, remained a central effect of the most accessible and arresting art form invented in the twentieth century.

That the "world wants to be deceived, has become truer than had ever been intended," wrote the German philosopher Theodor Adorno in the "Culture Industry Reconsidered." A pioneering founder of the Frankfurt School for Social Research, Adorno was a Jewish refugee who like Murnau and Mann had incongruously found himself in chipper Los Angeles. Because of his strong distaste for what he understood as the dangerous superficiality of American popular culture, Adorno developed a critique of the burgeoning film industry which understood movies and pop culture more generally as a dangerous form of enforcing ideological group think, whether in Nazi Berlin or capitalist Hollywood. What makes Adorno's analysis fascinating is that he speaks of the dangers of such pop culture in specifically Faustian terms, as the embrace of illusions of power at the cost of one's soul, only the soul that was in danger was a collective one, not just that of a single perfidious wizard.

"People are not only, as the saying goes, falling for the swindle," wrote Adorno, "if it guarantees them even the most fleeting gratification they desire a deception which is nonetheless transparent to them." Faust knows that Helen of Troy is just a chimera, yet he still desires that kiss. Adorno writes that people "force their eyes shut and voice approval, in a kind of self-loathing, for what is meted out to them, knowing fully the purpose for which it is manufactured." Today, Adorno can read as an elitist, a temperamental conservative who often got it wrong more than he got it right (his music criticism about jazz is tone-deaf to imbecilic). The philosopher may have been an elitist, insomuch as he was the beneficiary of a classical German education, but he was also a committed Marxist who thought that in the phrase "pop culture" the first word was indicative of the subject's dangerous superficiality and the second word was a contradiction. After all, even seemingly "progressive" contemporary critics celebrating the latest Marvel motion picture because of the producers' pose as seemingly tolerant of "inclusion" and "representation" seem to forget that the movie business is first and foremost a *business*. So, who better to fricassee the golden calves of the entertainment industry than a Marxist?

Remember that Adorno was not critiquing American culture from the vantage point of rarefied Europe, but rather from within his Santa Monica home, the professor a vital member of the German émigré community. Adrift from their home nation in the process of immolating itself and Western civilization more generally, these German intellectuals, artists, and leftists nonetheless had trouble footing themselves in the New World, especially in the simulacra of Los Angeles. For the task of Hollywood, according to Adorno, was the manufacture of not just dreams, but delusions, the propagation of more than fantasies, but of conformity. Hollywood produces propaganda no less than any other authoritarian state, work dedicated to obscuring the contradictions of capitalism and of making inequities and injustices appear pleasing, just as a demon can come disguised as a great beauty.

Bertolt Brecht, the Marxist playwright briefly turned studio screenwriter, decried in a poem how the "city is named for the angels, / And its angels are easy to find. / They give off a lubricant odor, / Their eyes are mascara-lined / At night you can see them inserting / Gold-plated diaphragms; / For breakfast they gather at poolside / Where screenwriters feed and swim." Attuned to the ways in which culture, even high culture (maybe especially high culture), can be used as part of a totalitarian project, Adorno's denunciation of Hollywood had nothing to do with the content of films. He was not a prude or a puritan, whether an actress flashed some flesh or a gangster got shot on screen was irrelevant to Adorno.[6]

Rather for Adorno it was the medium itself, later joined by television, and the way in which illusion could be used to obscure material reality, to flummox and cajole an audience into their alienation. Movies, it turns out, are the opiate of the masses (along with television and the internet). "Capitalist production so confines them, body and soul, that they fall helpless victims to what is offered them," writes Adorno with his colleague Max Horkheimer in their seminal *Dialectic of Enlightenment*. Steadfast materialist though the Marxists may have been, Adorno and Horkheimer still draw from a resolutely theological vocabulary, a mythic rhetoric. They speak of the "soul" and of a mass of "victims" falling prey to that which is "offered them," an obvious Faustian turn, except that all who are enraptured by mass media (all of us) are those who risk damnation.

What makes the capitalist dream industry so insidious, but also vampirically brilliant, is that it subsumes and cannibalizes all cultural critiques; any rebelliousness or even revolutionary sentiment can be harnessed to sell T-shirts and televisions, Alexa and androids. American pop culture, yoked to its master, industrial production, is sustained on trillions of gallons of bullshit derived from those two iconic streets, Madison Avenue in the east and Sunset Boulevard in the west. Authoritarian regimes extol the virtues of conformity in their propaganda, but capitalist propaganda is much more subtle, convincing people that they're rebels when they sustain the status quo, what Adorno describes as the "manipulation of taste [through] . . . the official culture's pretense of individualism." *Think different*, after all.

Don't misinterpret my pretense as being one of moral superiority, I'd gladly sign a Hollywood contract if one was before me, and I spend hours streaming television just like everybody else. Whether or not there is such a thing as ethical consumption under capitalism—or at all—is a question I have no means to answer, but I do know that we're all cosignatories of the Faustian contract. Maybe even more so when it comes to great art, or even mediocre art, whether watched on the big screen or the smart phone. When considering the mutual spiritual incriminations of the entertainment-industrial complex, there are Devil's bargains aplenty.

———

During the Golden Age of Hollywood, studios like Metro-Goldwyn Mayer, Paramount, Warner Brothers, Twentieth Century-Fox, and RKO had a monopoly on film production, a parsimonious model of corporate vertical integration where every aspect of making movies—of making *dreams*—was controlled by the system. Actors and actresses indebted to the studios often had little creative freedom. Clark Gable, Jimmy Stewart, and Judy Garland effectively owned by MGM, Shirley Temple and Betty Grable in the stable of Twentieth Century-Fox, working-class Warner Brothers with tough guys like Edward G. Robinson, James Cagney, and Humphrey Bogart, RKO dancing with Fred and Ginger and then Dietrich to Paramount. What was sold was glamor and elegance, bravery and toughness, wealth and beauty.

Not that performers were the only people within the industry to be enticed by such promise, for what writer wouldn't want the opportunity to see such a thankless art elevated into the Hollywood hills, as William Faulkner, F. Scott Fitzgerald, and even the communist Brecht understood. "Every day, I go to earn my bread / In the exchange where lies are marketed" writes Brecht, "Hoping my own lies will attract a bid." Not that implicated art which is still brilliant should be understood as anything less than still brilliant—were it so easy to conflate aesthetics and ethics (or the latter's debased sibling mere politics). But that filmmaking is a business—that must never be forgotten when signing on the dotted line. "It's Hell, it's Heaven," writes Brecht, "the amount you earn / Determines if you play the harp or burn."

The Faustian narrative has always evoked commerce; the central conceit of the fable is the signing of a contract after all. Yet even if Mephistopheles is riven through all of capitalist interaction, from the manager to the laborer, the producer to the consumer, eternally buying and selling back-and-forth for profits gained and souls lost (and biomes destroyed along the way), the nature of the entertainment industry can't help but feel even more on point. It's a bit abstract to say that the production of lug nuts and gears is Faustian (even if it is), but the manufacture of *fantastical, dream-like illusions* rendered on celluloid two stories high or available anywhere on earth via the silicon oracle in your pocket would have been rightly judged as powerful magic by our ancestors.

Far more than the ways in which Hollywood Babylon
ensnares everyone from screenwriter to performer, director
to moviegoer, is the undeniable, luminescent splendor of the
entire endeavor. Watch Lloyd Bacon's fluffy 1933 musical
Footlight Parade, in which James Cagney plays a Broadway
theater director who turns toward movies when they
threaten his livelihood (nobody interrogates Hollywood
quite like itself). *Footlight Parade* features the stunning
sequence remembered as "The Human Waterfall," cho-
reographed by Busby Berkeley. Over three hundred lithe,
synchronized swimmers in spangly, rhinestone-encrusted
bathing suits tumble off twenty different platforms into a
massive pool. Berkeley's dance sequences are captured by
Bacon's camera shifting from forward to above; dancers
are seen swimming between a regimented row of their colleagues' legs, while linking arms the swimmers make various complex geometric shapes within the pool as seen from
a bird's-eye view, at one point appearing as if an opening
flower whose petals are composed of beautiful women,
all of it culminating in a massive, rotating pyramid of the
dancers rising from the water.

Glitz and glamour, beauty and elegance, all captured
on celluloid forever, miraculously still viewable nearly
a century later. Even Faust's phantoms dissipated after
a few minutes. The cost of a ticket to *Footlight Parade*
was a quarter, coincidentally the same percentage of the
population then unemployed. Per Adorno, was something
like Bacon's movie merely a means of anesthetizing the

populace during the Great Depression? Or was it a glimpse of transcendence in the dross, an intimation of a utopia, a paradise, a heaven? It can be both. Remember that in Murnau's *Faust* the wizard gains the ability to cure the plague. We need not always condemn the bargain.

Naturally the Faustian contract itself has always been a popular subject for film. In Stanley Donan's 1967 comedy *Bedazzled* a loser played by Dudley Moore exchanges his soul to the Devil for several wishes that naturally unravel. Some thirty-two years later the remake replaced the modish Satan played by Peter Cook with a sexy Elizabeth Hurley. Taylor Hackford's 1997 *The Devil's Advocate* features several Faustian bargains in a supposedly serious horror film which reads as an extended lawyer joke, in which Al Pacino at his most Al Pacino-y plays an attorney with the spot-on-name of John Milton, predictably the Devil trying to ensnare a young, idealistic public defender performed by Keanu Reeves affecting an amazingly awful grits-and-biscuits Southern accent. The Coen Brothers' 2000 masterpiece *O Brother, Where Art Thou?* is a retelling of Homer's *Odyssey*, but a side-plot features their associations with the historically based bluesman Tommy Johnson, and a silent and terrifying Devil in the form of a taciturn Southern sheriff in aviator glasses who stalks them across the kudzu grassed landscape.

—

No film since Murnau, however, most fully exemplifies all the Faustian themes implicit in the art form than Roman Polanski's magisterial 1968 adaptation of Ira Levin's airport novel, *Rosemary's Baby*. Moving into the stately Dakota apartments on Central Park West when it was still conceivable that regular people could afford to live at such an address, struggling actor Guy Woodhouse as played with smarmy efficacy by John Cassavetes agrees to allow a Satanic witch's coven secretly operating in their building to impregnate his drugged wife, brilliantly performed by an ethereal Mia Farrow, all in exchange for his own professional stage success.

Farrow's Rosemary skulks through the streets of an increasingly claustrophobic Manhattan, privy to strange nightmares and the seeming sound of occult chanting through her thin apartment walls. Polanski imbues the bustle of New York with an insular paranoia, as Rosemary begins to (rightly) distrust her neighbors, her doctor, her husband. Flashing back to the night of her unborn child's conception, Rosemary has visions of clawed hands upon her naked body, of blood-red inhuman eyes staring unblinkingly at her. "This is no dream, this is really happening!" she screams as Satan writhes above her, the Devil seen by the audience only in parts, for his entirety is presumably too horrific to portray.

Rosemary has been traded without consent to this unnoticed coven operating within the crowded city, everybody using her for their own gain (not a terrible metaphor for the ingenue in Hollywood). Throughout *Rosemary's Baby*, Polanski embraces a distressing ambiguity as to whether her emotions are merited or the ephemera of a diseased consciousness, at least until the disturbing conclusion wherein Rosemary finally sees her baby and asks what has been done to make his eyes look so bestial, so inhuman. "He has his father's eyes," one of the members of the coven at this "christening" says, as Rosemary finally walks over to the baby with an unmistakable maternal affection.

Psychologically horrific in large part because of what the director doesn't show on screen, the infamous grifter and self-declared Pope of the Church of Satan Anton LaVey claimed that he had been hired by Polanski as an expert consultant, and that indeed it was his hands within the fur-covered claws grasping at Farrow's breasts and his eyes staring at the actress. Such a claim would appeal to a certain conspiratorial-minded understanding of Hollywood Babylon, yet nobody involved in the production of *Rosemary's Baby*, least of all Polanski, has confirmed LaVey's assertion. The shaved headed and vandyke-bearded devil in a magician's cape, LaVey appeared every bit a Satan from central casting, the best evidence against him being the demon in the conception scene from *Rosemary's Baby* is that nothing about the huckster was scary enough for that role. Besides, the admitted child rapist Polanski was a far more terrifying creature than LaVey, because actual evil has no need for pentagrams or icons of the goat-headed Baphomet.

For a brief period LaVey gained notoriety hosting Black Masses at his San Francisco church, which featured celebrities from Sammy Davis Jr. to Jayne Mansfield, and from where he promulgated in such works as *The Satanic Bible* an infantile philosophy cobbled together from Nietzsche, Ayn Rand, H. L. Mencken, and Aleister Crowley. Perhaps celebrities were drawn to LaVey's injunction within his *Bible* that the "highest of all holidays in the Satanic religion is the date of one's own birth." Despite the pyrotechnics offered at the Church of Satan, and the fevered imagination of Christian fundamentalists who believed LaVey's group to be an actual coven, the church was essentially a vanity performance art project combined with a pyramid scheme. LaVey was far more in the American tradition of the carnival barker than anything really nefarious.

The truth is always more mundane than any Black Mass or witches' Sabbath; how we're all implicated in the disorder of this fallen world, because evil is always far more banal. If LaVey had any insight, it was in his commandment that the "Satanist believes in complete gratification of his ego," for that is also the axiom on which our entire society depends, the calculus of supply-and-demand stoked by advertising and reflected in entertainment. Which is why *Rosemary's Baby* remains the foremost Faustian narrative about entertainment itself—Woodhouse after all trades his wife's body and his own soul for success as an *actor*. However the most cognoscente of Faustian explorations of the American ethos in its entirety is a far different film.

American director Robert Eggers's folk horror triumph, the 2015 movie *The Witch: A New-England Folktale,* made the same year that Murnau's skull was filched, seems unimaginably distant from Hollywood glamour, yet in running the American dream backward from Sunset Boulevard to the colonial city on a hill it fully excavates the Faustian bargain which birthed our civilization, with popular culture being but the most potent manifestation of that contract. Unlike *Rosemary's Baby,* Eggers' film doesn't feature elegant interiors or mid-century chic, but rather a Puritan family consigned to the howling wilderness of Massachusetts in the 1630s, punished for some unspecified heresy. There the fervent farmer William, his wife, their two young twins, his pre-teen son, and his adolescent daughter Katherine must live out their sentencing, struggling to survive in the harsh and unforgiving New World of blizzards and heatwaves, Nor'easters and draughts.

In the bleached and gnarled New England countryside, there are intimations of the supernatural, indications of William's beliefs in the unseen forces which conspire to tempt a man to perdition. Much is made by Eggers of the family's goat Black Philip, the slit-pupiled, horned, and bearded animal as ominous as any other goat, which is to say a bit. Like Polanski's film, *The Witch* engages a studied and coiled ambiguity; throughout the movie we're to consider that the paranoia and terror which the family experiences results from William's Puritan self-abnegation, their entire religious cosmology born from repressions projected outward. By the end, the audience discovers that the family's fears are justified, all members of the brood slaughtered in various violent ways except for Katherine, played by an otherworldly Anya Taylor-Joy who in her beauty evokes Farrow in *Rosemary's Baby*. Black Philip finally reveals himself to be if not the Devil, than certainly a demon, his croaking off-camera voice asking "Dost thou enjoy the taste of butter?"

What a temptation for the body-denying Puritan, what a prosaic enticement! Despite the old-timey inflection, Black Philip's question could almost be the tagline for a Madison Avenue commercial. "Dost thou wish to live deliciously?" Black Philip asks Katherine, before she disrobes and signs her name in the Devil's book, levitating alongside the coven she has joined. Popular culture then offers a particular American Faustian contract, not the wisdom of Marlowe or the power of Goethe, but simply the "complete gratification of . . . ego," as LaVey claimed, the promise to "live deliciously" as Black Philip said. Returning to our beginnings, Eggers's *The Witch* bluntly states that simple American maxim, whereby the national birthright is traded for a mess of pottage, the soul exchanged for butter, or Coca-Cola, Levi's, McDonald's, and the latest bit of Hollywood escapism.

CHAPTER THIRTEEN

THE DESTROYER OF WORLDS: CONDEMNED TO APOCALYPSE IN THE FAUSTOCENE

Just as Faust faces unintended consequences from his interactions with Mephistopheles, AI systems can have unforeseen outcomes.
—Chat GPT-3 (2023)

John Dee, the court astrologer to Queen Elizabeth I and the possessor of the largest library in the entirety of England, believed that a pitch-black obsidian scrying mirror in his possession, originally used as a ritual object by the Aztecs, was a powerful tool of divination.[1] Staring into the smooth surface of the flat circular stone, seeing his own face with his long tapered white beard and black skullcap reflected back at him—every bit the Prospero, or Faustus—Dee believed that he was able to contact the angelic realm, speaking to spirits fluent in Enochian, a language older than creation itself and spoken in the astral realms.

In his 1570 treatise *The Mathematical Preface to Elements of Geometry of Euclid of Megara*, Dee claimed that he was dealing in a "science whose subject is so ancient, so pure, so excellent, so surrounding all creatures, so used of the almighty and incomprehensible wisdom of the Creator." This is not how "science" would come to be understood. Dee's science wasn't inductive or empirical, it didn't trade in peer review or rigorous experimentation, it didn't test hypotheses or build mathematical models, it didn't construct predictive theories. Truths ascertained by Dee were derived from mystical experience of unseen forces, from the assortment of hermetic symbols and numerological calculation, from magical ritual.

Science as it's understood today, derives from a philosopher who lived a generation after Dee. Francis Bacon argued that knowledge is acquired through "simple sensuous perception," from the observation of material reality. According to Bacon in his 1620 tract *Novum Organum*, there is a single unassailable methodology for "searching into and discovering truth," which involves the derivation of "axioms from the senses and particulars, rising by a gradual and unbroken ascent, so that it arrives at the most general axioms last of all." Dee sought truth—like Prospero, like Faustus—in the "metaphysics of magicians," as Marlowe wrote, from the manipulation of ancient symbol and by staring into the black abyss of an Aztec mirror. Bacon, instead, believed that truth could be found in the careful design of experiments and their replicability, in the measurement of results and the refinement of data, for this "is the true way," as he argues, while mournfully concluding that it is "yet untried." But it would be.

Bacon has been the victor over Dee, for while the latter may have concurred with Marlowe's Faustus that "necromantic books, are heavenly," the former had the benefit of results. Wizards like Dee held to a faith that from their scrying mirror they were speaking to angels, that Enochian truths were imparted through arcane rituals, but Baconian empiricism led to the entire technological revolution. Dee wrote in poetry and prophecy, but those in Bacon's wake invented the steam engine and the telegraph, the airplane and the space shuttle, the computer and the internet—and the atom bomb. Technologies that Dee would have thought indistinguishable from the magic.

The partisans of Bacon are Kepler and Newton, Maxwell and Rutherford, Einstein, Bohr, and Oppenheimer. Those who work in the tradition of Dee are charlatans and weirdos, grifters and hacks, cranks and quacks. The world in which we live is very much Bacon's, even if our dreams are those of Dee. What this can obscure, however, are *just how similar Dee and Bacon were*. Both believed that ours was a world of unseen forces and that the adept could manipulate those forces, giving humanity tremendous power. "Human power and human knowledge meet in one," Bacon enthused, and if that describes a necromancer's vocation, the philosopher can't be faulted for having predicted such figures, albeit today we call them scientists.

Protons, neutrons, and electrons are measurable; gravity, electromagnetism, the nuclear forces are tangible; quantum fluctuations and singularities are verifiable, all these natural phenomena circumscribed by deductive mathematics and inductive observation, but in the intrinsic essentials of their nature, what they are—their *thing-in-itself* being—is as inscrutable as angels and demons. An atomic nucleus has a more measurable effect, more oomph if you will, than do the creatures which Dee believed himself to be communicating with, and while that's not unimportant, it's also not everything. Physics has about it a spookiness, for no less a partisan of empiricism than Newton could describe that his mechanics were as if "sacred Prophecy . . . [with] light for glory, truth, and knowledge, wherewith great and good men shine and illuminate others."

Perhaps then the greatest difference between Dee and Bacon wasn't in perspective, faith, or even interpretation, but merely in efficacy. Now our demons aren't chimeras, but machines—Mephistopheles in the guise of a computer, a locomotive, an atom bomb.

———

There is a different scrying mirror now, no longer the smooth black obsidian of Dee, but the altogether darker surface of our computer and cellphone screens. Our contracts are written not in blood but silicon, and Mephistopheles is now named artificial intelligence, his illusions called simulations, virtual reality, deep fakes.[2] During the period I wrote this book, journalists and online denizens became enraptured with the possibilities of artificial intelligence, of entire novels penned by a computer or movies and films generated from the subconscious ephemera of the digital ghost in machine. Seemingly realistic photographs of people who never lived gestated by prompts fed to computers, often hard to distinguish from that which actually exists. An uncanny tell however, as artificial intelligence is unable to properly render hands as of now, so smiling partygoers and beautiful models dreamt from the digital demon can have seven, or eight fingers per hand. In Medieval folklore, it was said that you could identify the Devil passing as a man by looking at his bestial feet. Both AI and Satan seem to be lacking in that particular expertise of illusion.

Mephistopheles' traces can be detected in the thought experiment known as "Roko's Basilisk." First appearing on the internet community board Less Wrong in 2010, a site devoted to techno-utopian thought, this hypothetical creature was named after the commentator handle of its author and the legendary, deadly, medieval reptilian monster known as the basilisk. Roko posited the idea that at some future date, after what futurists call the "Singularity" occurs, when artificial intelligence has completely outstripped humanity and achieved omnipotent powers, that an AI might exist which will punish anyone who has not actively worked toward its eventual existence and that we refuse to enter into covenant with such a being at our own peril. Furthermore, Roko's basilisk is capable of generating completely realistic virtual reality simulations where even after you're dead it can resurrect and punish you for not having done your technological due diligence in ensuring its creation. What caused horror among some of the contributors to Less Wrong was that knowing about Roko's basilisk but choosing not to work toward its incarnation was what ultimately threatened your (simulated) immortal soul, like a potential convert rejecting the one true God.

Equal parts Satan and John Calvin's god (though those are perhaps the same deity), Roko's Basilisk is clearly a being born of faith and not of reason. Atheists may be rife among the techno-utopian set, yet whether a believer in the Singularity identifies as an atheist, the fear and trembling before Roko's Basilisk is undoubtedly religious in nature, despite Less Wrong's claims to rationality.[3] Because the digital Calvinists of Less Wrong, and other assorted communities awaiting the technological Singularity, very much do fear Roko's Basilisk.

Eliezer Yudkowsky, the founder and moderator of Less Wrong and a respected figure in the AI research community, took the step of banning discussion of Roko's Basilisk from the message board, writing of Roko that "You have to be really clever to come up with a genuinely dangerous thought. I am disheartened that people can be clever enough to do that and not clever enough to do the obvious thing and KEEP THEIR IDIOT MOUTHS SHUT" (capitalization in the original). The concept itself became an internet meme, a technological urban legend like Slender Man or the stories of creepypasta willed into a type of reality. Elon Musk and Grimes supposedly kindled their (now dead) romance over an affinity for the thought experiment. And meanwhile, the subject remained banned on Less Wrong.

Roko repented for any offense caused and to the community whom he infected with his infernal *Gedankenexperiment*, contritely writing that he wished "very strongly that my mind had never come across the tools to inflict such large amounts of self-harm." What then is this other than Faust abjuring his magic books because he fears damnation?

We need not believe in an absurdity like Roko's Basilisk to see how a whiff of sulfur has comingled with silicon, how the leaders of the tech-industry have both embraced a quasi-mystical form of thinking while also trading away our human sovereignty in favor of digital capitalism which is itself a variety of sublimated faith. These are the penitents before the Singularity, the aforementioned collection of thinkers who believe that we're on the precipice of a massive technological, and thus psychological, cultural, social, and economic shift, as the computational powers of our machines completely surpass the abilities of their creators.[4]

For these figures, including respected scholars like

Ray Kurzweil and Hans Moravec, as well as robber baron
industrialists like Musk and Peter Thiel, the Singularity
looms, a messiah in silicon that will completely alter consciousness once our machines begin to think. Theirs is a
creed which holds that we'll be resurrected as immortals
in a future computer simulation, ushered into eternal life
by the apocalyptic arrival of a messianic moment. Whether
through Christ or computer, the theology isn't hard to
spot, even if it comes from avowed materialists.[5] For all the
mockery and criticism heaped on transhumanism, they're
not wrong to sense something of the sacred in technology.
Old gods must be continually born again, even as we assume secularity has killed them.[6]

From the strange case of Roko's Basilisk, I draw a number of conclusions. The fervency of those transhumanists
who imbue technology with a sense of the sacred (regardless of whether they'd identify it as such) shows the sturdy
endurance of the religious dimension. Even as it was long
taken as a given among some historians and political scientists that faith would somehow wither away in the modern
world, there can be no abolishment of any category called
"Religion," for that category merely refers to meaning
making, and as long as there are people (or artificial intel-
ligences) there will be a need for meaning.

From the supercomputers all of us carry in our pockets and that have rendered humans veritable cyborgs, to
the massive web of influence that we call the internet and
the often-detrimental effects of social media, the current

technological revolution is arguably its own type of Great Awakening. As much as Roko's Basilisk as a concept deserves disdain, the reality is that self-aware Artificial Intelligence, whether malevolent, benevolent, or something else, will surely be developed sooner rather than later. Such a development requires a cognoscente religious response. The ghost is very much in the machine, and it's impervious to exorcism.

Great moments of technological change often herald religious changes; by the nineteenth century connections were already being drawn between evangelicalism and technological change. A new religious enthusiasm arrived with the steam-locomotive and the telegraph, so that in 1829 Jacob Bigelow, a Harvard professor of Physical and Mathematical Sciences, could remark that "Next to the influence of Christianity on our moral nature," it was the new innovations which most had a "leading sway in promoting . . . progress and happiness." Whether true or not, it was clear that faith spread over the wire and preachers traveling by train had altered America's religious landscape once again. Is it any wonder that the digital revolution will bring about similar shifts in religion, and new Faustian bargains to consider?

———

The Fitchburg Railroad ran a little under fifty miles between its origin in Boston and its terminus. At the Concord station, a bit before the halfway point, the train glided along the western edge of Walden Pond. By the time in 1845 that the celebrated Transcendentalist Henry David Thoreau had gone to the "woods because I wished to live deliberately, to front only the essential facts of life," and had made his home in that small cabin, the Fitchburg Railroad had been operating for a year, built by underpaid, exploited Irish immigrant labor. Making its daily devotionals every day of the year, the Fitchburg thundered alongside the glacial kettle pond during chill New England winter with its frost-tipped pines and the pleasant cool summer days with oak's greenness, past spring's blooming lilac and dogwood and the autumnal maples' red, orange, and brown.

Having conditioned himself to listen to the black-capped chickadee and the song sparrow, to rain lashing against his cedar timber roof or the squalls of winter nor'easters, Thoreau's reveries were interrupted twice a day by the bestial whistle of the Luciferian locomotive as it made its way west and east. He did not like it. "We do not ride the railroad," Thoreau wrote in his 1854 *Walden; or, Life in the Woods*, "it rides upon us." Contemplating industrial capitalism's effect on the globe in the seventeen decades since, Thoreau didn't know the half of it.

Remembering *Walden* only as the account of an eccentric, quasi-hermit living on the edge of a Massachusetts bean field in the woods outside of Concord obscures how much of Thoreau's book is about not nature, per se, but the *transformation* of nature. Massive changes were underway on this continent that from the Atlantic to the Pacific had been valorized as Edenic since the first European saw land which didn't belong to them; steamboat and train, telegraph and factory all refashioned a very different landscape.[7] Were this an interruption only of the countryside's quietude that would be one thing, but the train signaled the beginning of our Anthropocene, when humanity's rapacious consumption of the earth for material gain altered the geology, ecology, and biology of the planet.[8]

It's estimated that because of the mass burning of coal—a nineteenth-century train's engine is powered by coal after all—the average temperature throughout the world rose a single degree Celsius during the nineteenth century, from when steam locomotives became common about three decades before the Fitchburg Railroad rumbled through Massachusetts (the average temperature rose almost another degree in the last century). Victorian scientists were aware of this connection; physicist Joseph Fourier, writing in an 1837 edition of *The American Journal of Science and Arts* hypothesized that industrial exhaust "must produce variations in the mean temperature for such places," while in 1856—two years after *Walden*'s publication—and Eunice Newton Foote wrote in *The American Journal of Science* that "An atmosphere of . . . [carbon dioxide] would give to our earth a high temperature." Steamrolling toward a distant apocalypse, and Emerson, on whose land Thoreau resided, writes in his journal about how he hears the "whistle of the locomotive in the woods . . . it is prophetic." More than they could have realized, for such progress over the past century-and-a-half now threatens to push the world toward an irrevocable climate catastrophe.

As the Intergovernmental Panel on Climate Change concluded in their 2021 report, we are at "code red for humanity," with one of the coauthors telling the American Association for the Advancement of Science that there's "really one key message that emerges from this report: We are out of time."[9] Rather than merely the punctured idyl of a Concord evening, the Anthropocene's dark promise is ever-rising temperatures and disappearing shorelines, massive raging wild fires and blighted crops, vicious new pandemics and billions of refugees, ocean acidification and the earth's sixth great extinction. More than just a whistle in the dark, the more potent image of what the train might represent was expressed by Thoreau and Emerson's contemporary Connecticut Senator James Lanman, who in his survey *Railroads of the United States* called locomotives "iron monsters . . . dragons of mightier power, with iron muscles . . . breathing smoke and flame through their blackened lungs," these demons which leap "forward like some black monster, upon its iron path, by the light of the fire and smoke which it promises forth." Lanman understood the attraction, for despite their sulphury breath, locomotives are "triumphs of our own age, the laurels of mechanical philosophy, of untrammeled mind, and a liberal commerce!"

That is the great paradox of the Anthropocene, the

knowledge that industry and technology are killing our world but that we remain addicted. Such irrationality can't be explained away by recourse to simple economic analysis, to the materialist's fantasy that reason, logic, and utility explicate the ways of humanity. What it requires is the theological imagination, the poetic imagination, the vocabulary of avarice, greed, and vaingloriousness. If there is any myth which has spoken to modernity, especially regarding this ecological precipice, then it's that master poem of the Romantic period (of which Transcendentalism was only one small branch), Goethe's *Faust*, begun in 1790 and completed in 1831, the decade before Thoreau moved into his little cabin.[10]

Thoreau's landlord was abundantly aware of Goethe's opus, if conflicted about its merits, Emerson noting in his 1863 *Historic Notes of Life and Letters in New England* that "the great poem of the age is the disagreeable poem of Faust." Yet writing at the dawn of the Anthropocene, with his *Faust* in part a critique of the rationalist Enlightenment instrumentalism which would literally fuel the coming industrial revolution, Goethe's work speaks to this moment of rising temperatures and sea levels. Even more than during Emerson's century, Faust is the operative myth for today.[11]

Faust is our operative myth because it expresses the madness of a culture collectively endeavoring to bring about the apocalypse all for the piddling convenience that a fossil fuel economy provides. Through his infernal contract, Faust is given certain abilities—he can transport himself anywhere in the world instantly, he has access to all knowledge, he can spy on people unseen—but of course the cost is his soul. What use would he have of Mephistopheles in our century, when Faust could affectively have the same abilities imparted through his smart phone, social media, and the twenty-four-hour convenience of Amazon shipping? "Him will I drag through life's wild waste, / Through scenes of vapid dullness," Mephistopheles says, and it might as well describe the experience of endlessly perusing Twitter, anesthetizing yourself from calamity to calamity as you doom scroll.

Our days are marked by a litany of Faustian contracts whose central incantation is the "terms of service," in which the relationship is non-negotiable, pre-drafted, and standardized. We click "Accept" on the multitude of apps and platforms which dominate our consciousness, our realities, and unlike Faust we don't even pause to consider the affect it has on our souls. All our personal information, exchanged for the dopamine rush of the "Like" or the "Retweet," our digital soul uploaded to Facebook and Twitter and Instagram, so that the basest and most superficial aspects of our identities can be unnervingly re-created by the Mephistophelean algorithm, our very selves translated into a homunculus of Big Data that could very well exist long beyond our mortal bodies. So omnipresent is social media, especially considering its disturbingly short history, that we too often glibly click our assent when Big Data asks for our souls. In exchange we receive the excitement of adoration and rage, of blinkered self-importance and of being able to shout into the simulacra's void, celebrities in our own estimation, for the algorithm tells us that we're important. "Ah, what a sense of your own greatness must / You have," Faust's servant Wagner says to him, an apt description of our own ever narcissistic, ever insular perspectives which retreat into microscopic granularity, even while the world burns (though that does provide opportunity for a great Instagram background). Mephistopheles remains the animating spirit of modernity as it had emerged in the nineteenth century, his motivating principle a utilitarian doctrine which sees both nature and other people as tools in the furthering of the individual's own desires. "Ich bin der Geist der stets verneint!" the demon tells Faust—"I am the spirit of perpetual negation."

Faustian spiritual malaise and our ongoing tragedy of the Anthropocene are not distinct, they are mutually reinforcing. A reduction of the earth's resources to something that provides mere convenience for us and unimaginable wealth for a corrupt few requires a jaded worldview, a denial of the blessedness of the earth (and of those who inhabit it).[12] Few adjectives more clearly describe such a situation as much as "Faustian," since as the magician foolishly gives away something of infinite value for the transient and illusory pleasures offered by Mephistopheles, so too does industrial capitalism sacrifice the environment for idols of wealth and myths of progress. The necromancer's individual negotiation yielded him the appearance of omniscient powers for a time, and the price was damnation; we've been collectively offered oil, gas, and coal, and the cost is nothing less than apocalypse. What makes Faust such a potent myth is that, no matter how corrupted his rewards may have been, his all-too-human desires for power, meaning, significance, and intimacy, are immaculately understandable. He is not without sympathy.

Merely identifying the spirit of our age with a term from cultural mythology clearly won't reduce the carbon dioxide in the atmosphere and transition the global economy toward one more humane and sustainable. Yet if there is any central proposition of demonology, it's that even if you can't control them completely, there is still a power in knowing the names of those creatures which bedevil you, whether Mammon, Moloch, or Mephistopheles. One need not literally believe in such entities—I don't—but mythopoesis does allow us to measure the enormity of that which we're up against.

Even more important, to understand the Anthropocene's negotiations as Faustian is a reminder that much like the good doctor, we shouldn't take those partisans of supply-side orthodoxy at their word that this system is "rational." Anything which proposes unsustainable and dangerous growth to the detriment of the biosphere is the exact opposite of rational, courting apocalypse for the benefit of imaginary numbers on a computer screen just like Faust falling in love with chimerical illusions conjured by Satan.

What the designation of "Faustian" does is identify liber-tarianism, neo-liberalism, and all manner of capitalistic en-thusiasms as what they are—not economics, but religion. The relationship between free markets and faith has been noted since Max Weber's 1905 *The Protestant Ethic and the Spirit of Capitalism*; he was abundantly aware of the irrationality at the core of a system in which economic "striving becomes understood completely as an end in it-self—to such an extent that it appears as fully outside the normal course of affairs and simply irrational."[13] The only way to understand the irrationalities of capitalism, espe-cially at this point in our history, is to comprehend that it's the dominant religion of our world and age: the Lord is the Invisible Hand, its priests are those titans of industry, the liturgy is commercialism, and the rites are sacrificial—a dark ritual with the entirety of the biosphere upon the altar. Capitalism is now no longer simply a means of orga-nizing labor and money, distributing commodities and as-signing them monetary value, but rather a dark faith unto itself. The goal is unlimited growth and ever more capital for a smaller and smaller group of people, even while all our futures are endangered.

Moloch, the Lord of utilitarian reductions and blood sacrifices, has been slowly wakening over the past five cen-turies. We see him in the thought-experiment of the eigh-teenth-century physicist Pierre-Simon Laplace, a demon who is aware of the position, trajectory, and velocity of every single particle in the universe, and thus according to the mathematician can predict every aspect of a predestined future with perfect accuracy, all of consciousness, intentionality, and freedom now mere numbers on a ledger. We see Moloch in the grim scholasticisms of Calvin who prayed to a God which existed purely for Himself, every bit the same fatalistic tyrant as Laplace's demon. And now Moloch reaches his apotheosis with Adam Smith's invisible hand around all our necks. Such men, puritans and positivists alike, valorized the word "rationalism" as a kind of shibboleth which masked something malignant at the core, envisioning economics, the universe, and God as a type of hyper-efficient and carefully assembled steam engine, but now the boiler is overheating and the entire thing threatens to explode.

"Storms, earthquakes, fire and flood assail the land" says Mephistopheles, though he sounds like somebody reading their newsfeed. Should the Anthropocene reach its terminus when, despite its name, it becomes impossible for the planet to sustain human life, then capitalism will have revealed itself as the most disastrous ideology in history. Or, perhaps more accurately, not capitalism or technology per se, but those powerful individuals which view both of those things as an end unto themselves rather than as a means unto an end. Right now we're at an impasse— there is a new, global, political, and spiritual reawakening from the movement Extinction Rebellion to Pope Francis's encyclical *Laudato sí* which attempts to imagine a more equitable future—but there's also the enthusiasms of the Lords of Capital, none more so than the confidence men of Silicon Valley who like Jeff Bezos shoot octogenarian actors into space or like Musk tinker with monkey brains, praying to Moloch's final incarnation in the form of the techno-utopian Singularity, their creed being nothing less than Faust's injunction "Bin ich ein Gott? Mir wird so licht!"—"Am I a god? Light fills my mind."

Few political movements have been more effectively tarred than the Luddites who agitated among the textile mills of England a generation before Thoreau, men who understood that mechanization signaled their economic obsolescence, and thus under capitalism their extinction. Far from being antiquated bumpkins, they were radicals attacking the instrumentalism of unfettered technology. It's not technology that's the problem—it's the doctrine that it's something more than a tool, that in fact we're tools for *it*. When Thoreau heard the locomotive's whistle, his fear was that rather than riding the train the train was riding upon us. The central economic, political, ethical, and spiritual question of the remainder of this century—no matter how much time we actually might have left—is how to stall that engine so that we're able to get off of the tracks. How to finally void the contract that our ancestors signed.

———

So then, still another scrying mirror, though more in how it was created than anything, reflecting back modernity to its own necromancers working in the baking New Mexican desert in the spring of 1945. Trinitite, a glass which unlike obsidian was made not by God, but only by humanity, first appeared on this earth in the last months of the most destructive war which had happened yet. Composed from an alchemy of quartz and feldspar, calcite and augite, plagioclase and arkose which constituted the fine white sands of Alamogordo, trinitite was produced on July 16th of that year when the first plutonium-based atomic bomb detonated, fusing those ingredients at temperatures of a hundred million degrees Celsius, the hypocenter of the device briefly five times hotter than the sun.

Mostly a shade of green reminiscent of the jade implements used by the Aztec priests who were the original possessors of Dee's device, trinitite rained down from the aftermath of that nuclear explosion in irregularly shaped globoids and spheroids, a shattering of vessels which existed for a few seconds within the intense white hot promethean light of that instant when humanity acquired the curse of being able to finally call Armageddon upon ourselves. This was the ultimate apotheosis of Bacon's method, which Dee could have scarcely imagined in his dingy alchemical cabinet—the manifestation of a false dawn upon the earth.

The taxonomic identifier for that material, scooped up from the resultant crater as thousands of broken green glass shards, was in homage to the code name for the site of this first test; that location was christened "Trinity" by the scientific director of the Manhattan Project, the physicist J.

Robert Oppenheimer, a cultured New Yorker fluent in five languages, who read Plato in Greek and Dante in Italian and would borrow the designation for the site of the first atomic bomb explosion from a sonnet by Dee's contemporary John Donne. "Batter my heart, three-personed God," reads the first line of that poem, now forever associated with the Trinity site. More appropriate might be a later turn of phrase in which Donne prays that he must "break, blow, burn, and make me new." Examining the trinitite as Oppenheimer and the other physicists surveyed the ruin wrought by their device in the incantatory heat of the southwestern desert, did the physicist see his own face reflected as Dee once had in his obsidian? Oppenheimer's gaunt, angular, handsome features beneath short black hair starring emptily through the shattered green visage of this element that he'd just created, a remainder of that nuclear creature which he and his colleagues had called forth into our reality?

What we do know, what everyone who knows anything about the Manhattan Projects knows, is that anecdote in which Oppenheimer recounted in a 1965 NBC interview that in the immediate aftermath of the explosion a "few people laughed, a few people cried. Most people were silent. I remembered the line from the Hindu scripture, the *Bhagavad Gita* . . . 'Now I am become Death, the destroyer of worlds.' I suppose we all thought that, one way or another."

Who can say that at that moment Oppenheimer hadn't

silently recalled the original Sanskrit phrase in which
Vishnu transforms into an avatar of oblivion, but according to others present at Trinity, in the seconds following
the test he'd actually said something rather different, if
ambiguous—"It worked!"

So much of how we interpret Oppenheimer's initial
reaction depends on if that declaration was whispered
or shouted, whether he was melancholic or ecstatic. The
Manhattan Project's director was oft criticized for availing
audiences of the full benefit of his classical education, but
whether the reference to the *Bhagavad Gita* was creative
misremembering, if it were pretension, it was at least accurate pretension. July of 1945 was an existential hinge in
human history, as if Sinai and Calvary unified in one terrifying blast. Humanity at that moment had inaugurated this
fearsome coiled, latent, potential violence hidden within
all matter, so that now apocalypse is always a single mad
decision (or computer error) away. Millennia of knowledge,
of the miraculous understanding of how mass and energy,
time and space, are unified to harness the power of the sun,
had finally yielded this—the most terrifying weapon ever
created.

By 1949, the Soviet Union had conducted their first nuclear test; in 1952, the first hydrogen fusion bomb would
be detonated by the U.S. in the paradisical Marshall
Islands; three years later the USSR would do the same in
Kazakhstan. With the trinitite still cooling at Alamogordo,
a group of physicists in 1945 concluded in a secret report

that it "would only require in the neighborhood of 10 to 100 [superbombs] of this type"—that is hydrogen bombs detonated in war—to irradiate the planet, to trigger nuclear winter and the eventual extinction of human life. Before the end of the decade, the United States would have at least ten bombs; by the end of the first year of the following they'd have a hundred. Today it's estimated that nine countries collectively have around 12,500 nuclear bombs, spread across continents and oceans, but the vast bulk of such weaponry is still shared between the United States and the Russian Federation.

Oppenheimer's claim that he interpreted that initial flash of white-hot nuclear light and the sonic boom which followed through Vishnu's terrifying transformation makes sense, because he was trying to impose narrative on the bomb. The bomb, unfortunately, refuses logic or reason. There is no narrative at the hypocenter of the nuclear explosion, it broaches no explanations. The spoken atom bomb is not the real atom bomb; her truths are unutterable, ineffable. The madness which makes possible the nuclear sword of Damocles can perhaps be circumscribed in myth and metaphor, poetry and allusion (as I've done here, as Oppenheimer did), but ultimately it can't be conventionally interpreted or conveyed. The bomb exists beyond all comprehension.

Within that hundred-million-degree fireball—shortly to be unleashed on the people of Japan, for whom the lucky were incinerated or burnt into shadows and the unfortunate

experienced literal hell—there was either the abolition of
meaning or the creation of a new one. Either way it signaled a resounding and deep cosmic silence after the shock
wave had subsided, a terrifying null-point, a demonic singularity. Adorno said that after Auschwitz, poetry was impossible; in opposition, I'd claim that after the first nuclear
test, only poetry is possible—because Trinity both killed
God and birthed a new god, our barely tamed chimera.
That is why it's the most occult of human creations, and
the men who invented it are the most Faustian of men.

Most who signed contracts with the Manhattan Project
did so because of patriotic duty or scientific curiosity, but
in the aftermath of Trinity virtually all became steadfast
advocates for disarmament.[14] Leo Szilard, who convinced
Albert Einstein to write the letter to President Franklin
Roosevelt which initiated the Manhattan Project became
an advocate for peace, while Einstein himself, whose theory of relativity was necessary to understand how nuclear
fission and fusion work, would infamously claim that he
wished he'd become a cobbler. Nobel laureates and project alumni Niels Bohr, Hans Bethe, and Enrico Fermi—
respectively he who uncovered the structure of the atomic
nucleus, the man who discovered how stars shine, and the
engineer of the first fission chain reaction—all came to op-
pose the proliferation of atomic weapons.

Such sentiments were shared by Oppenheimer, who
advocated for disarmament while director of the Institute
for Advanced Study in Princeton, but his last years were

unhappy. Hounded by the House Un-American Activities Committee for his youthful communist sympathies and haunted by the ghosts of Hiroshima, America's nuclear Faust crawled deep within a whiskey bottle, spending his days shakily wandering the sylvan grounds of the IAS. There he engaged the poet T. S. Eliot, that prophet of *The Wasteland* who had chanted in bangs and whimpers, in discussion of prosody rather than physics. A habitual smoker and alcoholic, Oppenheimer succumbed to throat cancer in 1967. Among the most brilliant physicists of the twentieth century, surrounded by men who had discovered the composition of matter and how stars shined, Oppenheimer would be remembered as the necromancer who figured out how the world could immolate itself. For all his humanistic learning, perhaps Oppenheimer's reaction to Trinity would have been better summarized not by the *Bhagavad Gita*, but by his young colleague Richard Feynman, who told a reporter "We scientists are clever—too clever—are you not satisfied?"

———

"Are you not satisfied?" could be the wry, mocking slogan of our own Faustian age. Satisfied by massive cars and plentiful guns, chill air conditioning and delivery on-demand, nonstop entertainment and bespoke simulated human interaction. Call our epoch what you will, and it's been called different things, most of them unsettling. For ecologists,

it's the Anthropocene because of the ways in which humanity has altered the environment; among some economists
and political scientists it's referred to as the age of "neo-
liberalism" or "late capitalism"; theorists and philosophers
speak of "post-modernism," while journalists following
Hiroshima and Nagasaki pretty unassailably called it the
"nuclear age."

Let me again suggest that our moment is best described
as the "Faustocene," for never have the immoral negotiations and intransigent capitulations of our broken society
been clearer, never has the light of our illusions and the
sound of our spectacles been more entertaining even as the
temperature rises and as the shoreline disappears. Riven
by its own catastrophic contradictions, the Faustocene is
an age of cold rationality and fervent occultism, of unfeeling irreligiosity and zealous fundamentalism. An age
marked by the ability to change and alter the world, to
create illusions and demonstrate the illusions of reality itself, to finally call God's bluff, but to establish a hell in
the interim, where magic and technology become indistinguishable. "Half the hour is past," Marlowe's Faust cried,
and it grows very close to midnight, indeed. Everything
in Western hubris has been leading to this moment, our
age of Chat GPT-3 and deep fakes, of wildfire and heat-
bulbs. All the overweening arrogance, rapacious hunger,
and wrathful domination, the desire for power disguised
as a thirst for knowledge driving us toward this final act of
our Faustian play.

The Faustocene's patrimony is death, and its child is apocalypse. This cankered age's charter could be divided into four separate sections, one devoted to industrial capitalism, another to positivism, a third to technological idolatry, and the final to military authoritarianism. Each are intricately linked and bolster one another, though they're not synonymous either. As an interlocking system, the pillars of the Faustocene are riven through all aspects of our globalized world, where incalculable power and wealth has been generated by many, but where it very much appears to anyone paying attention that the Devil will be arriving soon to collect his due.

Industrial capitalism provided the cannibalistic hunger that mined the bowels of the earth and smelted her innards while poisoning the air and water. From positivism came the idolatrous enshrinement of cold materialism over the vitality of life that has reduced human beings to data, instrumental to those dark wizards of unceasing technological power who replaced emotion with algorithm and reality with simulacra. Now the final aspect of the Faustocene is manifested in the growing international movement toward authoritarianism and fascism just as the biome collapses. Not just our souls, but indeed our entire planet traded for comfort and capital, a contract signed by you and me. The Los Alamos National Laboratory provided the mechanism, ExxonMobil and Gazprom the method, and the sweet illusions imparted to us by Google, Apple, Amazon, Meta, and Twitter, who also took time to write down our names, forever saved on the contract stored in the servers.

Whither our end—by locomotive, bomb, or computer? How will the Devil come to fulfill our contract, to collectively gather our souls for perdition?[15] In the miasma of simulation and artificial reality both warned about and desired by our digital prophets in Silicon Valley? With carbon dioxide rising to an untenable degree, our planet condemned to a runaway greenhouse effect and rendered all but unlivable? Or perhaps in the final conclusions of the bomb itself, our demonic face which launch'd a thousand missiles and burnt the topless towers of New York and Beijing, of Washington and Moscow, of Regensburg, Wittenberg, Cologne, Kongisberg, Prague, those nuclear flames proving the ephemerality of this shadow world and making the modern world vanish as if mere illusions, like so much smoke ascending to the rafters? All which we've accomplished destroyed with the breaking of those ancient seals, those antique jars, a shower of golden flaked papyrus dust briefly shimmering in the intense heat of that final war, until we're all no more.

NOTES

INTRODUCTION

1   Now, naturally, when you write about religion, as I have been for more than a decade now, and when you specifically have an interest in the darker facets of faith, you get asked about what you really believe, if you think any of it is "real." My answer to this question, I suspect, has often seemed a dodge, and an unsatisfying one at that. Yet I'm not being cagey or cute when I respond that the question itself has no interest to me, I think the "reality" of the Devil (or God) is the least interesting thing about him. Philosophy has long been dominated by two subdisciplines, epistemology and metaphysics. The first refers to theories of knowledge, the answer to the question of how we know what we know; the second discipline is about what the ultimate nature of reality is. When it comes to the Devil, I don't think we can answer our questions about metaphysics until we've settled our epistemology, and it's already been a few millennia of trying to do that now. I know not of the "science" of Faustus, but surely I understand its poetry, and what I'm saying is this—Faust's is a poetry which we'd do well to heed right now.

CHAPTER ONE

1   As Elaine Pagels writes in her classic study *The Gnostic Gospels,* this corpus contained "myths, magic, and instructions for mystical practice," all predicated on this belief which affirms that "self-knowledge is the knowledge of God; the self and the divine are identical."

2   Historian Bart Ehrman writes in *Lost Christianities: The*

Battles for Scriptures and the Faiths We Never Knew that "during the first three Christian centuries, the practices and beliefs found among people who called themselves Christians were so varied that the differences between Roman Catholics, Primitive Baptists, and Seventh-Day Adventists pale by comparison."

3   Nag Hammadi is far from the only reference to Simon Magus, for he flits uneasily through early Christian history, referenced by Church Fathers contemporaneous with the Gnostics, including Justin Martyr, Irenaeus, Hippolytus, and Epiphanius, along with the Jewish historian Josephus (not incidentally one of the secular sources who confirmed the existence of Jesus Christ as well).

4   The German religion scholar Hans Jonas writes rather floridly in *The Gnostic Religion* about Simon and Helen's cryptic influence on the later Faust legend, claiming that "Surely few admirers of Marlowe's and Goethe's plays have an inkling that their hero is the descendant of a gnostic secretary, and that the beautiful Helen called up by his art was once the fallen Thought of God."

5   For example, another heretic named Montanus in the second century preached that he and his two partners, a pair of women named Priscia and Maximilla, were typological of the Trinity, and that all were manifestations of the Holy Spirit in physical form. Even Paul, that infamous misogynist, is said to have traveled with a woman named Thecla whom he was partnered with in a celibate relationship, though references to her were assiduously expunged, this female apostle's image chiseled away from multicolored Byzantine mosaics and smashed from statues placed in the naves of Roman catacombs.

6   Two notable examples of these apocryphal scriptures include *The Acts of Peter* and *The Acts of Peter and Paul*.

7   "The very fury against Simon and his followers by orthodox Christians" writes Willis Barnstone in *The Other Bible: Ancient Alternative Scriptures* "proves the importance of this supposed contemporary of the apostles."

8   Owen Davies notes in *Magic: A Very Short Introduction* that "organized religion provides a culturally acceptable framework

for rationalizing the continuation of magical thinking."

9   Pagels writes that the Gnostics maintained that their beliefs, scriptures, ethics, and rituals were all to further resistance to "the demiurge who reigns as king and lord, who acts as a military commander, who gives the law and judges those who violate it."

CHAPTER TWO

1   The two different stories combined into one justify the plural in the painting's title.

2   The synoptic gospels of Matthew, Mark, and Luke are bare-bones (and in their nature contradictory) when it comes to describing the vision of Satan which Christ had while fasting and meditating in the Judean Desert for the period between his baptism in the Jordan River and the beginning of his ministry.

3   "Synoptic" refers to the first three of the four New Testament gospels—Mark, Matthew, and Luke—all of which share certain narrative features that show a common origin and orientation, the latter of which the Book of John radically departs from.

4   "How much confidence does Jesus have in himself?" asks the former Jesuit priest Jack Miles in his *Christ: A Crisis in the Life of God*. "We cannot know how fully he accepts his own identity . . . or at what point he first fully understands it," noting that Christ never denounces Satan in His own name, but only in that of the Father.

5   For those drawn to the correspondences between different religious traditions, there is a pleasing melodic congruence between Christ in the desert and the story of Siddhartha Gautama meditating beneath the Bodhi tree when he too is tempted by Mara. That god of illusions wished for Siddhartha to abandon his search for enlightenment which will culminate in his becoming the Buddha. Tempted by Mara's nubile daughters and threatened by hordes of demon soldiers, all such illusions are ultimately dust. "I sally forth to fight," says the future Buddha in the Pali Canon, "that I may not be driven from this post." The dramatic echoes are noticeable, but there is a crucial theological difference between if Siddhartha or Jesus would finally

give into such desires and bow down before their respective dark lords—the Buddha never claimed to be God.

6   The concept of a messiah is radically different between Judaism and Christianity, and for that matter with the earliest of Christianity and how it would come to develop. The fourth-century Apostles and Nicene Creed explicate a complex Trinitarian theology which relates God the Father to Christ the Son and the Holy Spirit, where the second person of that arrangement incarnated as a human and redeemed the earth through his sacrificial death. As understood in Judaism and the earliest of Christianity, by contrast, the messiah was not a god so much as an exemplary human.

7   *Paradise Regained* was printed alongside the closet drama *Samson Agonistes*. Joe Moshenska notes in *Making Darkness Light: A Life of John Milton* that the pair of *Samson Agonistes* and *Paradise Regained* made a "strikingly odd diptych . . . paired works [that] contrast jarringly with one another: Old Testament verse New Testament, violence and destruction verses peaceful and detached triumph," though this contrast is obviously intentional, an argument about different types of power.

8   Alexander is traditionally understood as having died at the same age of 33 as that which Christ was crucified.

9   The Grand Inquisitor is never identified as Torquemada, but it's implied as such, though he could possibly also be based on the notorious Dominican interrogator Bernardo Gui.

10   Dostoevsky's Russian soul countenances more than a bit of anti-Catholicism in *The Brothers Karamazov*, but it would be wrong to read the cynical disputation which the Grand Inquisitor will indulge in as mere sectarian agitprop on behalf of the Orthodox author.

11   It's fair to mention that the reference to the Society of Jesus is entirely anachronistic.

12   Eugene McCarraher in *The Enchantments of Mammon: How Capitalism Became the Religion of Modernity* argues that "modern capitalism rests on a metaphysical fault line: a profane, inanimate, external world given over to calculate and control," where the marker (or "Market") replaces divinity.

CHAPTER THREE

1   A renaissance which included immaculate versifiers like Julian
    of Norwich, the ecstatic poet Marie de France, and the autobi-
    ographer Margery Kemp.

2   As Jeffrey Burton Russell writes in *Lucifer: The Devil in the
    Middle Ages,* this idea of the "pact fit into both the tradition
    of Christian baptism and that of feudal homage," a rational
    document that embodies how to the "twin pillars of Christian
    faith . . . Scripture and tradition . . . Scholasticism [had] added a
    third pillar—reason—the analytical interpretation of Scripture,
    tradition, and observation."

3   "Much that was most cherished about Mary was not to be found
    in scripture," writes Miri Rubin in *Mother of God: A History
    of the Virgin Mary,* and so her admirers, including Hrotsvitha,
    "devised ways to make palatable and authoritative stories of pu-
    rity, nurture and miraculous birth, which were not contained in
    scripture."

4   The "Hail Mary" didn't become a popular Catholic prayer until
    a century after the nun was dead.

5   Theologian Mary Daly in *Gyn/Ecology: The Radical Metaethics
    of Radical Feminism* writes of her namesake that "despite all the
    theological minimizing of Mary's 'role,' the mythic presence of the
    Goddess was perceivable in this faded and reversed mirror image."

6   As translated in Thomas Cranmer's 1549 Anglican *Book of
    Common Prayer.*

7   Such language is what Jordan Kirk in *Medieval Nonsense:
    Signifying Nothing in Fourteenth-Century England* describes
    as "articulate, verifiable, meaningless."

8   Owen Davies writes in *Grimoires: A History of Magic Books*
    that Al-Andalus, close to the Catalan monastery where Gerbert
    was able to explore tomes gifted from Islamic libraries just to the
    south, was the home of this "Moorish tradition . . . [that brought]
    a fusion of Near Eastern cultural contacts, which for the first
    time filtered into the Western formulation of natural magic."

9   Despite no direct mention in the Hebrew Scriptures, there are a
    few glancing allusions to Lilith, such as to the "night hag" in Isaiah.

10 "It is obvious that in her mythological and magical capacity, Lilith was meant to represent that which distracted man from the right path, and all the related dangers befalling him," claims Felicia Waldman in a lecture entitled "From Demoness to God's Partner" held at the University of Bucharest in 2011, as was the circumstance with Sylvester and Meridiana.

11 Russell explains how during the Middle Ages, particularly during its later centuries, thought was "characterized by a strict and formal application of reason to theology, philosophy, and law."

CHAPTER FOUR

1   As his mentor Eliade—at least until the two fell out over the older scholar's past far-right membership in the Romanian fascist Iron Guard—wrote in *The Sacred and the Profane: The Nature of Religion*, "for those who have a religious experience all nature is capable of revealing itself as cosmic sacrality," and in terms of experiences which remain wholly and holy Other, there are few moments in life more sacred than death, wherever it should visit us.

2   "As fiction, it makes uncanny tragedy," writes Anton, but the "tragedy is, it's not fiction."

3   As Culianu's colleague Anthony Yu told Anton, the restroom was "ritually significant . . . It conveys symbolic and physical humiliation, stain, impurity, a most profane site to end a life," while again hypothesizing about the "cult killing" possibility, though that's been dismissed more as of late.

4   "The figure of Faust is—after Christ, Mary, and the Devil—the single most popular character in the history of Western Christian culture," writes Jeffrey Burton Russell in *Mephistopheles: The Devil in the Modern World*.

5   From the ashes of Münster came the heretical sect of the *Familiasts,* an occult group who in the following generation embedded themselves in royal courts from Philip of Spain to Elizabeth of England.

6   "Magic was a dominating factor," writes Dame Frances Yates in *The Rosicrucian Enlightenment,* "working as a

mathematics-mechanics in the lower world, as celestial mathematics in the celestial world, and as angelic conjuration in the supercelestial world." In the twentieth century Yates almost singlehandedly made the historical study of Renaissance occultism respectable through her extensive inventory of London's eccentric Warburg Library, the world's largest extant collection of grimoires.

7   During the same century as Bacon, though a bit younger than the estimable friar, was the Majorcan philosopher Ramon Llull, of the same monastic order as his English colleague, and equally promiscuous in his intellectual interests. Though Llull did write about both Kabbalah as well as alchemy, among other topics, it was the innovations in his *Ars Magna,* his "Great Art," for which he is most valorized, in which he invented a combinatorial system using diagrams and moveable wheels placed into the manuscript to generate answers to metaphysical queries, and which some have claimed is the nascent dawn of computer science. Like Bacon, Llull was a pious and reverential Christian (going on pilgrimages to try and convince Muslims to convert, for example), but despite the fervency of such faith his more esoteric concerns encouraged the image of him as a sorcerer.

8   As Llull's editor Anthony Bonner makes clear in the anthology *Doctor Illuminatus: A Ramon Llull Reader,* intellectuals in the Medieval and early modern worlds "did not make our neat divisions between philosophy, 'real' science, and the 'occult' science."

9   Though as Bruce Moran notes in *Paracelsus: An Alchemical Life,* the occultist justified his vocation against Faustian accusations by claiming that "human beings needed to know what the Devil knew," better to deploy the "kind of knowledge that the Devil misapplied."

10 Philip Ball writes in *The Devil's Doctor: Paracelsus and the World of Renaissance Magic and Science,* empiricism and "rationalism do not compete with mysticism and superstition but blended with it, producing a vision of the world that now seems at the same time wonderful and bizarre."

CHAPTER FIVE

1   Excluding, of course, during the Catholic interregnum of Queen Mary.

2   "The strangers who do inhabit this land . . . We'll cut your throats, in your temples praying/Not Paris' massacre so much blood did spill." A reference to the infamous St. Bartholomew's Day Massacre of twenty-one years previous, when as few as 5,000 and as many as 30,000 French Protestants were slaughtered over the course of a few days through several cities, most notably in Paris. The event was a traumatic touchstone for English Protestants.

3   Regardless of reasons, as David Riggs writes in *The World of Christopher Marlowe* this was a "talented young playwright [who] thrilled his audience with stunning representations of epicurean and underclass values; then, just when Marlowe became visible as a figure of opposition, he was silenced."

4   Riggs writes that the "intriguing question of who Marlowe was remains to be answered."

5   "In England, sacramental theater is now obsolete," writes Sarah Beckwith in *Signifying God: Social Relation and Symbolic Act in the York Corpus Christi Plays.*

6   Beckwith writes that "our received, deeply entrenched oppositions between church and theater, while fully comprehensible as the product of the particularities of English history, are themselves extraordinarily critically disabling" but for Medieval performers and audiences "sacraments are best understood as actions and not things."

CHAPTER SIX

1   The "primary purpose of powwowing is to heal physical and spiritual illness," writes David W. Kriebel in *Powwowing Among the Pennsylvania Dutch: A Traditional Medical Practice in the Modern World.* "It can therefore not only cure diseases and heal would but also remove curses, or hexes placed on a victim by a witch,"

2   A book which Davies describes as having the "greatest influence

on the modern world of magic and religion."

3   "In the serene world of mental illness," writes Michel Foucault
     in *Madness and Civilization: A History of Insanity in the Age
     of Reason,* "modern man no longer communicates with the
     madmen."

4   Carlo Ginzburg explains in *The Night Battles: Witchcraft and
     Agrarian Cults in the Sixteenth and Seventeenth Century* how
     "there are obvious differences between the gatherings described
     by the benandanti and the traditional popular image of the dia-
     bolical sabbat. It appears that in the former, homage was not
     paid to the devil. . . . There was no abjuration of the faith, tram-
     pling of crucifixes, or defilement of sacraments."

5   John Demos in *The Enemy Within: A Short History of Witch-
     Hunting* writes that his subject is "hardly confined to any single
     part of the world. In fact, it rises virtually to the level of a cross-
     cultural universal; witches of one sort of another are, or previ-
     ously have been, 'hunted' just about everywhere."

6   Ginzburg writes in *Ecstasies: Deciphering the Witches' Sabbath*
     that such an event is "formulated in its own values in the nega-
     tive. The darkness enveloping the gatherings of male and female
     witches expressed an exaltation of light; the explosion of female
     sexuality and the diabolical orgies, an exhortation to chastity;
     the animal metamorphosis, a sharply defined border between
     the feral and the human."

7   Ginzburg emphasizes that there would be "banquets, dancing,
     and sexual orgies."

8   Concepts like the Witches' Sabbath may have been "mere fic-
     tions," writes Norman Cohn in *Europe's Inner Demons: The
     Demonization of Christians in Medieval Christendom,* "but
     they were not necessarily regarded as such; and it is not surpris-
     ing that when witch-hunting began in earnest, the notion of the
     diabolic pact should have found a practical application."

9   This number is according to Lyndal Roper's study *Witch Craze.*

10   "Normally, strange things circulate discreetly below our streets,"
     writes the French philosopher Michel de Certeau in his twenti-
     eth-century study *The Possession at Loudun.*

11   Considering the ways in which the trial and execution was an

eruption of the chthonic, a transference of the persecutions which normally marked the witch trial to a man of relative privilege, and de Certeau asks "Is this the outbreak of something new, or the repetition of a past?"

12 "Like scars that mark for a new illness the spot of an earlier one," writes de Certeau, "they designate in advance the signs and location of a flight (or a return?) of a time."

CHAPTER SEVEN

1 Roger Shattuck writes in *Forbidden Knowledge: From Prometheus to Pornography* how by the Enlightenment art was "no longer [seen] as a traditional practice tied closely to notions of craft," but rather was interpreted as "an individual creative activity springing from original genius, reliant on a disinterested 'aesthetic' attitude, and free of social constraints."

2 The consummate Renaissance humanist, influenced by the Neo-Platonism which held that the truth of things, their actual form, was hidden within and transcendent of our mere world of shadows. This was the doctrine by which Michelangelo could claim that all he did when making a sculpture was merely to chip away the excess marble and reveal that which was always truly within. Platonism, that ancient and venerable philosophy which holds that all which we can see, hear, touch, taste, and smell is but a pale imitation of a higher and truer realm is also the fundamental axiom of all magic, so that the artist Michelangelo isn't so distant from the necromancer Faust.

3 "The occult in its common acceptance is not a special category under forbidden knowledge," writes Shattuck, "but a vast catch-all collection of religious, secular, psychic, and magical lore," artistic as well.

4 This affirmation of the artistic genius's ability to harness the generative abilities of divinity was the philosophy of a "whole generation of Romantic artists," claims Shattuck, "After his fashion, Faust belongs to this legacy."

5 Critic George Steiner in *The Grammars of Creation* writes that the "creative act and that which it engenders is . . . an enactment

of freedom. It is integrally liberty . . . 'creation,' properly understood and experienced, is another word for 'freedom.'"

CHAPTER EIGHT

1 Rüdiger Safranski in his massive biography *Goethe: Life as a
   Work of Art* explains how the poet "was determined to give his
   life the character of a work [of art] . . . Something that rises out
   of the flow of time, has a beginning and an end and, between
   them, a clear form: an island of significance in the sea of inchoate contingency."
2 The Auerbach was Goethe's favored tavern and already associated with the historical necromancer (the Devil supposedly
   helped Faustus ride a beer keg out the front door as if it were a
   pony).
3 "With the wager between Faust and Mephisto and the resulting
   dynamic action, the momentous transformation of metaphysical furor into an engine for civilization's conquest of the world
   unfolds," writes Safranski. "Aided by Mephisto, Faust has good
   fortune with women, reforms government finance, provides
   bread and circuses, becomes a successful military commander,
   and finally a colonizer on a grand scale."
4 With worrying future connotations, in German the word is
   "Volk."
5 Philosopher Isaiah Berlin explains in *The Roots of Romanticism*
   that for the women and men who were the vanguard of the
   movement, it was defined by "the familiar, the sense of one's
   unique tradition, joy in the smiling aspect of everyday nature,
   and the accustomed sights and sounds of contented, simple, rural folk—the sane and happy wisdom of rosy-cheeked sons of
   the soil."
6 Such "traces bear witness to a struggle with the Devil that is
   at the same time a struggle with ambivalence, a struggle with
   ambiguity, a struggle with words," writes Kimberly Ball in the
   scholarly journal *Western Folklore*.
7 Margaret Atwood notes in her study *In Other Worlds:
   Speculative Fiction and the Human Imagination* that "Once

upon a time there weren't any scientists, as such, in plays or fic-
tions, because there wasn't any science as such, or not science
as we know it today." In place of computers, there were scrying
mirrors; rather than centrifuges, there were alchemical glasses;
no robots, but homunculi. These "alchemists and Faustian
magicians certainly form part of the mad scientist's ancestral
lineage," writes Atwood, but Shelley introduced something entirely new.

8   Far from being simply ignorant of science, Shelley rejects total-
izing dogmas of positivism, so that, as the science writer Philip
Ball notes in *Unnatural: The Heretical Idea of Making People*
that it is only "on the surface" that *Frankenstein* is "wholly secular." Ball writes that the novel's "insight owes more to theological than to scientific tradition" and that *Frankenstein* "expresses
ambivalence towards procreation itself."

CHAPTER NINE

1   The earliest substantiated paintings, red ochre smeared across
rough granite walls, dates back 45,000 years to a cave in
Indonesia. Evidence of music, however, predates that by a stunning fifteen centuries, a bone flute bored with four holes spaced
for fingers discovered at a site in Slovenia, appropriately not far
from where Tartini would be born and raised. Carved from the
thigh-bone of a juvenile bear, the Slovenian flute is unequivo-
cally an instrument, proof of the propensity for music even in
the most distant reaches of what it means to be human. That
should be taken literally, as archaeologists believe that the instrument was crafted for Neanderthal hands, our close cousins
but genetically not Homo sapiens.

2   "It's worth noting how rarely myths describe music originating
as entertainment or works of artistic expression," writes Ted
Gioia in *A Subversive History of Music,* for "our oldest ancestors knew something we ought to remember . . . music is power."

3   Isabel Fonesca writes in *Bury Me Standing: The Gypsies and
their Journey,* when they "first appeared in Europe in the four-
teenth century the Gypsies presented themselves as pilgrims and

they told fortunes: two winning protestations in a superstitious age," winning protestations that ultimately became an albatross.

4   Both Paganini and Johnson were conjectured to have had Marfan syndrome, their extra-long fingers perhaps as responsible for their skill as the Devil was.

5   Elijah Wald writes in *Escaping the Delta: Robert Johnson and the Invention of the Blues* that "it is long past time for music journalists to get over the cliché of always linking Robert Johnson and the Devil," quipping that such sentiments "tells us less about the realities of Johnson's music than about the romantic leanings of his later, urban white listeners," and it's a point well-taken.

6   "Every culture has its legends . . . Robert Johnson selling his soul at the crossroads is one of ours," writes Wald, the "'us' being present-day, urban, literate, mostly white fans." Though Wald admits that it's a "potent and intriguing legend" that says "a great deal about our yearnings and dreams."

CHAPTER 10

1   Tituba was most likely part Taino Indian from the Caribbean and part Black.

2   Of course this "Proctor" is really just Miller speaking, a secular left-wing Jew castigating not just the barbarities of the seventeenth century, but of the McCarthy Era.

3   A New Light Presbyterian minister, Edwards would have been associated—ironically—with liberalizing aspects of worship in Calvinist churches during the First Great Awakening of the eighteenth century.

4   "The New-Englanders are a people of God," wrote Mather yet again in *The Wonders of the Invisible World*, who had settled in this country which "were once the Devil's Territories," with the divine warning that the prince of this world desired that once again "He should have the Utmost parts of the Earth for his Possession," and so the minister and his associates deigned to do all that they could to prevent such a thing from transpiring, though obviously they only facilitated that land-grant. If

Mather's fear came to pass, than it was partially because of the unforgiving, inhumane, nightmarish Calvinism which defined their project, a theology which so valorized the Devil and prepared his throne for him.

5   Supposedly delivered aboard the Arbela in 1630, though forgotten for nearly two centuries before a copy of Winthrop's sermon was rediscovered in the archives of the New-York Historical Society.

6   Note how typologically auspicious the name of his wife is.

CHAPTER 11

1   Designed by the architect Julius Ralph Davidson and now owned by the German government as a cultural center.

2   Worth mentioning that this is also the exact same time-period during which Mann is writing the novel, the outcome of the Second World War still uncertain.

3   "I am perfectly aware that with the foregoing paragraph I have seriously compromised this new section as well, which I really had hoped to keep shorter," etc. ad nauseum.

4   Despite initial enthusiasm for regrettable positions such as those espoused in *Reflections of a Nonpolitical Man.*

5   Men such as Hjalmar Schact, the Reich Minister for Economics, leader of the German National Peoples' Party Alfred Hugenberg, and Chancellor Paul von Hindenburg.

6   "In the middle of Europe in the middle of the twentieth century," writes historian Timothy Snyder in *Bloodlands: Europe Between Hitler and Stalin,* "the Nazi and Soviet regimes murdered some fourteen million people. The place where all of the victims died, the bloodlands, extends from central Poland to western Russian, through Ukraine, Belarus, and the Baltic States."

7   Bulgakov renders Christ in Hebrew as Yeshua Ha-Nostri.

CHAPTER 12

1   In this regard, *Nosferatu* must be included alongside fellow silent film director Robert Wiene's nightmarish 1920 *The Cabinet of*

Dr. Caligari and Fritz Lang's dystopian 1927 movie *Metropolis*.

2   "Scripts," in the parlance of silent film, would refer to the title cards.

3   The distributor in question being Universum-Film Aktiengesellschaft.

4   Something which Lang's *Metropolis* was also guilty of.

5   None of these productions are at the level of a Murnau, obviously, much less a Leni Riefenstahl.

6   Adorno was, after all, writing during the height of the Hays Code when studios self-censored their productions to a uniform conservatism.

CHAPTER 13

1   His collection consisting of heavy, leather-bound vellum manuscripts of occultism was held in the dark wood-lined environs of his rural Mortlake estate; the Aztec mirror's ownership history before Dee is obscure, but he somehow procured it from Spanish colonials. The mirror still exists and can be seen at the British Museum.

2   I hold to the British philosopher John Gray's argument in *Black Mass: Apocalyptic Religion and the Death of Utopia* that the "history of the past century is not a tale of secular advance," for even ostensibly materialist or positivist dogmas are still "myths, which answer the human need for meaning."

3   Science journalist Sally Adee notes in *The Last Word on Nothing* there is a contradiction in the fact that the "kind of rationalist who would propose a future technological superintelligence is not the kind of person who has any patience with religious tropes."

4   Writing in *Slate,* technology journalist David Auerbach explains that for them the "singularity brings about the machine equivalent of *God itself.*"

5   Anthropologist Beth Singler, in conversation with Adee, tells the latter that "This narrative is an example of implicit religion . . . It's interesting that this explicitly secular community is adopting religious categories, narratives and tropes."

6   Ed Regis in his *Great Mambo Chicken and the Transhumanist Condition,* which despite its curious title and its 1991 publication date remains the best general introduction to their thinking, writes that the transhumanist goal is a "temporal, corporal, quite this-worldly way of escaping all the same ills and limitations of the flesh, just exactly as it had been envisioned by the greatest saints." With the appropriate amount of snark, Regis explained that thinkers like Moravec are "at bottom, interested in the same thing [as religion], which is to say, true immortality, life ever-lasting in the form of pure consciousness."

7   Men like Thoreau and Ralph Waldo Emerson alternated between despairing and triumphant, and as Leo Marx claimed in his classic study *The Machine in the Garden: Technology and the Pastoral Idea in America,* a studied ambivalence marked the intelligentsia on these subjects, noting that "nothing quite like the event announced by the train in the woods had occurred before."

8   Regarding that metal shriek outside of Concord, Marx catalogues numerous other instances as recorded by men like Nathaniel Hawthorne and Emerson, with the train representing how the "great world is invading the land, transforming the sensory texture of rural life . . . and threatening, in fact, to impose a new and more complete dominion over it."

9   As claimed by atmospheric scientist Kim Cobb.

10   "If Henry Thoreau was impressed by *Faust,* he has unfortunately left no record of his enthusiasm," writes Joel Porte in *The New England Quarterly.*

11   "Like Faust, torn between his earthly lusts and his spiritual strivings, they were dualists; yet they yearned for unity," explained Porte in his consideration of the spiritual conflict at the heart of the nineteenth century, and if true while Emerson and Thoreau were alive, how much more accurate today?

12   Pope Francis writes in his encyclical *Laudato sí: Care for Our Common Home* that "Economic powers continue to justify the current global system where priority tends to be given to . . . the pursuit of financial gain, which fail to take the context into account, let along the effects on human dignity and the natural

environment. Here we see how environmental deterioration and human and ethical degradation are closely linked."

13 Weber's thesis concerned the connections between religion and economics, but Eugene McCarraher argues something even more radical and certainly more reflective of the dire state of the world during the Anthropocene in *The Enchantments of Mammon: How Capitalism Became the Religion of Modernity*, arguing that "Under capitalism, money occupies the ontological throne from which God has been evicted."

14 With the notable exception of Edward Teller, Stanley Kubrick's inspiration for *Dr. Strangelove.*

15 "Divinity, adieu!" —Kit Marlowe.

Mephistopheles appearing to Doctor Faustus, from a 1631 edition of
Tragical Historie of D. Faust, the play by Christopher Marlowe.
© World History Archive / Alamy

ACKNOWLEDGMENTS

Devil's Contract is a book which I first envisioned twenty years ago. Along the way I've worked with and learned from innumerable teachers and scholars who helped refine my knowledge, my research, and my thinking. A few of them include Carolyn Kyler, Lauren Mayer, Linda Troost, Dana Shiller, Robert Vande Kappelle, Peggy Knapp, Michael Whitmore, Jonathan Sawday, Ruth Evans, Jonathan Drakakis, Willy Maley, Jonathan Hope, Mark Poteet, Lyndon Dominque, Seth Moglen, Edward Galagher, Edward Whitley, and Barbara Traister.

A huge portion of my gratitude for this book of course has to go to the incredible team at Melville House who have been amazing to work with. Special thanks to Sammi Sontag, Pia Mulleady, Hanna Lafferty, Katrina Weidknecht, Janet Joy Wilson, Dan O'Connor, and Sofia Demopolos. In particular, I have to thank my editor Mike Lindgren, whose vision, erudition, and humor have been invaluable in this project. A good editor is worth their weight in gold, and Mike isn't just a good editor, he's a brilliant one.

Finally, the absolute bulk of my gratitude must always go to my family. Thank you to my mother Janet, my brother Jacob, and my father Matt. Though my father has been gone for nearly a decade, he lives on in my sons Finn and Milo, who share his curiosity, humor, and kindness. Above all, thank you to the love of my life, my wife Meg.

ED SIMON is the executive director of Belt Media Collaborative and editor in chief of literary journal *Belt Magazine*. A staff writer for *LitHub*, his essays and criticism have appeared in the *New York Times*, the *Atlantic*, the *Paris Review* Daily, the *New Republic*, and the *Washington Post*. He lives in Pittsburgh, Pennsylvania with his family.